HYPERTENSION IN PRACTICE

PRACTICAL PROBLEMS IN MEDICINE

HYPERTENSION IN PRACTICE

D. G. Beevers, MD, FRCP

*Reader in Medicine, University of Birmingham
and Honorary Consultant Physician, Dudley Road Hospital, Birmingham*

G. A. MacGregor, FRCP

*Senior Lecturer, Charing Cross and Westminster Medical School
and Honorary Consultant Physician, Charing Cross Hospital*

Foreword by
Sir Raymond Hoffenberg
President of the Royal College of Physicians

MARTIN DUNITZ

First published in the United Kingdom in 1987
by Martin Dunitz Ltd, 154 Camden High Street, London NW1 0NE

British Library Cataloguing in Publication Data

Beevers, D.G.
   Hypertension in practice.—(Practical
   problems in medicine)
   1. Hypertension
   I. Title   II. MacGregor, G.A.   III. Series
   616.1'32   RC685.H8

   ISBN 0–906348–94–3

Phototypeset in Garamond by Input Typesetting Ltd, London SW19 8DR
Reproduction by Adroit Photolitho Ltd, Birmingham
Printed and bound in Singapore by Toppan Printing Company (S) Pte Ltd

Contents

Foreword

Sir Raymond Hoffenberg, KBE, MD, PhD
President of the Royal College of Physicians

Few subjects give rise to greater controversy and dispute than the management of hypertension. The problem starts with its definition and proceeds through a consideration of its risks, how best to identify individuals who need treatment, and what form of treatment should then be given. In the face of so much disagreement, dogmatism must be avoided. Drs Beevers and MacGregor have wisely recognized this and their book presents a fair, detached and pragmatic approach to the topic.

On its own or in conjunction with other risk factors, especially cigarette smoking, hypertension is associated with serious morbidity and high mortality. The size of the problem is immense. The authors conclude, for instance, that a single casual blood pressure of 160/95 or more would be found in over 7 million people of all ages in England and Wales. The resource implications of identifying those at risk and instituting effective treatment are frightening. Yet the problem has to be tackled. For this to be done sensibly, the nature of the disease and its implications must be properly understood.

The authors of this text have considerable experience of managing hypertension clinics. Their familiarity with the disorder becomes apparent in their emphasis on practical points, such as the correct way to measure blood pressure, and how best to assess a new hypertensive patient.

Most new patients are found to have high blood pressure during routine examination; they seldom have symptoms or signs to go with it. Which of these subjects should be investigated and how fully? This difficult decision is dealt with clearly and helpfully.

Most doctors will appreciate the chapters on treatment. The authors sensibly deal first with non-pharmacological ways of lowering blood pressure and then consider the staged introduction of anti-hypertensive drugs. This is rapidly shifting ground. As they write – more or less – views are changing about the choice of first-line drugs: beta-blockers? ACE inhibitors? calcium-entry antagonists? The authors pursue a relatively unaligned course, simply emphasizing the relative strengths and weaknesses of the various groups of anti-hypertensive agents.

This book will, I am sure, prove invaluable to students and newly qualified doctors as it will give them a sound perspective of a difficult topic. If they follow its advice, the management of this common and serious disorder should be considerably improved.

PART 1: THE CAUSES AND CONSEQUENCES OF HYPERTENSION

1
The importance of hypertension

BACKGROUND

Diseases of the arterial system are responsible for more premature deaths than all other causes, including cancer and infections combined. Now that infective diseases and malnutrition, have largely been controlled in Western societies, the modern epidemic can best be described as 'atherothrombotic'. Large-scale population follow-up studies have identified three major risk factors for arterial disease: high blood pressure, high blood lipids and cigarette smoking (see Figure 1.1). Of these, high blood pressure is the most potent predictor of life expectancy, after taking into account the age of the individual, and his or her family history.

Hypertension is a treatable chronic

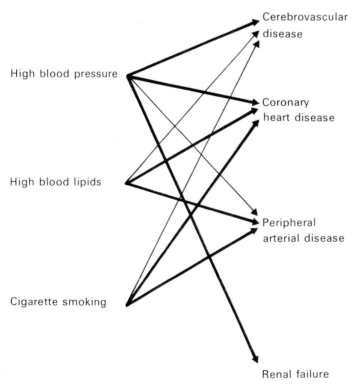

High blood pressure

High blood lipids

Cigarette smoking

Cerebrovascular disease

Coronary heart disease

Peripheral arterial disease

Renal failure

Figure 1.1 The three major cardiovascular risk factors and their disease manifestations (the thickness of the lines denotes the strength of the association).

disease which affects up to one quarter of the adult population. During the last thirty years its importance has become more widely understood, yet there still remains too much ignorance about it among both doctors and patients. Perhaps the main reason is that there is still no universally recognized definition of the condition. Each specialist tends to have his or her own criteria relevant to a particular interest. Attempts to provide a universal definition have been unsuccessful. In a book devoted to clinical hypertension, it is most useful to employ a practical view, relevant to clinicians.

THE DEFINITION OF HYPERTENSION
The best clinical definition can be taken as the level of blood pressure above which investigation and treatment is of proven benefit to the patient.[1] While following this pragmatic approach, however, it is crucial that the clinician should be fully up-to-date on the proven usefulness of treatment in a field where new information is constantly becoming available. Several major multicentre trials have been published recently (see Chapter 9) and more information about them will follow, so it is possible that the criteria for treatment of the milder grades of hypertension and also of elderly patients will change.

The pragmatic definition
The pragmatic definition of hypertension at the present state of knowledge is a diastolic blood pressure in patients below the age of seventy years measured at the fifth phase (disappearance of diastolic sounds, see page 62), which on two occasions exceeds 95 mmHg. In older patients there is less clarity as to the level, but hypertension might be defined as a diastolic blood pressure greater than 100 mmHg (see Chapter 15). Patients whose blood pressures are at or above these levels need

elementary investigation and follow-up and in some cases detailed investigation is necessary to identify underlying causes. Below this level drug therapy has not yet been shown to be useful, and in some cases it might even be harmful, by virtue of the patient's anxiety or the side-effects of antihypertensive drugs.

Systolic versus diastolic blood pressure
The definition used here takes no account of the height of the systolic blood pressure. The reason for this is that to date there are no clinical trials published that have examined the benefits of treating systolic hypertension when the diastolic pressure is not raised. However, there is good evidence that the clinicians' concentration on diastolic pressures is not logical. Population surveys and studies of hypertensive patients have shown that the height of the systolic blood pressure is actually a better predictor of death than the diastolic pressure.[2] It is possible to calculate from insurance company data that a man aged thirty-five with a blood pressure of 160/90 has a shorter life expectancy than a similar man whose blood pressure is 150/100. Although the diastolic pressure of the former is lower, his higher systolic pressure means that he is at greater risk.[3]

Decisions on the level of systolic pressure worth treating have to be based on extrapolations from clinical and epidemiological data which is largely concentrated on diastolic pressures. Usually both systolic and diastolic pressures are raised so the diastolic definition of hypertension is sufficient. There are, however, a great many people, particularly in the older age groups, whose systolic pressures are raised to above 200 mmHg but whose diastolic pressures are normal. This condition is known as isolated systolic hypertension[4] and is found in about 15 per cent of the population aged sixty years or more. The prognosis is poor, and the benefits of drug therapy are uncertain, and a multicentre therapeutic trial is being established in the USA. In view of the high risk in patients with systolic pressures over 200 mmHg, an attempt at reduction probably is desirable even if the diastolic pressure is not raised (see Chapter 15).

The main reason why elevation of systolic blood pressure has a greater prognostic value than that of diastolic pressure is that it rises more sharply with advancing age, and this rise may in part be caused by the development of thickening of the brachial artery, owing to the chronically raised intra-arterial pressure. This implies that raised systolic pressure may be a reflection of arterial end-organ damage. The presence of other evidence of end-organ damage, for example, left ventricular hypertrophy or a vascular complication such as a stroke is not surprisingly a powerful prognostic feature in an individual patient. It might thus be inferred that the level of the systolic pressure would be more closely related to life expectancy than that of the diastolic pressure.

WHO criteria

The World Health Organization (WHO) has determined that hypertension begins at a systolic blood pressure of 160 mmHg or more or a diastolic blood pressure of 95 mmHg or more (see Table 1.1).[5]

These criteria are frequently used in the world literature, and have the advantage that they include systolic as well as diastolic pressure and therefore are closely related to the prognosis. As the value of reducing systolic pressure is still uncertain, the WHO criteria cannot be used as a guide to the correct level for starting antihypertensive therapy. Neither do they take account of the age of the subject and the number of blood pressure readings, even though blood pressures rise with advancing age and tend to fall on repeated measurement.

The concept of borderline hypertension is particularly dubious as it implies there is some sort of border or clear-cut dividing line between normal and abnormal pressures. The epidemiological view of hypertension clearly negates this belief.

	Systolic blood pressure		Diastolic blood pressure
Normal	less than 140 mmHg	with	less than 90 mmHg
Borderline	140–159 mmHg	and/or	90–94 mmHg
Definite	160mmHg or more	and/or	95 mmHg or more
Mild hypertension	160–179 mmHg	and/or	95–104mmHg

Table 1.1 WHO criteria for hypertension. It is important to note that these take no account of the age of the patient, the number of blood pressure readings or the presence of pre-existing vascular complications of hypertension.

Blood pressure in population

An understanding of the epidemiological approach is important if the clinician is to manage his patients properly. The epidemiologist sees blood pressure from the point of view of its impact on the health of the whole population rather than individual patients. Sir George Pickering pointed out that hypertension should be seen as a quantitative rather than a qualitative entity. In the general population, blood pressure is distributed in a roughly normal manner in a bell-shaped curve, with a slight skew towards higher readings (Figure 1.2). There is no evidence of any sub-group of hypertensives distinct from normotensives and no dividing line between normal and raised blood pressure.[6]

The risk of death is directly related to the height of the blood pressure.[7] Even people whose blood pressures are exactly average for their age in Westernized societies have a higher cardiovascular risk than those with lower pressures (see Figure 1.3). Again, hypertension appears to be a disease of quantity rather than

quality. In general, the higher the pressure, the worse the outlook, and again there is no evidence of any dividing line between pressures that carry a low risk and pressures that are associated with premature death. It is apparent that with the exception of hypotension due to autonomic neuropathy or associated with severe generalized illness, Addison's disease or heart attack, it is not possible to have too low a blood pressure. Unlike hypertension, which is associated with premature death, low blood pressure on its own is not a diagnosis of any significance or meaning.

Blood pressure and age In Westernized societies average blood pressures tend to rise with advancing age.[8] This rise starts soon after birth and continues until the age of about six weeks (see Chapter 17). Blood pressures then level off until the age of about four years, when they start rising again, and continue to do so up until the age of about sixty (see Figure

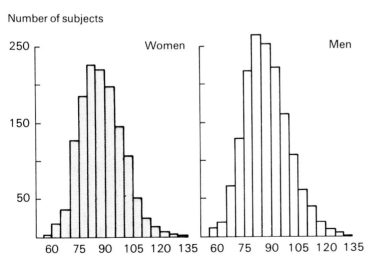

Figure 1.2 The distribution of blood pressure in middle-aged men and women in Renfrew, Scotland.[6]

Diastolic blood pressure (mmHg)

1.4). Above this age there is relatively little rise in diastolic pressure and some studies have even demonstrated a slight fall, but systolic pressures do continue to rise.[9] Any definition of hypertension has to take into account the relation of blood pressure and age, and clearly no single blood pressure level is satisfactory.

The epidemiological definition This states that hypertension is a disease of quantity alone, which affects the whole population, and not just those patients whose pressures are above the presently accepted therapeutic dividing line. The phenomenon of the rise in blood pressure with increasing age is not seen in most primitive or rural populations, and hypertension is very rare. The epidemiologist would thus like to see a reduction of blood pressure for the whole population, and not just for the minority of people with high pressures.

Complicated hypertension

High blood pressure has been called the hidden killer as it may be symptomless until an advanced stage, yet one disastrous definition of hypertension is based solely on symptoms or complications. If this definition alone were to be employed there would be even more potentially preventable strokes, heart attacks and other vascular crises than at present. It is too late to wait for ECG evidence of left ventricular hypertrophy, let alone clinical evidence of end-organ damage.

HOW COMMON IS HYPERTENSION?

In men and women aged between thirty-five and sixty-five years severe hypertension with diastolic pressures of 130 mmHg or more is found in about 0.5 per cent of the population.[6] If left untreated these people have a prognosis which is rather worse than grade II carcinoma of the breast. A small proportion of patients with even higher blood pressures have malignant hypertension (see Chapter 2). Its untreated prognosis is worse than that of stomach or lung cancer, with an 80 per cent chance of death within one year. The syndrome is, however, fortunately rare. In a busy district hospital serving a population of 300,000, about five or six new cases of malignant hypertension are seen each year.

Diastolic blood pressures between 110 and 129 mmHg are found in about 4 to

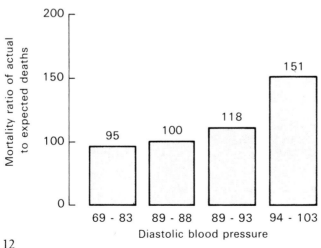

Figure 1.3 The mortality rate (ratio of actual to expected deaths) in relation to diastolic blood pressure in men (data from the Actuarial Society of America).

5 per cent of the adult population. This represents about twice the incidence of diabetes mellitus. The combined prevalence of moderate and severe hypertension is therefore about 5 per cent. In the average primary health care practice with about 2500 patients per doctor, about ten patients below the age of sixty-five will be found with diastolic pressures of 110 mmHg or more.

It will be seen from the bell-shaped curve that the milder grades of hypertension are the most common. Diastolic blood pressures between 90 and 109 mmHg are found in about 20 per cent of the middle-aged adult population. In younger adults the prevalence is lower, and in the elderly it is correspondingly higher. A casual blood pressure of 160/95 or more is found in roughly 50 per cent of Western populations aged seventy years or more. It is possible to calculate that in the population of England and Wales of 49.6 million, 7,196,000 people (14.5 per cent) of all ages have a single casual blood pressure of this level. An

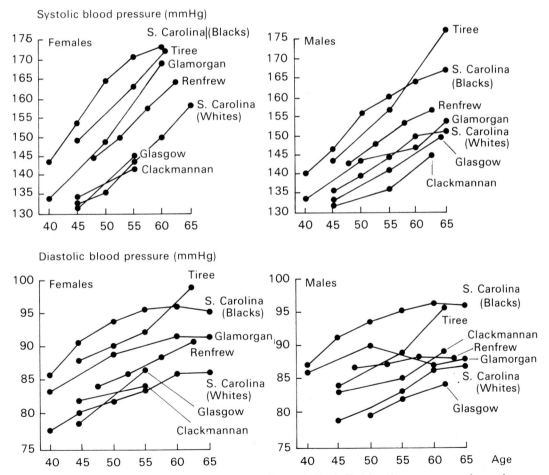

Figure 1.4 The relationship between systolic and diastolic blood pressure and age in men and women in several British and USA population surveys.

average British general practitioner should expect to have 360 registered patients of all ages with a single casual blood pressure of 160/95 mmHg or more (see Table 1.2).

Similarly, in the USA blood pressures exceeding 160/95 have been estimated to be present in 23.2 million people, this representing 15 to 19 per cent of whites aged eighteen to seventy-four years and 27 to 29 per cent of blacks. If the criteria for diagnosing hypertension are lowered to include cases with diastolic pressures between 90 and 95 mmHg then around 40 per cent of the population would be considered hypertensive. If isolated systolic hypertension is also included, hypertension would be found in more than half of the population over the age of sixty years.

The above figures obtained from population screening surveys are based on single casual blood pressure readings only. On rechecking many of these high blood pressures fall.[10] This is due partly to familiarization of individuals to the screening survey techniques, with reduction of the fear or defence reaction, and partly to the statistical trend for initially high values

(and initially low values) to move towards the mean for the population on resampling. After two or three readings, the prevalence of hypertension falls. In one recent massive American study, only 6.9 per cent of a screened population had diastolic pressures that were persistently 90 mmHg or higher.[11]

All the above statistics are based on population surveys which have employed diastolic pressures measured at the disappearance of sounds (fifth phase, see page 63). A higher prevalence would be found if the muffling of sounds (fourth phase) were used. Variations between surveys may be due to this, and also to the number of readings, the age, sex and ethnic distribution of the population. Other factors influencing pressures are the manometer cuff size and the position of the arm in relation to the heart, the amount of training of the observers, the time of day and time of the year, the ambient temperature, the anxiety of the subject and the waiting time before the pressure is measured (see Chapter 6).

The risks of hypertension
High blood pressure is the commonest

Age	Men	Women
0–19	7 (2%)	4 (1%)
20–39	25 (7%)	8 (3%)
40–59	70 (25%)	52 (18%)
60–79	66 (35%)	93 (37%)
80+	10 (50%)	26 (50%)
Total	178	183

Table 1.2 Estimated number of patients who are registered with an average British general practice who have a single casual blood pressure of 160/95 mm Hg or more. Figures in brackets denote the percentage of people in that age band with hypertension.

risk factor for the commonest cause of death. The two-year survival rate for malignant hypertension if left untreated is around 10 per cent (see Figure 1.5). Patients with diastolic blood pressures above 130 mmHg have a 40 per cent two-year survival rate if left untreated. Moderate hypertensives with diastolic pressures between 110 and 129 mmHg have an 80 per cent two-year survival rate. However, these statistics, the only ones available, are based on information obtained thirty years ago, before the advent of effective antihypertensive drugs.[12] Such patients now receive drug therapy and their mortality is correspondingly reduced, although not normalized. In the milder grades of hypertension, where diastolic blood pressures are between 95 and 105

mmHg, the annual mortality rate at the age of forty-five years is about three times higher than in people whose pressures are nearer the average for the population. While this increased relative risk is marked the absolute risk, that is, the chance of dying within five years, is fairly small, and many people with mild hypertension survive to a normal life expectancy.

Even people whose blood pressures are just about average for the population have an annual mortality at the age of forty-five years of about four per thousand, so that within ten years 4 per cent will die. By contrast, the mortality in people whose blood pressure is well below the population average have an annual mortality of only three per thousand.[7]

In practical terms, the clinician should

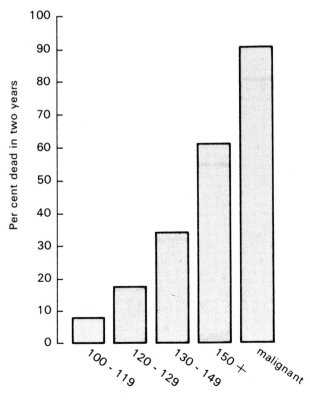

Figure 1.5 Survival rate for untreated patients with high blood pressure.[12]

Per cent dead in two years

Diastolic blood pressure (mmHg)

be aware that a man aged thirty-five years with a blood pressure of 150/100 mmHg has an odds-on chance of dying before he reaches the age of sixty years unless active steps are taken to reduce the pressure. With advancing age, the risk for a given level of blood pressure increases. Clinical hypertension, which represents about the top quintile of the blood pressures of the population aged forty-five years, carries a 3 per cent annual death rate. The same pressures at the age of fifty-five years carry a 5 per cent annual mortality, and at the age of sixty-five years annual mortality rises to 8 per cent.

Multiple risk factors

As stated earlier, there are two other important cardiovascular risk factors in addition to raised blood pressure. These are cigarette smoking and raised blood lipids. It is important to note that all three factors have a multiplicative or synergistic effect on each other (see Figure 1.6).[13] A person with two risk factors is much worse off than a person with only one. It is possible to define high, moderate or low-risk hypertensives on the basis of the measurement of blood lipids and assessment of smoking habits (see Table 1.3).

By any criteria, hypertension is important; it is also neglected. The prime considerations in this chapter have been the risk of the disease itself as well as the risk from hypertension in the whole population. Most heart attacks and strokes occur in people whose pressures are either only very mildly raised, or are just about the average for the population. Although the risk of death to the individual from near average blood pressures in Western countries is small, because this very mild hypertension is so common, the numbers of vascular complications is large

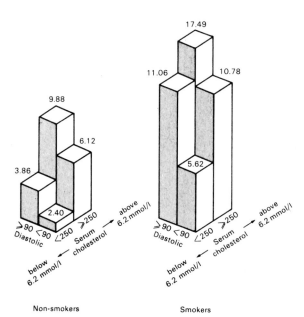

Figure 1.6 Five-year age adjusted coronary heart disease death rates per thousand for 325,384 white males aged thirty-five to thirty-seven in the Multiple Risk Factor Intervention Trial programme (from M. G. Marmot, 'Epidemiology and the art of the soluble', *Lancet 1*, 1986, 897–900).

Systolic BP	Cholesterol	Non-smoker	Ex-smoker	Smoke 1–14	Smoke >15
SBP >190	>8.7	H	H	H	H
	7.0 – 8.6	M	H	H	H
	<7.0	L	M	H	H
SBP <190	>8.7	M	H	H	H
	7.0 – 8.6	M	M	H	H
	<7.0	L	L	M	H

Table 1.3 Risk score for hypertension based on blood lipid measurement and smoking habits (H = high, M = medium, L = low). (Data from Professor Lars Wilhemsen.)

(see Table 1.4). Clinicians need to be concerned with blood pressures that are high enough to require antihypertensive drug therapy, but they should also be concerned to see a lowering of blood pressure in all their patients. The goal of good medical care should be not only successful management but also primary prevention achieved with a relevant education programme.

The underdiagnosis of hypertension
The term 'The rule of halves' (see Figure 1.7) was first coined in the early 1970s in the United States, and population studies in Europe and elsewhere have reported

Diastolic blood pressure	Percent of men with this level of blood pressure	Death rate per 1000 in 10 years from cardiovascular disease
<75	19	81
75–84	33	85
85–94	26	101
95–104	13	108
105–114	6	178
>115	3	201

Table 1.4 The prevalence of different levels of diastolic blood pressure in the Whitehall study in relation to the death rate in the following ten years.

the same findings. The rule of halves means that, unless special efforts are made, only half of the hypertensives in the population will ever be diagnosed. Furthermore, of those cases that are diagnosed, only half receive treatment, and of those only half have adequately controlled blood pressure. The end result is that only between 10 and 15 per cent of hypertensives receive good medical care – a situation that constitutes a national and international scandal.[14] If a fully laden jumbo jet were to crash killing all its passengers every six weeks, there would be a public outcry. In the UK as many people die of preventable hypertension-related disease, and this goes without comment even from the medical profession.

Dangerous myths

The climate producing the rule of halves is due in part to a series of dangerous myths and misconceptions. Doctors, administrators, politicians and patients are remarkably ignorant of the true priorities of medical care and the relative importance of various diseases.

Myth 1 Cancer is a more important health hazard than all other diseases.

Not so

While cancer may seem a more terrifying and urgent medical problem, hypertension-related diseases kill more people than all other causes combined, including cancer. Furthermore, although hypertension is treatable and premature deaths can be avoided, there is scant evidence that medical care can influence cancer mortality.

Myth 2 Severe hypertension is a more important hazard to health than mild hypertension.

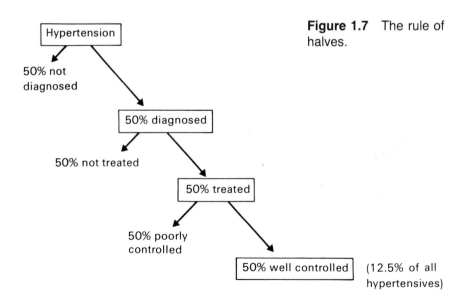

Figure 1.7 The rule of halves.

Not so

Although severe hypertension is commonly a fatal condition, it is relatively rare. Mild hypertension with its lower risk, by contrast, is very common so its prevention or cure could lead to a massive reduction of cardiovascular disease and premature death.

Myth 3 Hypertension is characterized by symptoms including headache and tiredness.

Not so

Until recently practically every medical textbook stated that hypertension causes these symptoms. In fact, no symptoms, not even headache or epistaxis, are related to mild to moderate hypertension. If they were, hypertensives could be relied upon to present to their doctor with diagnostically useful symptoms before the development of vascular complications.

Myth 4 Mild elevations of blood pressure are often due to some recent psychosocial stress and can be ignored.

Not so

Single casual measurements of blood pressure during insurance medical examinations, for example, are a very potent predictor of risk. A man aged thirty-five with a single casual diastolic blood pressure reading of 100 mmHg is unlikedly to survive to retirement age unless something is done to reduce his pressure.

Myth 5 Among patients receiving drug therapy, once blood pressure is well controlled, therapy can be stopped.

Not so

Many patients have the mistaken belief that antihypertensive drugs are like antibiotics, requiring only a short course of treatment. This dangerous misconception is often the fault of the doctor who has failed to explain the nature of the disease and its treatment to the patient. Very rarely and only under close medical supervision is it possible to stop therapy in treated hypertensives.

Perhaps the biggest single reason for the rule of halves is that the system of primary and secondary health care in most countries is not oriented towards the management of chronic diseases. Usually the doctor's role is rather like a shopkeeper's. The patient describes a symptom and is given the appropriate treatment, frequently as a commercial transaction. The onus is on the patient to present and to seek follow-up. The solution to the rule of halves is to reverse the patient–doctor relationship so that the initiative is in the hands of the doctor to seek out hypertensive patients and supervise the longterm control of their blood pressure.

Solutions

There are remarkably few diseases for which the mass screening of healthy people is justified. The general criteria for well population screening are:

- The disease must be sufficiently common to justify the effort of examining millions of healthy people.
- The disease must be detectable at an early presymptomatic stage.
- The disease must be worth treating at this early stage, contributing to prevention of death or disease.
- The screening technique should be cheap, simple and acceptable to healthy people.
- Screening and follow-up must be

continuous and feasible within the existing health care resources.

By all these criteria, hypertension is a suitable case for some form of screening. It affects up to 20 per cent of the adult population, it is easily detectable and is worth controlling. The main problem is the organization of detection and follow-up programmes. In Chapter 11 we show how this can be managed. This is one of the major contributions that the primary care team can make to the reduction of life-threatening levels of high blood pressure.

PRACTICAL POINTS

- Hypertension is an important risk factor for premature death from cardiovascular disease.

- Existing definitions of hypertension cannot be relied upon for effective detection in a normal practice.

- Outdated ideas and myths about the nature of the disease are responsible for the lack of action in treating hypertension.

- The clinician should aim to reverse the present doctor–patient relationship, concentrating more on prevention through monitoring and early detection.

2
The complications of hypertension

BACKGROUND

Raised blood pressure gives rise to several different forms of damage to arterial walls. The resultant diseases, including heart attack, stroke and intermittent claudication mean that many different clinical specialists must understand the consequences of raised pressure and be aware of the value of blood pressure reduction.

THE VASCULAR LESIONS OF HYPERTENSION (see Figure 2.1)

Most of the vascular lesions in hypertensive patients are related directly to the height of the blood pressure. They may lead to the development of either haemorrhagic or ischaemic tissue damage. At very high pressures the risk is serious and the outcome if no treatment is given is almost invariably fatal. In mild hypertension the arterial damage is less and many patients suffer no complications at all, even though their risk of dying prematurely is increased.

- **Arteriolar necrosis** This is the hallmark of the malignant phase of hypertension. Microvascular necroses are found in the arterioles of the brain, heart, kidneys, retina and many other sites, but not in skeletal muscle or skin.[1]

- **Arteriolar thickening** The basic lesion of hypertension is increased peripheral resistance due to arteriolar vasoconstriction associated with thickening of the vessel wall. As the peripheral resistance is raised and cardiac output remains normal, the blood pressure is elevated.[2]

- **Atheroma** Hypertensive patients are prone to develop atheroma in larger vessels due to lipid-rich deposits in the arterial wall. Cigarette smoking and hyperlipidaemia also increase this rate of deposition. Atheroma causes narrowing of cerebral and coronary arteries as well as of the aorta and leg arteries. In the renal arteries this can cause atheromatous renal artery stenosis.

- **Intravascular thrombosis** There is a tendency for intravascular thrombosis to develop in atheromatous vessels, particularly in the cerebral and coronary arteries. This may lead to complete occlusion of the vessel, with infarction of the tissue supplied by that vessel.

- **Aneurysm** Large vessel aneurysms are commoner in hypertensives, who also have an increased chance of developing aortic dissection.

- **Charcot–Bouchard aneurysms** These are microvascular aneurysms of the intracerebral arteries, and are almost specific to hypertension.[3] When they rupture, they cause intracerebral haemorrhages.

- **Berry aneurysms** Aneurysms of the arteries of the Circle of Willis are common in severe hypertension, particularly if it is associated with polycystic disease of the kidneys.

- **Fibromuscular hyperplasia** This

lesion shows up as an irregular lobulated narrowing of the renal arteries, which can cause raised blood pressure. Its aetiology is unknown.

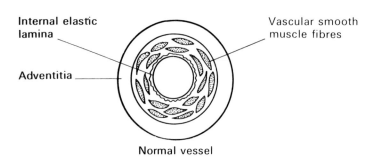

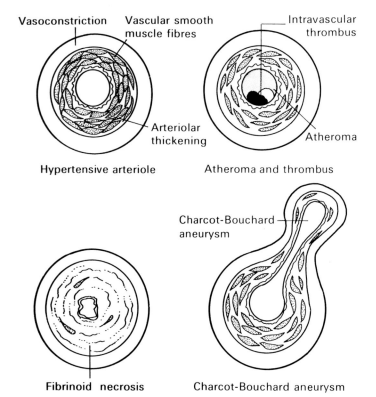

Figure 2.1 The vascular lesions of hypertension.

VASCULAR COMPLICATIONS

The types of arterial damage listed above give rise to a variety of complications in many different systems of the body.

The heart

Myocardial infarction Coronary heart disease is twice as common in hypertensive patients as in the remainder of the population (see Figure 2.2).[4] The risk is closely related to the height of the blood pressure. About 1 per cent of hypertensives suffer a myocardial infarction each year, whereas the figure is only about half this number in people with diastolic pressures below 90 mmHg (see Figure 2.3). A

Figure 2.2 Heart with infarct.

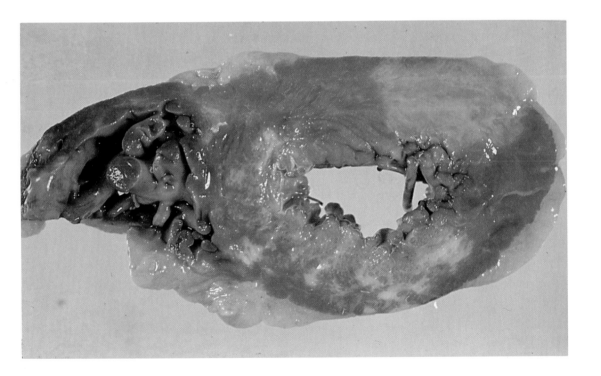

patient with a myocardial infarction who has had previous hypertension has a worse prognosis than a similar patient with no such history. Hypertensive patients who also smoke cigarettes have an even worse prognosis, particularly of sudden death, their risk being about half as much again. Similarly, the risk is increased if there are also raised blood levels of LDL and VLDL cholesterol and lower HDL cholesterol levels.

Angina pectoris Angina is about twice as common in hypertensives as in normotensives. This may partly be due to atheroma of coronary arteries causing ischaemia but may be compounded by the relatively larger left ventricular mass. Lowering the blood pressure with reduction of left ventricular load may relieve angina even if beta-adrenoceptor blockers are not used.

Heart failure Left ventricular failure may occur in a hypertensive patient following a myocardial infarction. It may also develop in severe hypertensives who have gross left ventricular hypertrophy (see Figure 2.4). This form of heart failure should therefore be readily reversible.

The diagnosis of hypertensive heart failure is less common nowadays, and this

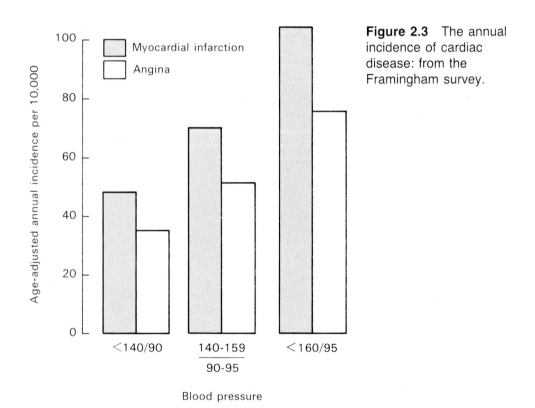

Figure 2.3 The annual incidence of cardiac disease: from the Framingham survey.

may represent a real fall in the incidence owing to more effective control of raised blood pressure. Alternatively the reduction may be due to previous under-diagnosis of painless heart attacks in hypertensive patients. Now with more sophisticated myocardial enzyme measurements, myocardial infarcts are more easily detected.

Left ventricular hypertrophy ECG evidence of left ventricular hypertrophy is closely correlated to the height of the blood pressure. About 50 per cent of patients with moderate hypertension (diastolic pressures between 110 and 120 mmHg) have the ECG criteria for definite hypertrophy. When left ventricular hypertrophy is present the prognosis is bad.[5] A hypertensive patient with hypertrophy has four times the chance of developing a heart attack compared to a patient with a similar blood pressure level but no hypertrophy. Such a patient also has a risk of stroke increased twelvefold, and a threefold higher risk of intermittent claudication. For this reason the routine ECG in a new hypertensive patient is a very powerful predictor of outcome.

Cardiac output In hypertensive patients the cardiac output is normal. It does fall

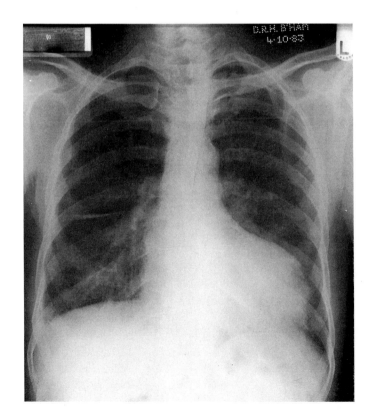

Figure 2.4 Chest x-ray showing left ventricular enlargement and pulmonary oedema with upper lobe diversion indicative of left ventricular failure.

as heart failure develops, or following a myocardial infarction. Elderly hypertensives do, however, have a lower cardiac output than younger patients and they also have a greatly increased peripheral resistance.

Cardiomyopathy It has been suggested that some hypertensive patients tend to develop left ventricular hypertrophy out of keeping with the height of the blood pressure. It is thought that this may be due to a hypertensive cardiomyopathy. Some hypertensive patients with big, poorly contracting hearts, often with atrial fibrillation, are in fact heavy drinkers. High alcohol intake can cause a congestive cardiomyopathy as well as hypertension.

Figure 2.5 Brain showing intra-cerebral haemorrhage.

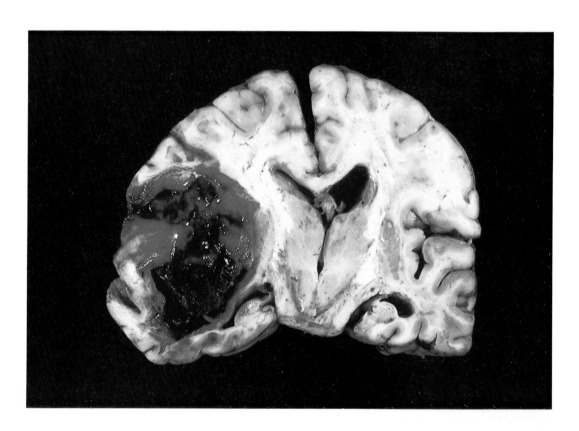

The brain

Subarachnoid haemorrhage About 50 per cent of patients with subarachnoid haemorrhage have pre-existing hypertension,[6] and about 30 per cent do not have berry aneurysms of the Circle of Willis. Cigarette smoking is also associated with subarachnoid haemorrhage. When a vessel ruptures the patient develops acute meningeal irritation with severe headache and usually rapid loss of consciousness. About half all patients die after their first haemorrhage, but this figure may be reduced by surgical clipping of an aneurysm. There is some evidence that beta-blockers reduce the recurrence rate, but rapid reductions of blood pressures may be hazardous.

Cerebral haemorrhage This is a common complication of severe hypertension. It is the most frequent cause of strokes in blacks, but not in whites.

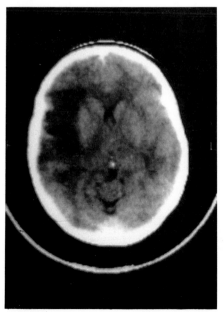

Figure 2.6 CT scan showing cerebral infarct.

Cerebral haemorrhages occur as a result of high pressure in the intracerebral microaneurysms of Charcot and Bouchard (see Figure 2.5).

Cerebral infarcts In white hypertensives with less severe hypertension the most likely cerebral lesion is a cerebral infarct (see Figure 2.6). This is related to cerebral thrombosis associated with atheroma of the intracranial vessels. The overall risk of stroke in a hypertensive man is about half that of developing a heart attack. The incidence is about 2 per cent per year for patients with diastolic blood pressures of around 110 mmHg. In milder hypertension, where diastolic blood pressures are around 100 mmHg, the incidence is 0.5 per cent per year. Of patients under the age of seventy admitted to hospital with a stroke, about half have pre-existing hypertension. There is recent evidence to suggest that high alcohol intake may be an important precipitating factor in young strokes. This may be due to acute rises in blood pressure following heavy drinking or possibly to alcohol-induced cerebral vasoconstriction.

Cerebral embolus Embolization can occur from a left ventricular thrombus in patients with heart attacks or from a left atrial thrombus if there is also atrial fibrillation. Another source of embolus is from carotid artery stenosis. The clinical presentation is either a completed stroke or a transient cerebral ischaemic attack. Both are commoner if the patient is hypertensive.

Cerebral bloodflow The bloodflow to the brain is remarkably constant despite fluctuations in blood pressure. This state of cerebral autoregulation does however break down when pressures are either very low or very high, and also immediately

27

following a stroke. When blood pressure is reduced rapidly by more than about 35 per cent, cerebral bloodflow falls and cerebral ischaemia may develop. Conversely when blood pressures are very high, cerebral bloodflow rises and cerebral oedema may develop, leading to encephalopathy. In hypertensive patients the normal cerebral autoregulation is reset at a slightly higher level, but bloodflow remains constant as long as pressures are not lowered too rapidly.

The syndrome of encephalopathy is very rare but may be seen in association with the malignant phase of hypertension with papilloedema. If a hypertensive patient develops sudden onset of a focal neurological deficit, then it is more likely that the diagnosis is either a cerebral haemorrhage or infarction. In these circumstances rapid reduction of blood pressure is dangerous as it may cause a reduction of bloodflow to the surrounding undamaged brain and worsen the neurological lesion.

Very rarely, focal neurological signs may develop in a very severe hypertensive patient where there is no cerebral infarct or haemorrhage. This syndrome of encephalopathy is very difficult to diagnose unless a CT scan is performed to exclude structural brain damage. Encephalopathy can be considered to be present if there are fluctuating neurological signs with restlessness, confusion and sometimes generalized convulsions. Here rapid reduction in blood pressure is needed as cerebral bloodflow is raised, although blood pressures should not be lowered too rapidly (see Chapter 14).

Lacunae There is now increasing evidence from CT scanning suggesting that some severely hypertensive patients with no focal neurological signs do have small neurological lesions (see Figure 2.7). Clinically these patients have memory impairment and a reduction of cognitive skills. More extreme cases are encountered in which hypertension is associated with general deterioration of cerebral function, dementia, hyperreflexia and a steadily downward clinical progress.

The peripheral vessels

Aneurysm Atheromatous plaques develop in the aorta and the common iliac vessels and these may progress to aortic aneurysm or to aortic dissection.[7] Deaths from ruptured aortic aneurysms are three times as common in hypertensive patients as in normotensives.

Intermittent claudication This is twice as frequent in hypertensive patients as in people with normal blood pressure (see Figure 2.8). The other cardiovascular risk factors, cigarette smoking and hyperlipi-

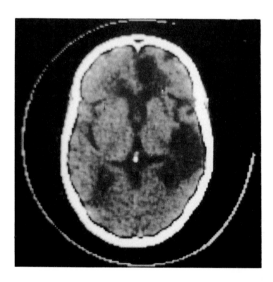

Figure 2.7 CT scan showing multiple cerebral infarcts in a demented patient.

28

daemia, are often present. It should be remembered that beta-adrenoceptor blockers used to control blood pressure may induce or aggravate claudication in patients with peripheral vascular disease.

The kidney

Hypertensive nephrosclerosis Mild symptomless haematuria and proteinuria are common in hypertension, even when it is not associated with the malignant phase or an underlying intrinsic renal disease. Hypertensive patients with blood urea levels of about 10 mmol/l die at twice the rate of those with no renal damage.[8] Uncontrolled hypertension causes progressive renal damage and irreversible renal failure may develop. The overall risk of dying from renal failure in a hypertensive patient is about five times higher than in normal subjects. The otherwise inexorable deterioration can be reduced or delayed if blood pressure is controlled. Frequently some underlying renal disease is present which may have initiated the raised blood pressure and a vicious cycle may follow in which the hypertension causes further renal damage. Hypertension is present in 70 per cent of patients undergoing chronic renal dialysis. Furthermore, hypertension complicates up to 70 per cent of cases with intrinsic renal disease, including glomerulonephritis. Even after bilateral nephrectomy and renal transplantation, hypertension may persist.

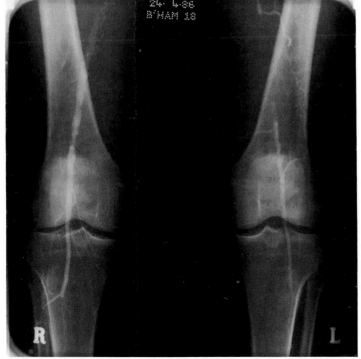

Figure 2.8 Femoral arteriogram showing atheroma.

Arteriolar necrosis In patients with malignant hypertension, arteriolar necrosis leads to a rapid deterioration of renal function. These lesions do heal if the blood pressure is controlled.

Renal artery stenosis Atheromatous renal artery narrowing or occlusion may occur as a consequence of high blood pressure in older patients. Sometimes, however, it is still worth diagnosing and treating as surgical repair of the renal artery may reduce the blood pressure or make it easier to control with drugs. In younger patients renal artery stenosis may be due to fibromuscular hyperplasia, which may be surgically remediable.

MALIGNANT HYPERTENSION

This is a multisystem disorder, characterized by arteriolar fibrinoid necrosis. Death is usually due to progressive renal failure, heart failure or stroke. If left untreated, most cases are dead within two years. While in the malignant phase underlying renal or adrenal causes of hypertension are frequent, still about 65 per cent of cases have essential rather than secondary hypertension. Malignant hypertension is the only form of hypertension which is directly associated with cigarette smoking. The ophthalmological features are retinal haemorrhages, cotton wool spots, hard exudates, particularly forming a macular star, and bilateral papil-

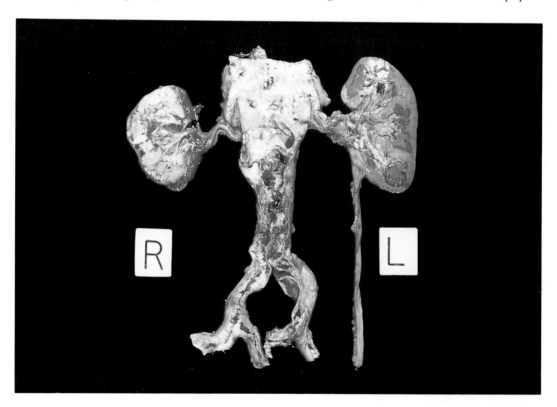

Figure 2.9 Gross atheroma of aorta and iliac vessels with renal artery stenosis.

loedema. Patients who have all the retinal features except papilloedema are sometimes labelled as accelerated hypertensives. The prognosis of those classified as accelerated hypertensives is about the same, so they too should now be regarded as malignant, requiring urgent therapy.

As part of the multisystem disorder, a microangiopathic haemolytic anaemia is common, and this feature is not seen in nonmalignant hypertension. About half of patients with malignant hypertension do not have cardiomegaly even on echocardiography. This implies that such cases are unlikely to have longstanding hypertension, but may instead have a relatively acute onset.

MULTIPLE RISK FACTORS

When the other cardiovascular risk factors, particularly hyperlipidaemia and cigarette smoking, are present the risk of a hypertensive patient developing arterial complications is much greater.[4] The effect of several risk factors combined is more than simply additive; there is a multiplicative or synergistic effect so that the presence of two risk factors is more than twice as bad as the presence of one only. A forty-five year old hypertensive patient who also smokes cigarettes has nearly twice the chance of developing a vascular complication. If he or she also has a high blood cholesterol level the risk is five to six times higher than in a patient with the same blood pressure with low cholesterol levels who does not smoke. It should be added that if this high-risk patient also has ECG evidence of left ventricular hypertrophy, he or she then has a 60 per cent chance of developing a vascular complication in the next eight years.

The implications of these statistics on the interrelation of cardiovascular risk factors are that clinicians should not concern themselves with the height of the blood pressure alone. Where relevant, efforts to control smoking and hypercholesterolaemia are quite as important as antihypertensive therapy.

PRACTICAL POINTS

- The major vascular complications of hypertension are
  —heart attack
  —stroke.

- Malignant hypertension is the only form directly associated with cigarette smoking.

- Accelerated hypertensives, with retinal features, have a prognosis similar to malignant hypertensives.

- Multiple risk factors have a synergistic effect on the chances of developing arterial complications.

- Efforts should also be made to reduce smoking and blood cholesterol levels.

3
The cause of hypertension: epidemiological clues

BACKGROUND

The epidemiologist's view of hypertension differs from that of the clinician. When seen from the point of view of national mortality and morbidity statistics, hypertension and hypertension-related deaths assume enormous proportions. This is due mainly to the large numbers of mildly hypertensive people, rather than to the few with severe or malignant hypertension. It is in this field that the general practitioner has an important role: most practitioners have few severe hypertensives on their list, but a great many mild cases who need detection, follow-up and counselling.

When investigating blood pressure in the general population, the epidemiologist is concerned with levels well below those where antihypertensive drug therapy is usually considered necessary. In theory at least, a downward shift of the average blood pressure of the population by no more than 5 mmHg could prevent more heart attacks and strokes than any new wonder drug given to severe hypertensives.

Epidemiological evidence also provides clues to the aetiology of raised blood pressure which are relevant to clinical practice. Large population surveys with follow-up are able to identify cardiovascular risk factors and their interrelations. The object of this chapter is to discuss the information available.

BLOOD PRESSURE AND AGE
Western countries

In Western countries older people tend to have higher blood pressures than young

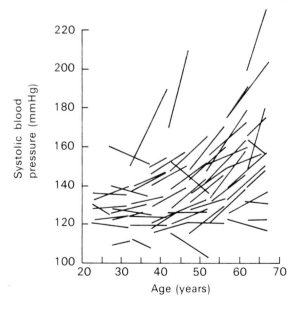

Figure 3.1 Changes in blood pressure in the population of Rhondda, South Wales, initially and on rescreening a decade later.[2]

people.[1] Follow-up studies have demonstrated two important trends. First, blood pressures rise with advancing age, and second, those individuals whose blood pressures start at a higher level tend to retain their place in the distribution and their blood pressures tend to rise faster (see Figure 3.1).[2]

This phenomenon of tracking is seen in all age groups, including infants. It implies that whatever environmental factors influence blood pressure, they start to exert their effect in early life. This is not to deny that genetic factors have a role, but they may represent an increased genetic susceptibility to environmental influences rather than a cause of raised blood pressure. The clear demonstration in population studies of a faster rise in people with higher pressures also suggests that there may be a vicious cycle effect, by which those individuals with higher pressures in early life tend to sustain minimal arterial damage, which causes a further rise, particularly in systolic blood pressure, and this then causes more vascular damage and further elevation of pressure.

Extreme old age

A slightly different picture emerges of blood pressure in extreme old age. Cross-sectional studies have shown that the average diastolic blood pressure of people over about seventy is lower than people below this age. Longitudinal population studies have also shown that some people do genuinely sustain a fall in diastolic pressure when they become very old. This may not necessarily be physiological but may be due to clinical or subclinical cardiac damage leading to a reduction in cardiac output. Other diseases may also be present and may contribute to a lowering of the blood pressure in association with weight loss and general ill

health. A further factor is that people with raised blood pressure may have died off, leaving only survivors with lower pressures. Against this hypothesis is the fact that while diastolic pressures are lower in elderly people, raised systolic pressures become increasingly frequent with advancing age, so that isolated systolic hypertension is a common problem in the elderly.

Primitive societies

Whatever the mechanisms are that produce a rise in blood pressure with age, there is no reason to suppose that they are physiological. Studies of non-Westernized rural populations have shown that hypertension is unknown in these groups, and blood pressures show only a tiny rise with age. By contrast, genetically identical people and even relatives living in urban communities do have a marked rise in pressure with age. The effect of age on the blood pressure of these people must therefore be due mainly to environmental factors. The possible influences are differences in the diet and other socio-economic factors including environmental stress.

BLOOD PRESSURE AND GENETICS

Family history

High blood pressure tends to run in families, so that the normotensive blood relatives of hypertensive patients have a greater chance of developing raised blood pressure themselves (see Figure 3.2).[3] While the familial concordance of blood pressure may be due in part to shared exposure to environmental influences, for instance, diet or stress, there remains a large genetic component. It has been suggested that as much as 50 per cent of the variation of blood pressure within a population may be due to genetic factors.

Genetic susceptibility

The genetic component of high blood pressure may not itself necessarily cause hypertension as it is probably only a genetic predisposition to develop raised pressure in response to various environmental factors. It has been suggested that normotensives with positive family histories of hypertension may be more susceptible to the pressor effects of high salt intake, environmental noise, isometric exercise, mental arithmetic and even high alcohol intake.

Many studies of normotensives with or without a family history of hypertension are confounded by the unreliability of data on their parents' blood pressures. Also normotensives with a positive family history tend to have higher blood pressures than age-matched normotensives with no family history. It is possible that the cause of raised blood pressure may be found by investigating children in order to identify the initiators of later clinical hypertension in those with and without family histories.

RACE AND BLOOD PRESSURE

Most studies of blood pressure in black and white people in the USA have reported higher average blood pressure in blacks, with a higher prevalence of hypertension. By contrast, rural blacks in Africa have low blood pressures although hypertension is common in black people living in African cities (see Figure 3.3).[4] Some studies in the UK have not shown such clear-cut differences in blood pressure between blacks and whites. The higher blood pressure in some black people probably reveals a genuine genetic effect, producing a tendency to develop hypertension in response to various environmental factors, including high salt, low potassium diets, increased environmental stress and, especially in women, a higher prevalence of obesity. It has been claimed that hypertension is somehow different in blacks. This difference may be less apparent after correction for socio-economic and dietary factors. In both Britain and America, blacks are more likely to be unemployed, poor or stressed, and they

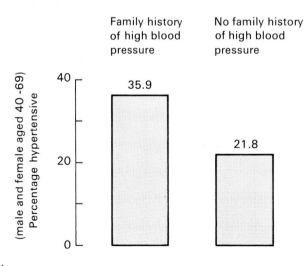

Family history of high blood pressure

No family history of high blood pressure

(male and female aged 40 -69)
Percentage hypertensive

40 — 35.9

20 — 21.8

0

Figure 3.2 The percentage frequence of hypertension in people with and without a family history of the condition.[3]

may also receive inferior medical care. Nevertheless, as discussed in Chapters 11 and 12, there are differences in response to antihypertensive drugs and the lower plasma renin levels in blacks remain unexplained.

Cardiovascular disease

Although hypertension may be commoner in black people, they do, in general have less heart disease than whites, but conversely they suffer more strokes (see Figure 3.4). The total mortality is there-

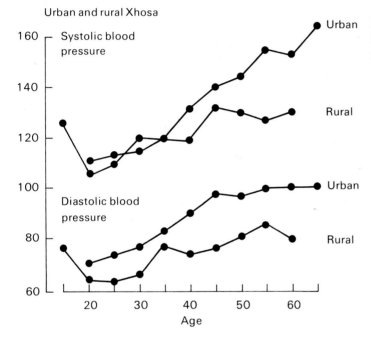

Figure 3.3 Blood pressure in relation to age in rural and urban South African blacks.[4]

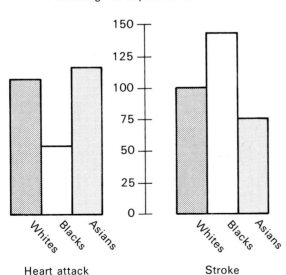

Figure 3.4 Admissions for heart attack and stroke in blacks, whites and Asians in Birmingham.[5]

35

fore much the same as for whites.[5] It is probably incorrect to believe that for a given level of blood pressure, blacks have a greater risk of death than whites.

Black people have lower serum total cholesterol and higher HDL cholesterol than whites, and this may explain their apparent relative protection from heart attacks. However, some population studies have led to the conclusion that the differences in coronary heart disease between blacks and whites cannot be explained by differences in the three known coronary risk factors, hypertension, cigarette smoking and hyperlipidaemia.

Other ethnic groups
There are few reliable studies of other ethnic minority groups in Western countries. It has been shown that hypertension is common in both Indian and Pakistani migrants to the UK. The prevalence is quite as high as in whites. This is interesting because many of the middle-aged immigrants from the Indian subcontinent arrived in Britain when they were aged about twenty, having come from rural areas of the Punjab and Pakistan.[6]

There is more information on the blood pressures of Japanese migrants to America compared with genetically identical groups remaining in Japan. Blood pressures are lower in the USA, but serum cholesterol levels are higher. Thus Japanese Americans have more heart attacks than Japanese in Japan, but they suffer fewer strokes.

DIFFERENCES IN BLOOD PRESSURE BETWEEN MEN AND WOMEN

Before the menopause
Below the age of about forty, women tend to have slightly lower blood pressures than men. This difference in early life may be due to the endocrinological events associated with the child-bearing years. Besides blood pressure being lower in younger women, so too is the cardiovascular risk for a given level of pressure. However, the gradient between blood pressure and risk holds true for women as much as for men, and it is wrong to believe therefore that high blood pressure is somehow less important in women.

Effect of childbirth
There is a weak tendency for women who have had pre-eclampsia in pregnancy to develop higher blood pressure in later life. The condition pre-eclampsia is most common in first pregnancies, and there is only a slight tendency for women who have had pre-eclampsia to develop it again in subsequent pregnancies. There is no evidence that women who have more than one child have higher blood pressures, and indeed the reverse may be so (see Chapter 16).

After the menopause
After the age of about fifty there are no consistent differences in the average blood pressures of men and women, although the risk for a given level of blood pressure is still lower in women than in men.

SOCIOLOGICAL AND DIETARY FACTORS

Weight
Fat people have higher blood pressures than thin people (see Figure 3.5). There is, however, an important confounding factor to be taken into account, namely the greater error when measuring blood pressure in obese arms. There is a tendency to over-read blood pressure in fat arms, and the fatter the arm the greater the error (see Chapter 6).

Even after correction for arm circumference, there remains a weak positive

36

relationship between body mass index and both systolic and diastolic blood pressures.[7] Recent statistical analyses have suggested that body mass index exerts its effects mainly on diastolic pressure, with little independent effect on systolic pressure, which is mainly related to age. There remains some doubt as to whether the blood pressure/body mass index relationship is due to adipose tissue only or whether it is partly explained by a contribution from high lean body mass. The relationship is further complicated because some obese people may eat more sodium, less potassium, more animal fats and more calories than thin people.

Obesity and risk of death Since obesity is associated with high blood lipid levels and a tendency to hyperglycaemia as well as with high blood pressure, it is possible after allowing for these factors that obesity may not itself be an independent cardiovascular risk factor. This is only a theoretical consideration as obese people do have many of these abnormalities, and a high cardiac risk. When people lose weight, their blood pressures tend to fall.

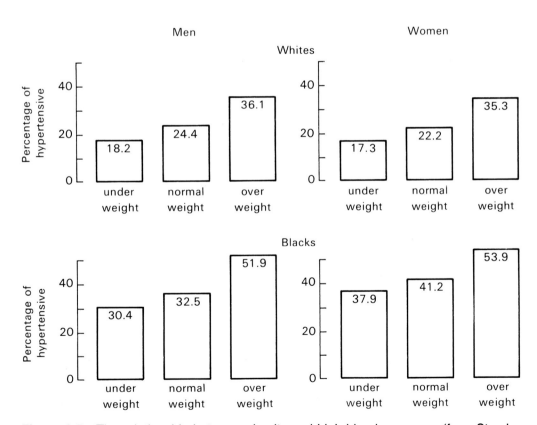

Figure 3.5 The relationship between obesity and high blood pressures (from Stamler, *JAMA 240*, 1978, 1667–70).

Salt

The first suggestion that a high salt intake gives rise to high blood pressure goes back four thousand years to the ancient Chinese Yellow Emperor, Huang Ti. He suggested that people who ate too much salt developed harder pulses. More recent epidemiological evidence is impressive, although the evidence by its very nature still remains circumstantial.

Primitive rural societies in Africa and the islands of the South Pacific consume very little salt (below 50 mmol per day) and they have hardly any hypertension, and no rise in blood pressure with age.[4] Conversely, northern European, American and Japanese populations who consume a lot of salt (200 to 300 mmol per day) have high average blood pressures (see Figure 3.6). In northern Japan, where the salt consumption averages 400 mmol per day, there is a close relationship between stroke incidence and salt intake.[8]

Unfortunately no international collaborative study has yet been completed in which directly comparable data have been obtained from different populations. Many of the early studies of primitive non-salt-eating populations were poorly conducted and do not bear close examination. There are, besides, other confounding differences between urban Westernized populations and primitive groups. The primitive populations have other common causes of death, mainly from infections and infestations, and in general they are thinner and have lower blood lipid levels.

There is some evidence that over the last fifty years dietary salt consumption has progressively fallen, and this has been paralleled by a fall in stroke incidence both in Europe and the USA.

While international comparisons and longterm follow-up data usually support the salt story, many national com-

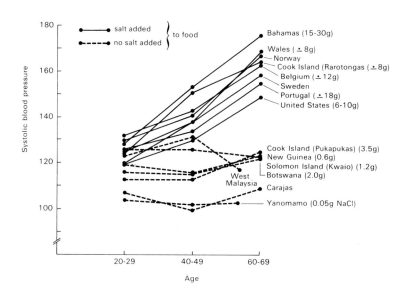

Figure 3.6 Comparative international data on salt intake and high blood pressure levels at varying ages (from J. V. Joossens, London: RSM International Congress & Symposium Series, 1980).

munity studies do not. When single populations are studied, only rarely are hypertensives reported to consume or excrete more salt than normotensives. This does not necessarily invalidate the salt hypothesis as it can be argued that these whole populations are salt loaded and have a high prevalence of hypertension. There is also strong reason to believe that it is not salt intake alone but a genetic tendency to retain sodium that causes hypertension to develop in susceptible people.

One of the difficulties with epidemiological evidence in this context is that dietary studies are hard to undertake, and often inaccurate. Salt questionnaires are difficult to standardize, and detailed studies by dietitians are few. Urinary sodium excretion shows marked variations from day to day and between individuals.

Potassium

The role of potassium in lowering blood pressure has received little attention until recently. International comparisons of blood pressure have shown, in addition to differences in salt intake, important differences in potassium intake. Hypertension tends to be associated with a low potassium intake as much as with a high salt intake. These factors cannot easily be considered separately, and in assessing their effect it is probably best to examine dietary or urinary sodium/potassium ratios. It is interesting to note that in the USA, where hypertension is commoner in blacks than whites, there are virtually no differences in urinary sodium excretion between these two groups but a marked difference in potassium excretion, blacks consuming and excreting lower quantities of potassium. It has been suggested that the potassium and blood pressure story may be partly due to social and economic

factors, as potassium-rich foods tend to be expensive.[9]

The international epidemiological data on blood pressure in relation to sodium and potassium intake is very unsatisfactory. To overcome many of the possible confounding variables, including obesity, social class and alcohol intake as well as local environmental factors such as ambient temperature, an international collaborative study of sodium and potassium intake as assessed by twenty-four-hour urinary excretion (Intersalt) is currently being mounted. The methods of measuring blood pressure are carefully standardized and it is hoped that many of the controversies about blood pressure and electrolytes will soon be resolved.

Alcohol

Many epidemiological studies have shown a direct relationship between alcohol consumption and blood pressure.[10] There is also mounting evidence for a close correlation between high alcohol intake and stroke mortality and morbidity in both community and clinical studies (see also Chapter 10).

There is a trend for the lowest blood pressures to be recorded in those who consume small amounts of alcohol. Strangely, teetotallers seem to have slightly higher blood pressures than moderate drinkers (see Figure 3.7). This may be because they are less healthy, having given up drinking for medical reasons. Alternatively, teetotallers may genuinely have slightly higher blood pressures, implying that small amounts of alcohol lower blood pressure but large amounts do not.

In heavy drinkers, hypertension is common, and the more they drink the higher are their pressures (see Figure 3.8).[11] Hypertensive patients have a higher frequency of raised liver enzyme levels (gamma glutamyl transferase and aspartate aminotransferase) and higher mean erythrocyte cell volumes (MCV), and they drink more than normotensives. It has been estimated that about 10 per cent of hypertensives have alcohol-induced hypertension. If this is so, then alcohol is the most frequent underlying cause for hypertension, being at least five times commoner than all other known causes.

Coffee

There is no consistent epidemiological data to link hypertension with high intakes of caffeine taken in tea or coffee.

Animal fats

With the exception of the north Japanese most populations with high blood pressures also consume large quantities of animal fat and dairy produce. It is not known whether this contributes to the blood pressure levels or whether the concomitant high salt intake is responsible. It has been shown that feeding a high-cholesterol diet to rats causes hypertension. In humans there is some evidence that a reduction in animal fat intake without any change in dietary salt causes a fall in blood pressure.[12] Vegetarian diets may therefore be antihypertensive. As with all dietary manipulations, it is difficult to be certain which mechanism is responsible for the change in pressure. There is some evidence that a high-fibre diet which has a high vegetable content may also be protective against hypertension, but again

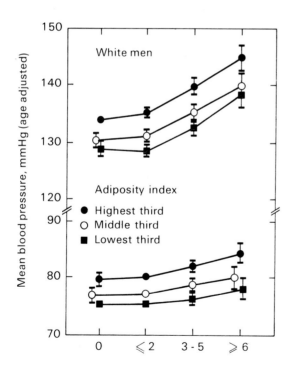
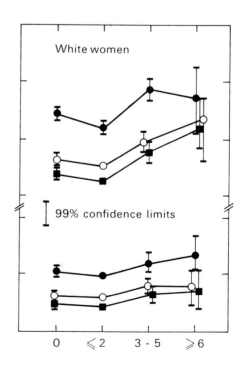

Figure 3.7 Blood pressure in relation to usual alcohol intake in the Kaiser Permanente Heart Program of 87,000 people.[10]

concomitant changes in sodium and potassium intake may be partly responsible.

Calcium

Populations consuming higher quantities of calcium, either in drinking water or in dairy produce, tend to have lower blood pressures. However, by contrast many studies also report a positive correlation between blood pressure and serum total calcium levels.[13] Reports of negative correlations between serum ionized calcium and blood pressure may be accounted for by problems with laboratory methods. This whole field is highly controversial.

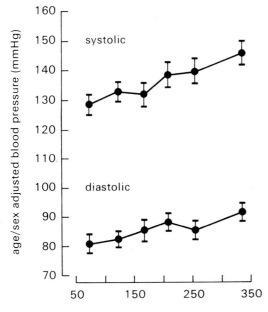

Figure 3.8 Relationship of systolic and diastolic blood pressure to mean daily alcohol intake for three months preceding admission in 136 alcoholic patients.

Smoking

After one or two cigarettes have been smoked, blood pressure may rise sharply. Despite this acute effect, epidemiological studies show no relationship or even a negative correlation between blood pressure and cigarette smoking. Non-smokers may have slightly higher blood pressures than smokers and people who stop smoking sometimes sustain a slight rise in pressure.[14] These differences may be due to changes in weight; heavy smokers are thinner, iller and more breathless, and when they stop smoking, they eat more and gain weight. Although smoking is not related closely to blood pressure, it is of course a potent independent risk factor for cardiac death. Furthermore, hypertensives who are also smokers have more than twice the risk of dying prematurely.

There is one rare but interesting exception to the rule that cigarette smoking and blood pressure are negatively associated. Malignant hypertension is closely related to cigarette smoking.[15]

Stress

Hypertension being a disease of Westernized and particularly of urban societies (although large urban/rural differences are not seen much in Europe and the USA), it is tempting to attribute high blood pressure to the stress of modern living. Certainly, acutely stressful stimuli raise blood pressure and may be more pressor in subjects who have familial hypertension. However, there must remain considerable doubt as to whether chronic stress raises blood pressure.

The investigation of environmental stress and high blood pressure is confounded by the other social factors including poverty, dietary fats, calories and electrolytes, alcohol intake and cigarette smoking.

Studies of various psychosocial indices including aggression, neuroticism and introversion have produced conflicting results. Many reliable studies have found no effect.[16] In individuals there is some evidence of the relationship between stress and hypertension. The Type A/Type B classification of personality has in general demonstrated — again with exceptions — that Type A (stressed) people have higher blood pressure and a higher relative risk of death than Type B people. But hypertensives may develop higher stress levels once they have been diagnosed and made to worry about their health. The term hypertensive personality is misleading and may only be an accurate description of people who are being called frequently to the blood pressure clinic and so are worried about their blood pressure.

Exercise

Dynamic exercise raises blood pressure and isometric exercise raises it a lot. Despite this, people who take exercise are healthier and may have lower blood pressures than those who take none. This may be because they are thinner and tend to have more sensible dietary, drinking and smoking habits.[17]

After exercise blood pressure falls, and people who take regular exercise may therefore have lower pressures for longer periods of the day.

Trace metals

Both cadmium and lead, which are environmental pollutants, have been claimed as causes of hypertension. The data in favour of these hypotheses are poor, and it is probable that other variables including cigarette smoking and alcohol intake explain the apparent relationship. After correction for these, there is no conclusive evidence that these elements are related to high blood pressure. However, a recent major American study has reported a close independent correlation between blood lead and blood pressure,[18] although the British Regional Heart study found no such effect.[19] The topic is controversial.

PRACTICAL POINTS

- Epidemiological studies of blood pressures in populations suggest that hypertension is strongly genetically inherited.

- There are major environmental influences: the role of salt, stress, alcohol, obesity, smoking and other factors have all received much attention.

- Environmental factors may be reversible and it would be hoped that the blood pressure could be reduced in whole populations and not just individual patients.

4
The cause of hypertension: clinical and biochemical clues

BACKGROUND
Studies in the community and also in general practice have shown that less than one patient in fifty with high blood pressure has an identifiable underlying cause. Even in hospital practice less than 10 per cent of cases have renal or adrenal causes for their hypertension. Hence for the vast majority of people with raised blood pressure we do not know the cause. Rather than call this 'hypertension of unknown cause' it is usually labelled 'primary hypertension', or more commonly 'essential hypertension'. This chapter discusses the mechanisms that are known to control blood pressure in normal people and those factors that may raise it, both in patients with essential hypertension and in the small minority of patients with an underlying disease. A great deal of research has been centred on the mechanisms of essential hypertension. If we could understand these, we might be able to prevent hypertension developing, rather than having to treat the condition at a relatively late stage.

THE MECHANISMS FOR MAINTAINING NORMAL BLOOD PRESSURE
In mechanical and haemodynamic terms, the height of the blood pressure is determined by the amount of blood that is pumped out by the heart and by resistance to flow in the peripheral arterial tree.

Surprisingly, the major resistance to flow is not in the large arteries or in the capillaries, but in the small arterioles of the vascular system. These arterioles are highly contractile and are at all times constricted to some degree; the amount of constriction determines the height of the blood pressure. Variations of the degree of constriction from one area to another also regulate regional bloodflow. There are many complex feedback systems governing both the degree of resistance and the cardiac output. For example, during exercise there is an increase in cardiac output but a large reduction in peripheral vascular resistance in the arterioles supplying the voluntary muscles. Blood pressure tends therefore to remain relatively constant. There is a small rise in systolic blood pressure but this is accompanied by a small fall in diastolic pressure. Clearly the balance is very finely tuned, although we do not fully understand all of the mechanisms.

Cardiac output
In patients with established essential hypertension cardiac output is normal, and their elevated blood pressure is due to a raised peripheral resistance (see Figure 4.1).[1] In very severe hypertension, when the heart is under strain, cardiac output falls and this leads to the clinical features of left ventricular failure.

43

It has been suggested that in the early phases of the development of essential hypertension, cardiac output is raised and peripheral resistance is normal. As blood pressure rises over the ensuing years, peripheral resistance gradually rises but cardiac output returns to normal.[2] This early transient elevation of cardiac output has been attributed to increased sympathetic drive or increased circulating blood volume. However, almost all hypertensive patients seen in clinical practice have normal cardiac output; and it is the peripheral resistance which is raised.

Peripheral resistance

The walls of the small arterioles contain smooth muscle cells which respond both to hormonal influences and to neural input through the autonomic nervous sytem. The degree of contraction of smooth muscle cells is thought to be determined by their intracellular free calcium content. Calcium is normally found in low concentrations in these cells compared with plasma, so in order to maintain this gradient there are several different calcium pumps on the cell membrane which extrude calcium. It is now thought that in patients with high blood pressure the free intracellular ionized calcium content of smooth muscle cells is increased. This has yet to be shown directly, but perhaps can be indirectly inferred by the use of calcium-entry antagonists such as nifedipine, diltiazem and verapamil, which block the inflow of calcium to the cell, reduce smooth muscle calcium concentration and lower blood pressure.

There is evidence that the prolonged arteriolar vasoconstriction and increased pressure lead to the development of structural changes within these vessels. The vessel walls become thicker, so that the lumen is further reduced and this leads to a further increase in blood pressure.[3]

The autonomic nervous system

The autonomic nervous system, particularly on the sympathetic side, can cause both constriction and dilatation of arteriolar smooth muscle. Surprisingly, the

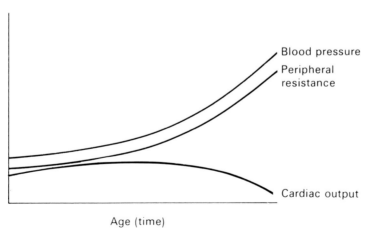

Figure 4.1 Schematic representation of blood pressure rise with age.

Blood pressure

Peripheral resistance

Cardiac output

Age (time)

circulating amounts of noradrenaline (norepinephrine) and adrenaline (epinephrine) under physiological conditions play only a small role in determining the degree of contraction of arterioles. Most circulating noradrenaline is derived from spillover from peripheral sympathetic ganglia or nerve endings where it is a neurotransmitter, and relatively little is derived from secretion by the adrenal gland. Drugs which block the sympathetic system, including the alpha- and beta-receptor blockers, lower blood pressure. The autonomic nervous system does have an important role in maintaining normal blood pressure in both hypertensive and normotensive individuals. However, a major problem in investigating the role of the autonomic system has been the difficulty of finding an accurate measure of its activity. Assays of plasma noradrenaline or adrenaline are technically difficult and, more importantly, reflect sympathetic activity rather poorly.

It has been suggested that, at least in part, overactivity of the sympathetic nervous system may be the cause of hypertension. Early papers appeared to show a relationship between plasma noradrenaline levels and blood pressure, but these did not take into account the rise in plasma noradrenaline levels with age.[4] More recently it has been suggested that circulating adrenaline levels may be impli-

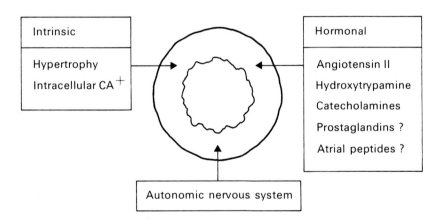

Figure 4.2   Factors influencing the degree of constriction of aterioles.

cated in the maintenance of raised blood pressure, but again the evidence is conflicting. While there is little evidence that increased sympathetic activity causes hypertension, the sympathetic nervous system has an important role in short-term variations of blood pressure in response to stress, exercise and changes in posture.

The renin–angiotensin–aldosterone system
The renin–angiotensin–aldosterone system, like the sympathetic nervous system, is an important mechanism which maintains normal blood pressure and both are closely integrated (see Figure 4.3). The activity of the renin system can be more easily measured than that of the sympathetic system. There are several types of drugs that block the effects of renin and reduce blood pressure, but it is now clear that essential hypertension is not caused by an abnormality of renin release.

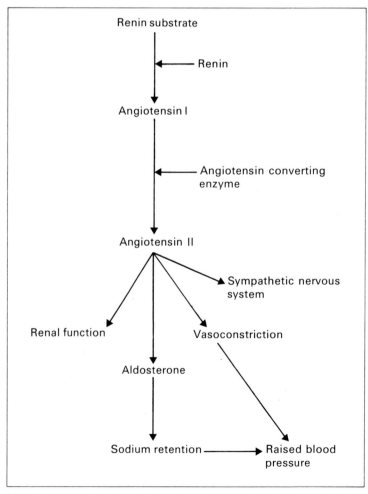

Figure 4.3 The renin-angiotensin system.

Renin is an enzyme secreted by the juxta-glomerular cells of the renal cortex. Its action is to cleave off the decapeptide angiotensin I from a large circulating protein (renin substrate or angiotensin-ogen) which is produced by the liver. Angiotensin I has no physiological action but is immediately converted in the pulmonary circulation and in other tissues to the potent pressor octapeptide angiotensin II. The enzyme responsible for the conversion of angiotensin I to angiotensin II is the angiotensin-converting enzyme (ACE); it is now possible to block this enzyme with ACE inhibitors like captopril and enalapril, with a consequent reduction in blood pressure (see Figure 4.4; also Chapter 12). Angiotensin II is the most potent vasoconstrictor known, causing contraction both of small arterioles and of veins. It can also stimulate the sympathetic nervous system by a direct effect on the brain and also indirectly by increasing peripheral neurotransmission.

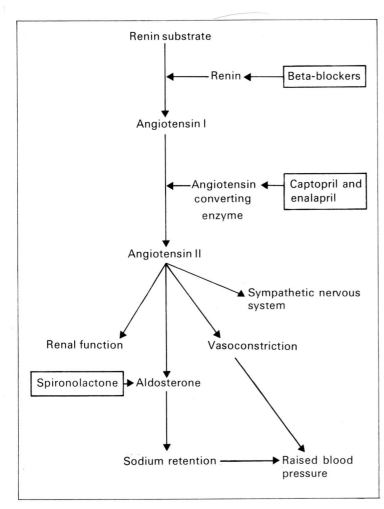

Figure 4.4 The renin-angiotensin system showing the site of action of drugs which block its effects

Angiotensin II is also an important stimulus for the secretion of aldosterone. Both aldosterone and angiotensin II are important in the regulation of sodium and water balance as well as peripheral arteriolar tone.

The activity of the renin angiotensin system is closely related to concurrent dietary salt intake. As more salt is consumed, the amount of circulating renin and angiotensin II decreases. If salt intake is reduced there is a large rise in renin and angiotensin II levels and a greater dependency by the blood pressure on the renin angiotensin system.[5] Other stimuli for the release of renin are the sympathetic nervous system and the baroreceptors within the renal arterioles, which directly respond to a fall in pressure by increasing renin release.

In many patients with essential hypertension, circulating levels of renin and angiotensin II are lower than in normotensive individuals of the same age. These people have been labelled as having low-renin hypertension.[6] The mechanism of this reduction in renin release is not clear.

Patients with low levels of renin do respond differently to some antihypertensive drugs. They have a small fall in blood pressure in response to ACE inhibitors and beta-blockers but a larger fall with salt restriction or the use of diuretics.

Aldosterone is a potent sodium-retaining mineralocorticoid hormone secreted by the zona glomerulosa of the adrenal cortex. It works directly on the distal renal tubules, increasing the exchange of sodium for potassium, thereby causing sodium retention at the expense of potassium loss (see Figure 4.5). It was once thought that abnormalities of aldosterone secretion might be important in essential hypertension, but recent evidence is against this concept.

Other hormones which may regulate blood pressure

Vasopressin (anti-diuretic hormone) is secreted by the posterior pituitary gland and is important in the control of water balance. Despite its name it probably has

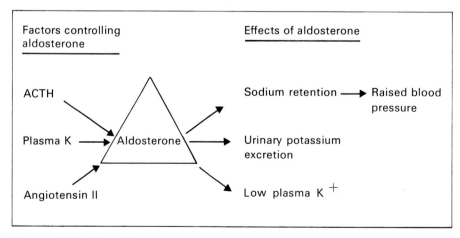

Figure 4.5 The aldosterone system.

48

little to do with blood pressure control in normal concentrations. When given in large amounts by intravenous infusion it is a direct vasoconstrictor but the quantities needed are much higher than those seen in physiological circumstances. It may, however, with angiotensin II, help maintain normal blood pressure in the presence of volume depletion. Patients with very high circulating levels of arginine vasopressin who have the syndrome of inappropriate anti-diuretic hormone excess (SIADH), usually associated with carcinoma of bronchus or myxoedema, do not have hypertension.

Cortisol In the syndrome of cortisol excess (Cushing's disease), blood pressure may be high. It is possible that a high concentration of cortisol has some mineralocorticoid effect. In addition, high cortisol levels cause a rise in circulating levels of plasma renin substrate and angiotensin II and also increase the sensitivity to circulating catecholamines. Each of these mechanisms could cause a rise in blood pressure. In adrenal failure (Addison's disease) both cortisol and aldosterone levels are low and patients often present with gross sodium and water depletion with low blood pressure and postural hypotension.

The prostaglandins are local tissue hormones that may be important in determining local arteriolar tone. When given

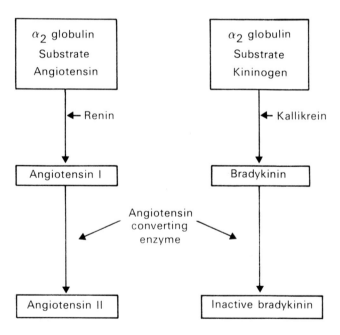

Figure 4.6 The renin-angiotensin and kallikrein systems.

by intravenous infusion some prostaglandins cause vasoconstriction and others cause vasodilatation. There is no evidence to suggest that there is any abnormality of prostaglandin metabolism in patients with high blood pressure. However, when indomethacin, an inhibitor of prostaglandin production, is given, some blood pressure lowering drugs, particularly the diuretics, become less effective.

The kallikrein–kinin system This is a cascade system which produces bradykinin, a local tissue vasodilator that could possibly lower blood pressure. Bradykinin is partly degraded by the same converting enzyme (ACE) which is responsible for the generation of angiotensin II (see Figure 4.6): thus ACE inhibitors such as captopril and enalapril could work both by reducing plasma angiotensin II production and by increasing bradykinin levels, although it is probably that the fall in plasma angiotensin II is more important.

ACTH This hormone controls circulating cortisol levels and to a lesser extent aldosterone. In patients with pituitary Cushing's disease, both cortisol and aldosterone are raised.

Other systems that are important in regulating blood pressure

Baroreceptor reflexes The baroreceptors in the carotid sinus and the aortic arch are sensitive buffers, smoothing out variations in heart rate, blood pressure and cardiac output. In patients with high blood pressure there is some resetting of these baroreceptors so that higher pressures are needed to activate the baroreceptor reflex. There is no evidence that abnormal baroreceptor tone is responsible for hypertension, and the abnormalities reported to date are more likely to be a consequence of chronically raised blood pressure.

Central nervous system It has been suggested that various neurotransmitters, including endorphins, are related to the development of high blood pressure. There have been no clinical findings as yet from which a direct cause and effect can be inferred.

Sodium transport

Despite our knowledge of the various mechanisms that maintain normal blood

---

1 Raised sodium concentration in red and white blood cells.
2 Diminished Ouabain sensitive Na^+ transport in white cells.
3 Increased Na^+—Li^+ counter transport—? genetic defect.
4 Increased plasma level of sodium transport inhibitor (structure not identified).
5 Increased plasma levels of atrial natriuretic peptides (ANP).

Table 4.1 Some abnormalities of sodium metabolism found in essential hypertension.

pressure, we know very little about the cause of essential hypertension, but various abnormalities are now emerging, particularly relating to sodium metabolism.

Intracellular sodium There is now general agreement that the intracellular sodium content of red and white cells is raised in many patients with essential hypertension (see Table 4.1). Furthermore, a similar abnormality is seen in a proportion of normotensive relatives of patients with essential hypertension. The reasons for this elevation are not known, and are the subject of controversy. However, it is possible that we are nearer now to understanding some of the mechanisms that may raise blood pressure in essential hypertension.[7]

Intracellular calcium It has been suggested that raised intracellular sodium can facilitate a rise in intracellular calcium (see Figure 4.7).[8] This in turn could cause increased excitability of smooth muscle

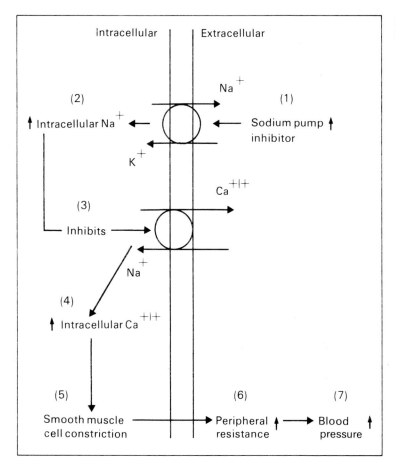

Figure 4.7 Blaustein's hypothesis.

cells, which would lead to constriction of peripheral arteriolar smooth muscle. The calcium content of smooth muscle cells is difficult to measure, and this hypothesis has yet to be fully tested.

The sodium pumps There are at least three pumps that regulate sodium transport across cell membranes. These are the sodium–sodium countertransport pump, the sodium–potassium cotransport pump, and the ouabain-sensitive sodium–potassium ATPase pump. This last pump is the most important. There is now evidence that this pump may be inhibited in many patients with essential hypertension and in some normotensive relatives of hypertensive patients.[7]

The kidney

In the early 1960s it was suggested that in essential hypertension there might be a primary abnormality of the kidney causing sodium and water retention.[9] This could give rise to an increasing amount of fluid in the extracellular space and an increase in plasma volume that would cause a rise in cardiac output. Subsequently, peripheral vascular resistance would increase by autoregulatory mechanisms and so blood pressure would rise. At this stage cardiac output would be expected to return to normal as the raised blood pressure itself would cause the kidney to excrete more sodium. The high blood pressure could then cause further structural thickening of the small arterioles, giving rise to further vasoconstriction and to a vicious cycle in the development of hypertension. This theory, while implicating the kidney as the cause of essential hypertension, has the disadvantage that no one has been able to demonstrate any evidence of plasma or extracellular fluid expansion in the early phase of hypertension.

52

However, the idea that the kidney may have an important role in the development of essential hypertension has been confirmed by elegant kidney cross-transplantation experiments in rats with genetically determined hypertension. If the kidney from the genetically bred hypertensive rat is transplanted into a hypertension-resistant rat, the animal develops raised blood pressure. In the reverse experiment, when the kidney from a rat that should remain normotensive is put into a rat that is genetically hypertensive, the animal fails to develop hypertension. This inherited renal abnormality of the different strains of rats may be related to a difficulty in excreting sodium.[7]

Human renal transplant recipients who receive a kidney from a donor with a family history of hypertension have been shown to have higher blood pressures. Patients who develop renal failure secondary to essential hypertension have normal blood pressures after renal transplantation. These two findings also support the concept that the kidney may carry the underlying abnormality that causes essential hypertension in man.[7]

The natriuretic hormone If the kidney is responsible for the development of high blood pressure in essential hypertension it is possible that the abnormality in the kidney is related to a difficulty in excreting sodium. In other words, subjects who are going to develop essential hypertension inherit a kidney that is less able to excrete sodium compared to subjects who do not develop high blood pressure. On a high salt diet, if there is a difficulty in getting rid of sodium there would be a greater stimulation of the mechanisms designed to unload this extra sodium and water. While the mechanisms for excreting sodium and water are not fully clarified, there is an increase in circulating levels of the recently described atrial natriuretic peptides from the heart and also of inhibitors of the sodium pump, probably from the hypothalamus.

These mechanisms could be largely successful in removing the extra sodium and water but the sodium transport inhibitor could also inhibit sodium transport in other cells, accounting for the abnormalities of the sodium pump that have been described. It might also inhibit sodium transport across the smooth muscle cell of the arteriole. This would cause a rise in intracellular sodium in the arteriolar cells and thereby increase intracellular calcium concentration, which, in turn, could increase their excitability and degree of constriction, leading eventually to the development of high blood pressure (see Figure 4.8).[8]

Much work is currently being done on the measurement both of the atrial peptides and of sodium transport inhibitors in plasma; while there is evidence that there may be a rise in a sodium transport inhibitor in the plasma of hypertensive subjects, the subject remains a matter of considerable debate.

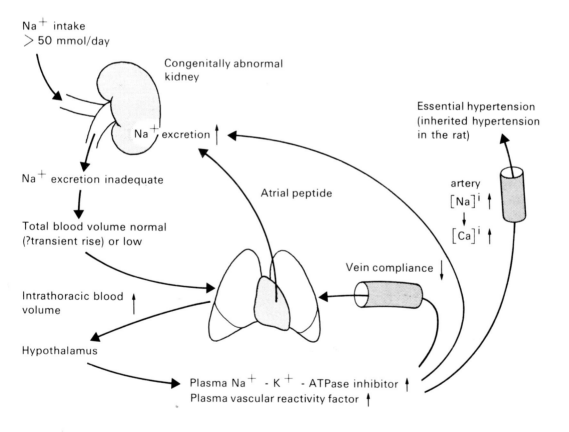

Figure 4.8 Hypothesis for the rise in arterial pressure in inherited hypertension.

The new epidemiological evidence of a link between low potassium intake and high blood pressure can also be linked with the sodium pump. There are several mechanisms whereby potassium might prevent the development of high blood pressure. It has been known for many years that potassium loading causes natriuresis, and this effect may be more marked in people who are receiving a high sodium intake. In addition, low circulating potassium levels might inhibit the sodium pump, and a rise in plasma potassium might cause the pump to be stimulated, thus reducing blood pressure.

If dietary sodium and potassium intake have such an important role in the development of hypertension, then an increased sensitivity to these electrolytes might be seen in people with a strong family history of essential hypertension, who are more likely to develop high blood pressure themselves. This hypothesis requires extensive prospective studies in children and young adults long before they develop hypertension.

SECONDARY HYPERTENSION

The nature and investigation of underlying renal or adrenal diseases that are major causes of secondary hypertension are discussed in detail in Chapter 8. In most, the mechanisms are not yet fully understood. Excess circulating levels of the various hormones described above can, however, cause high blood pressure.

Excess aldosterone (primary hyperaldosteronism) This is due to the autonomous oversecretion of the adrenal mineralocorticoid aldosterone, usually from an adrenal tumour, which causes sodium retention and potassium loss.[10] The reasons for the resulting rise in blood pressure are not known but are likely to be due to sodium retention. In this syndrome plasma levels of renin and angiotensin II are very low. After adrenalectomy or blockade of aldosterone by the specific antagonist spironolactone, blood pressure returns to near normal. Blood pressure is less satisfactorily controlled if there is concurrent renal damage caused by the hypertension.

Excess renin Hypertension due to excess renin secretion is very rare, but it does occur with renin-secreting tumours.[11] These lead to very high circulating levels of angiotensin II, which directly cause high blood pressure. After removal of the tumour, which is usually benign, blood pressure returns to normal. In malignant and renovascular hypertension, excessive secretion of renin may be the direct cause of the raised pressure. In most other forms of kidney disease there is some sodium retention, and plasma renin and angiotensin levels are either normal or raised. It is likely therefore that the high blood pressure is maintained by a combination of sodium and renin and not by one of these factors alone.

Excess of adrenaline or noradrenaline Excessive levels of these hormones are produced by phaeochromocytoma and other neuro-endocrine tumours.[12] If the tumour predominantly secretes adrenaline patients tend to have systolic hypertension with increased cardiac output, increased heart rate, sweating and flushing. Occasionally they also suffer from postural hypotension due to a disproportionate beta-adrenergic stimulation in the presence of a shrunken intravascular volume. Tumours that predominantly secrete noradrenaline cause both high systolic and diastolic pressures, but less tachycardia. However, most phaeochromocytoma secrete a combination of both adrenaline and noradrenaline.

Excess cortisol High blood pressure occurs commonly but not invariably in patients with both pituitary and adrenal Cushing's syndrome. It may be related to the mineralocorticoid activity of the excess circulating cortisol or possibly to the concurrent raised plasma levels of plasma renin substrate.

Other mineralocorticoids High blood pressure has been attributed in the past to increased circulating levels of deoxycorticosterone, 18-hydroxydeoxycorticosterone and several other obscure mineralocorticoid-like substances. The evidence for these syndromes is poor.

Implications

Essential hypertension is related to abnormalities of many homeostatic systems. Despite our lack of complete understanding of the mechanisms of raised blood pressure there are logical reasons to reduce pressure using sodium restriction, diuretics, drugs that block the sympathetic system, inhibitors of renin release, angiotensin generation, and calcium-entry antagonists. Only rarely, however, is it possible to reverse a single causative factor for raised blood pressure.

PRACTICAL POINTS

- Research into both neural and endocrine causes of essential hypertension has failed to reveal any single cause.

- An underlying cause for high blood pressure is found in fewer than 5 per cent of cases of hypertension.

- However, awareness of the possible mechanisms maintaining normal and high blood pressure may influence our method of managing individual patients.

5
Drug-induced hypertension

BACKGROUND

There are many drugs that have been shown to cause or aggravate hypertension. Others interfere with the response to some antihypertensive agents (see Table 5.1). Patients receiving any of these drugs should be monitored regularly for changes in blood pressure.

The oral contraceptive Nearly all women who take the oral contraceptive sustain a rise in blood pressure, but usually this is too small to be of any clinical importance.[1] Properly conducted prospective studies have confirmed that the rise is due to the oral contraceptive itself, as it does not occur in similar

Table 5.1 Drugs affecting blood pressure.

Chronic hypertension	
Oral contraceptives	About 5 per cent of women
Hormone replacement therapy	Not well documented
Oral corticosteroids	Only in high dose
ACTH	Poorly documented
Carbenoxolone	Mineralocorticoid-like action
Liquorice	Mineralocorticoid-like action
Antacids (high sodium content)	Theoretical hazard only

Acute rises in blood pressure

Noradrenaline

Angiotensin

Dopamine

Mono-amineoxidase inhibitors, taken with dietary amines

Cold cures – phenylpropanolamine

Clonidine withdrawal
Opiate and alcohol withdrawal

Interference with antihypertensive drugs

Nonsteroidal anti-inflammatory drugs (e.g., indomethacin) block thiazides

Tricyclic antidepressants block adrenergic neurone blockers (bethanidine)

Indirect effect on blood pressure

Nephrotoxins

Methysergide – retroperitoneal fibrosis

Drugs causing lupus syndrome (procainamide, hydralazine)

women using barrier methods of birth control.

About 5 per cent of women taking high-dose oestrogen pills develop diastolic blood pressures above 90 mmHg. More severe hypertension, and even malignant phase hypertension, have been reported in some patients, but this is rare (see Figure 5.1). Clinically significant rises occur more commonly in older women. There is surprisingly only a very weak link between hypertension induced by the oral contraceptive and previous hypertension induced by pregnancy, or pre-eclampsia. There is also only a very modest correlation between the rise in blood pressure from the pill and the gain in weight. Biochemically, the disturbances of the renin–angiotensin–aldosterone system are similar in pregnancy and with the oral contraceptive. In both situations, the renin–angiotensin system is altered with rises in the levels of plasma renin substrate levels and plasma angiotensin II. There is also some evidence that there is volume expansion, and the combination of raised plasma angiotensin II and increased circu-

lating volume may be the mechanism of the hypertension (see Figure 5.2).

Low-dose oestrogen pills also raise blood pressure, although possibly to a lesser extent. Women who develop hypertension from the high-dose oestrogen pill may sustain a fall in pressure when the oestrogen content is reduced. There remains some doubt whether progestogen-only oral contraceptives raise blood pressure. While the Royal College of General Practitioners study suggested an effect, a prospective controlled study from Glasgow could find no evidence that this type of pill raises blood pressure.

It is not known whether women who sustain a rise in blood pressure from the pill will develop hypertension in later life. Attempts to define which women are particularly susceptible to oral-contraceptive-induced hypertension have been disappointing. Results have shown only that older women are particularly at risk, and black women may have a lower risk than whites.

Normally women who develop hypertension should be advised to stop the oral

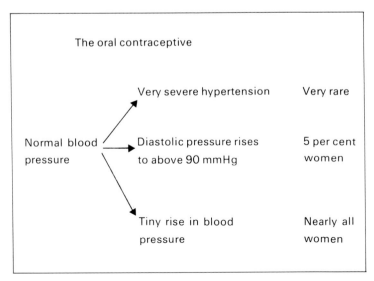

The oral contraceptive

Very severe hypertension — Very rare

Normal blood pressure → Diastolic pressure rises to above 90 mmHg — 5 per cent women

Tiny rise in blood pressure — Nearly all women

Figure 5.1 The frequency of raised blood pressure in women taking the oestrogen/ progestogen oral contraceptive. The lower the dose of oestrogen the lower the rise in blood pressure; progestogen-only pills may have much less effect.

contraceptive and change to alternative methods of birth control. However, there are some occasions when the cardiovascular or social risk from an unwanted pregnancy is so great that oral contraceptives have to be continued and antihypertensive drugs given concurrently.

Hormone replacement therapy (HRT) There is very little published information on the effects of HRT on blood pressure, but some reports have suggested that it may raise blood pressure. Usually if blood pressure rises it is best to discontinue this form of therapy. Sometimes there are overwhelming menopausal symptoms so that these agents have to be continued and antihypertensive drug therapy instituted in addition.

Carbenoxolone This is a liquorice–based drug sometimes used for treatment of peptic ulcers. It has biochemical prop-

erties similar to those of aldosterone.[2] It may cause hypertension with electrolyte abnormalities identical to those seen in Conn's syndrome (primary hyperaldosteronism). Oedema too is not uncommon. Potassium-losing thiazide diuretics are specifically contraindicated in hypertensive patients receiving carbenoxolone as they worsen the hypokalaemia and may cause muscle weakness and even paralysis. The potassium-retaining diuretic spironolactone can interfere with the ulcer-healing effect of carbenoxolone, but amiloride or triamterene are safe. Deglycyrrhizinized-liquorice ulcer-healing drugs do not have this aldosterone-like side-effect and do not cause hypertension.

Addiction to liquorice can cause hypokalaemia, and sodium and water retention, in a similar manner to carbenoxolone. In Europe many people eat combined liquorice and salt tablets, which frequently causes a rise in blood pressure.

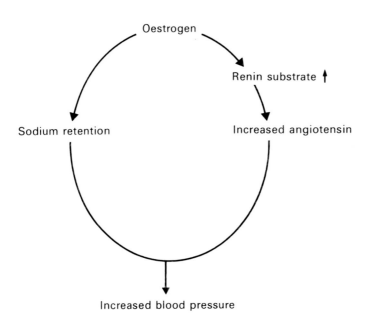

Figure 5.2 The mechanisms of oestrogen-induced hypertension.

Oral corticosteroids Acute high-dose oral corticosteroid therapy can raise blood pressure. This is probably partly due to a mineralocorticoid-like action of the corticosteroid with volume expansion, but plasma renin substrate levels are also increased and there may be increased sensitivity to circulating levels of angiotensin II. There may thus be a vasoconstrictor as well as a volume expansion element to this form of hypertension. Increased sensitivity to circulating adrenaline and noradrenaline has also been postulated.

Chronic low-dose steroid therapy with prednisolone in the treatment of rheumatoid arthritis or asthma does not appear to cause hypertension, even though plasma renin substrate levels do rise.[3] However, all patients receiving prednisolone, prednisone, triamcinalone or hydrocortisone therapy need regular checks of their blood pressure, serum sodium, potassium and glucose levels. There are reports of hypertension with the use of high-dose topical steroid preparations for skin, ear and eye conditions. Some topical steroids have marked mineralocorticoid properties causing sodium and water retention with hypokalaemia and renin suppression mimicking primary aldosteronism.

ACTH Blood pressure rises in response to ACTH therapy because this drug stimulates both the mineralocorticoid and glucocorticoid actions of the adrenal gland.

Purgatives Purgatives do not cause hypertension but they may induce hypokalaemia, which may suggest the presence of either renal or adrenal disease. Unexplained hypokalaemia in a hypertensive patient can occasionally be due to purgative abuse.

Cold cures and anorectics Many remedies for coughs and colds and also some slimming pills contain sympathomimetic amines. The phenylamine group (ephedrine, pseudoephedrine, phenylephrine and phenylpropanolamine) all cause vasoconstriction, and hypertension has been reported in some patients. The imidazoline derivatives resemble clonidine in their chemical structure and although normally they are used only topically, both hypertension and hypotension have been reported. Interestingly, oral or inhaled beta-agonists such as salbutamol do not cause hypertension.[4]

Nephrotoxins Any drug that damages the kidney may cause a rise in blood pressure. For instance, some antibiotics can cause renal failure, particularly the aminoglycosides (eg, gentamicin) and cephalosporins. This usually occurs only when they are given in high doses to patients who already have renal failure or are acutely ill. Phenacetin (an obsolete anti-inflammatory drug), when taken chronically, can cause renal papillary necrosis and eventually renal impairment. Because the damage is mainly in the medulla of the kidney, there is usually sodium loss. In general, patients with phenacetin nephropathy therefore have a low rather than a high blood pressure, often with postural hypotension.

Hydralazine and procainamide Both these drugs can cause a drug-induced lupus syndrome, which is usually reversible. However, if there is renal involvement, blood pressure may rise. Hydralazine-induced lupus is less common in fast metabolic acetylators and is rare if the total daily dose of the drug is below 100 mg.

Methysergide Fibrosis of the retroperitoneal tissues occurs with methysergide therapy for migraine. The ureters become obstructed and bilateral hydronephrosis and renal failure develop. Practolol also rarely causes a form of retroperitoneal fibrosis, but there is no evidence that other beta-blockers have this effect (see Chapter 11).

Monoamine oxidase (MAO) inhibitors These powerful antidepressant drugs are no longer widely used. When patients receiving MAO inhibitors such as tranylcypromine, phenelzine, iproniazid or isocarboxazid also consume amines such as tyramine in cheese, yeast extracts or in cold cures, a sudden and occasionally disastrous rise in blood pressure may occur.[4]

Tricyclic antidepressives These do not cause hypertension, but do interfere with the antihypertensive effects of some obsolete adrenergic neurone blocking drugs, such as bethanidine, guanethidine or debrisoquine, as well as clonidine. They may also cause serious arrhythmias. Their use in hypertensive patients should be discouraged.[5]

Indomethacin Indomethacin and other nonsteroidal anti-inflammatory drugs, relieve painful inflammation by blocking prostaglandin synthesis, but they may sometimes cause fluid retention and a rise in blood pressure. They can also block the antihypertensive action of thiazide diuretics as well as the actions of beta-blockers, vasodilators and captopril.[6] The anti-inflammatory agent, sulindac, may cause less interference with antihypertensive therapy than indomethacin.

Clonidine withdrawal Clonidine, a centrally acting alpha-stimulating drug, reduces blood pressure, but when high doses are discontinued suddenly a rebound rise in blood pressure occurs which may be very severe and mimic a phaeochromocytoma crisis. Rebound hypertension has been reported with other centrally acting drugs such as methyldopa and indoramin. In our opinion, clonidine has no place in modern clinical practice.

Trace metals Gold therapy can cause glomerulonephritis and hypertension. Both lead and cadmium as environmental pollutants have been implicated in causing hypertension. Recent evidence suggests that this is unlikely in the case of cadmium but there is still debate about lead as a cause of raised blood pressure.

Narcotic addiction During narcotic withdrawal blood pressure rises to high levels. This syndrome is very similar to that seen in alcohol withdrawal (see Chapter 10).

Drug-induced hypotension Apart from the antihypertensive drugs discussed in Chapter 11, some others may cause unwanted falls in blood pressure, and some, particularly in overdosage, cause circulatory collapse. All tranquillizers and sedatives, and many opiate analgesics, may cause idiosyncratic or dose-related hypotension.

PRACTICAL POINTS

- All hypertensive patients should have a detailed drug history taken.

- High blood pressure can sometimes be corrected simply by discontinuirg the pressor agent.

PART 2: INVESTIGATION

6
Blood pressure measurement

BACKGROUND

The height of the blood pressure is such an accurate predictor of a person's future morbidity and mortality that its measurement is far and away the most important observation made in clinical practice. As blood pressure measurement is simple and carries no hazard, it should be regarded as a routine check to be carried out on everyone.

Despite the importance of high blood pressure, there is considerable confusion over the correct method of measurement.[1] Insufficient care is often taken with the technique, defective apparatus is used and documentation is haphazard.

The first recorded measurement of blood pressure was in 1730 by The Reverend Stephen Hales, a distinguished biologist and curate of Teddington, Middlesex, England. He introduced a cannula into an artery in the neck of a horse and measured the height of the column of blood in a glass tube. He observed that when the horse struggled, the blood pressure rose.

The indirect method of measuring pressure was invented in 1898 by Scipione Riva Rocci. Using a mercury manometer he was able to measure the pressure needed to occlude the brachial artery and obliterate the radial pulse. Riva Rocci's original apparatus subsequently underwent several modifications but the basic principle remains to this day. One famous physician who made some improvements was Von Recklinghausen. The idea of listening below the occluded artery rather than just palpating it dates from 1905 when Nicolai Korotkov, a Russian army surgeon, wrote a thesis on the sounds that were audible as the mercury manometer was deflated. In honour of him the blood pressure sounds are called the Korotkov sounds.

The advent of electronics has made possible the production of a great many automatic devices with varying degrees of success. In normal practice, however, the Riva Rocci–Korotkov technique remains standard and is attractive if only because of its simplicity.

THE KOROTKOV SOUNDS

As the mercury column falls, the following phases are heard through a stethoscope applied over the brachial artery (see Figure 6.1). Their exact physiological significance is unclear, although their prognostic importance is undeniable. The Korotkov sounds are not transmitted heart sounds, but are caused by turbulence induced by constriction of the brachial artery.

- **Phase 1 The first appearance of sounds** Systolic pressure is usually recorded when the second beat is heard, as the first beat might have been due to some extraneous noise.

- **Phase 2 The softening or disappearance of sounds** This silent gap is usually no more than 5 mmHg. It is frequently not present, but when it is it may cause underestimation of the systolic pressure. It is thus important to inflate the mercury manometer to well above the pressure needed to occlude the brachial or radial pulse.

- **Phase 3 The reappearance of sounds** These sounds are sometimes difficult to hear at first, but they become louder after a few mmHg.

- **Phase 4 The muffling of sounds** This used to be taken by some as the level of diastolic pressure. Usually it is impossible to identify this phase.

- **Phase 5 Final disappearance of sounds** This is now regarded as the best measure of diastolic pressure. In some patients with hyperdynamic circulation (for example, in preg-nancy, thyrotoxicosis, after exercise and in children), sounds do not completely disappear, but continue to be audible down to 0 mmHg; sometimes the persistence of sounds is caused by tight clothing occluding the brachial artery above the cuff. More often than not, phase 4 and phase 5 diastolic pressures coincide. A difference of more than 5 mmHg is unusual.

BLOOD PRESSURE MEASUREMENTS

Systolic or diastolic pressures
Most clinical trials and studies have concentrated on the diastolic blood pressure. There is no really good reason for this. Epidemiologists have demonstrated that both systolic and diastolic pressure are potent predictors of risk.

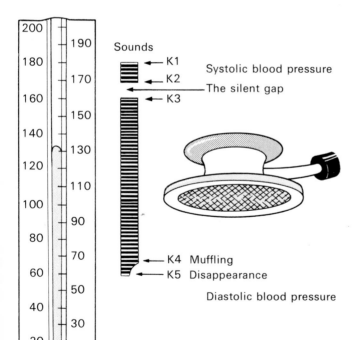

Sounds

K1 — Systolic blood pressure
K2
K3 — The silent gap

K4 Muffling
K5 Disappearance

Diastolic blood pressure

Figure 6.1 The indirect measurement of blood pressure: the Korotkov sounds.

Above the age of forty-five the height of the systolic pressure is a better predictor of risk than the diastolic pressure. This may be explained by the fact that a rising systolic pressure occurs partly as a consequence of arterial damage due to hypertension (see Chapters 1 and 2). A disproportionately high systolic pressure in relation to the diastolic pressure may thus be regarded as a vascular complication of hypertension, and a potent risk factor. In clinical practice systolic and diastolic pressures are both recorded and they are usually closely correlated.

Korotkov phase 4 or phase 5?

Both phase 4 and phase 5 are regarded as candidates for the best estimate of diastolic pressure. Neither represents the true diastolic pressure, which can be measured only by using an intra-arterial cannula and pressure transducer. The indirect diastolic pressures are usually higher than the intra-arterial pressure, so phase 5 is nearer to the true pressure.

In clinical practice, diastolic pressure should normally be taken at phase 5, the disappearance of sounds. The reasons for this are:

- Most epidemiological studies of populations and cardiovascular risk employ phase 5.
- All modern multicentre clinical trials of therapy to prevent complications employ phase 5.
- The inter-observer variation is less with phase 5, when this is tested with blood pressure training films. The intra-observer variation may, however, be less with phase 4.
- With exceptions phase 5 is nearer to the intra-arterial pressure.

Lying, sitting or standing

Normally diastolic blood pressure rises a little on standing; the systolic pressure may fall by a few mmHg. In some elderly patients and those with autonomic failure, as well as those receiving obsolete adrenergic neurone-blocking drugs, blood pressure falls on standing. Blood pressure should be measured with the patient either lying or sitting, and then standing at least once, but with modern antihypertensive drugs postural hypotension is not a problem, so lying or seated pressures are sufficient in most people.

Most large-scale epidemiological studies and clinical trials have employed the seated blood pressure. This is the most convenient position for routine clinical practice.

Mean arterial pressure

The mean arterial pressure can be calculated from the sum of the diastolic pressure plus one-third of the pulse pressure. It therefore takes into account both systolic and diastolic components. The calculated mean arterial pressure is closely related to the measured mean intra-arterial pressure. These readings are not, however, normally used in clinical practice.

Resting, casual or basal pressure

All blood pressures are variable and the higher the pressure the greater the variability. The data available from the insurance companies and from longterm population studies are based on single casual blood pressure measurements, and these are very accurate predictors of risk. When people relax in a quiet room, their pressures almost invariably fall and even very high blood pressures, associated with end-organ damage, may settle. Contrary to the original view, basal blood pressures are not better predictors of risk than casual readings. In the clinical environment blood pressures settle because:

- The patient becomes used to the procedure, the doctor and the environment (acclimatization).
- The patient is given placebos (placebo response); this is probably the same mechanism as the acclimatization response.
- When any biological parameter is remeasured, the extreme readings, either high or low, tend to return towards the average (regression to the mean).

Usually in mild hypertensive patients there is little further fall after the blood pressure has been measured at five consecutive clinic visits.

Sources of error

Errors in blood pressure measurement are easily made and should be minimized. They may be due either to the equipment or to the observer.

Errors due to the manometer

- **Insufficient or too much mercury in the manometer,** so that at rest the reading is not 0 mmHg.
- **The mercury column slopes away from the vertical** (see Figure 6.2) owing to damaged hinges on the manometer box. This causes falsely high readings. Some mercury manometers are manufactured with a built-in tilt. In these, correction has been made for the slightly longer glass column.
- **The mercury column becomes dirty** so that the mercury meniscus cannot be seen properly (see Figure 6.3). The glass tube should be cleaned about once a year.
- **The rubber tubing is leaky** so that cuff deflates too quickly. This causes falsely low readings.

Errors caused by the cuff

- **The cuff size is too small** When the cuff is too short, there is inadequate compression of the brachial artery (see below).[2] It should be 10 in (25 cm) longer than the internal rubber

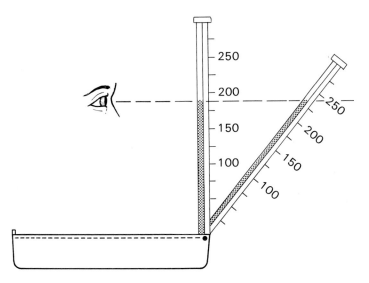

Figure 6.2 The effect of the manometer not being in an upright position.

bladder, with a tail of a further 24 in (60 cm). Velcro cuffs have shorter tails and are convenient but they do tend to lose their grip unless cleaned regularly. The rubber bladder inside the cuff should encircle at least 66 per cent of the arm circumference and preferably more. Bladders that are too small cause over-reading of pressure, yet most commercially available blood pressure cuffs have bladders that are too small. The cuff is labelled as 'normal' or 'large adult' by the size of the bladder and not the overall cloth covering. The minimum size for adult pressure readings is 5 in (13 cm) wide and 9 in (23 cm) long (see Table 6.1).

Figure 6.3 A dirty manometer tube (photographed when reading 0 mm mercury) in a hospital casualty department.

66

In patients with obese arms whose arm circumference exceeds 13 in (33 cm), a 'large adult' cuff should be used (see Figure 6.4). Every blood pressure clinic and practitioner should have ready access to large cuffs for obese people (see below).

- **The cuff is not at the same level as the heart** While it does not matter where the mercury manometer is in relation to the heart, it is very important that the forearm cuff is on the same level as the heart (see Figure 6.5).[3] If the arm is raised, falsely low blood pressure readings are obtained; falsely high readings result if the cuff is below heart level. It is also very important that the arm is supported, as the isometric exercise of holding the arm up can cause a rise in blood pressure.

- **Faulty or blocked inflation–deflation valves** These make it

Arm Circum-ference (cms)	Error with regular cuff			
	You under read		You over read	
	Syst	Diast	Syst	Diast
24	7	4		
26	5	3		
28	3	2		
30	0	0		
32			2	1
34			4	3
36			6	4
38			8	6
40			10	7
42			12	9
44			14	10
46			16	11

Table 6.1 Estimated error in mm Hg when blood pressure is measured in different arm circumferences with a normal-sized cuff.[2]

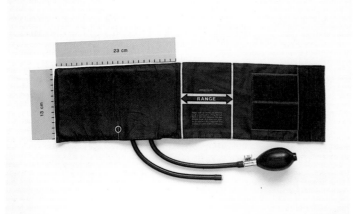

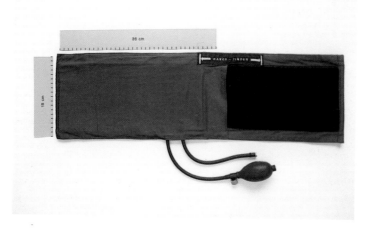

Figure 6.4 Different-sized cuffs: *top*, normal, *middle*, large adult, *below*, thigh.

impossible to lower the pressure in the cuff slowly enough to obtain an accurate reading.

Observer errors

- **Faulty technique** The column is deflated too quickly.

- **Parallax error** The mercury column is not level with the observer's eyes.

- **Terminal digit preference** The observer reads pressure either up or down to the nearest 10 mmHg. While this may not appear to matter too much in individual cases with moderate to severe hypertension, it can ruin multicentre studies where systematic differences may be obtained between observers which are not due to differences in the patients' pressures. In view of the importance of blood pressure in predicting a patient's survival, an accurate reading should be obtained.

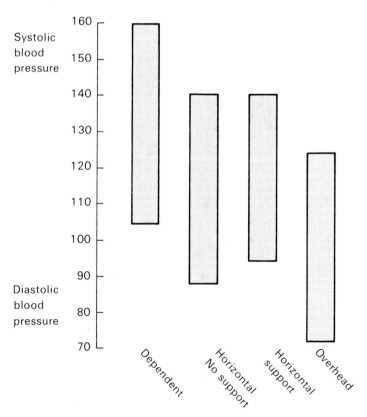

Figure 6.5 Blood pressure measured in four different arm positions.

- **Observer bias** The observer, aware of the patient or the treatment being received, may bias his or her reading to fulfil preconceived notions.

- **Hearing impairment** This may cause the observer to underestimate systolic pressure and overestimate diastolic pressure.

THE CORRECT TECHNIQUE FOR MEASURING PRESSURE (see Figure 6.6)

- Ensure the patient is comfortably seated or standing, and neither too hot nor cold. It is now known that blood pressures are lower in a warmer environment, and rise when it is cold. Try to avoid exertion and stressful discussions while pressures are being measured.
- Apply the forearm cuff neatly, with the rubber bladder covering the brachial pulse. The ϕ mark should be over the brachial artery. Many modern cuffs have the 13 in (33 cm) circumference marked out. If the arm circumference exceeds this range a large adult cuff should be used.
- Ensure that the manometer column is vertical, and connect it to the cuff.
- Ensure the forearm is supported, preferably resting on a desk, slightly extended and externally rotated.
- Inflate the cuff at a slow, steady rate to 30 mmHg above the level needed to occlude the pulse.
- Place the diaphragm of the stethoscope over the brachial artery. Do not press too hard. It does not matter if the diaphragm is partly underneath the edge of the cuff, although it should be noted that this can cause creaking noises which may confuse the observer.
- The observer's eyes should be at the

same level as the top of the column of mercury.
- Deflate the manometer cuff at the rate of 2 to 3 mmHg per second.
- Record the systolic blood pressure (phase 1) when the blood pressure sounds are first heard.
- Record the diastolic pressure at phase 5 (disappearance of sounds). If sounds can still be heard, even when the manometer reads 30 mmHg or less, then diastolic pressure should be taken at the muffling of sounds (phase 4).
- Blood pressures should be measured to the nearest 2 mmHg.
- Write down all the readings immediately.
- At first consultations check the blood pressure in both arms to ensure there is no discrepancy. If pressures differ significantly there is some narrowing of the subclavian artery, in which case the higher pressure is the more important.
- Measure the blood pressure at least twice at all consultations. The second reading is the one on which decisions are usually made.

Special situations
Atrial fibrillation may be due to coronary heart disease, alcoholic cardio-myopathy, thyroid disease or rheumatic heart disease. It renders blood pressure measurement difficult and at least three readings should be taken.

Aortic coarctation In this rare condition, which is usually diagnosed in children, blood pressure is raised in the arms but normal or low in the legs. Where coarctation is suspected, for example when palpation of the femoral artery simultaneously with the radial pulse suggests radio-femoral delay or when

69

femoral pulses are weak or absent, blood pressure should be measured in the legs. A cuff with a rubber bladder encircling two-thirds of the circumference is wrapped around the thigh with the patient lying prone. The Korotkov sounds are auscultated in the usual way over the popliteal artery in the popliteal fossa.

Children

The measurement of blood pressure should be an integral part of the assessment of a paediatric case. The principles are no different from those used in adults. In children over the age of two a conventional mercury manometer is used and the Korotkov sounds auscultated. If the Korotkov sounds prove inaudible, the systolic pressure can be measured by palpation alone. In infants in whom conventional measurements are impossible, special Döppler blood pressure measuring

Figure 6.6 The correct technique: (i) Ensure the mercury meniscus reads zero before use. The observer's eye must be level with the top of the meniscus to avoid parallax error.

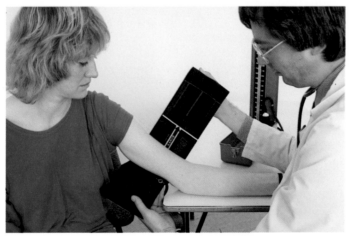

(ii) The ⏀ mark must be over the brachial artery.

devices should be used. If these are not available the 'flush' method of measuring blood pressure is used. This is described in Chapter 17.

Anaeroid sphygmomanometers

Anaeroid sphygmomanometers are useful, and when new they are usually accurate. They tend to deteriorate after two or three years, however, and there is no way of telling whether they are accurate except by checking them against a mercury manometer, with a Y-tube connection to a cuff wrapped around a bottle.

It is therefore best not to use anaeroid sphygmomanometers in hospital or in general practice health centres, where the mercury manometer is preferable. Anaeroid manometers are more portable and so are useful for home visits.

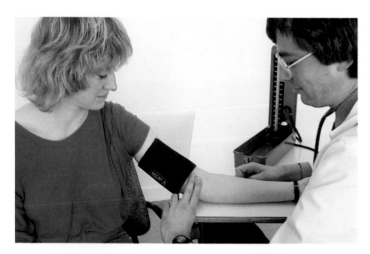

(iii) Ensure that there is enough space below the cuff so that the stethoscope does not come into contact with it.

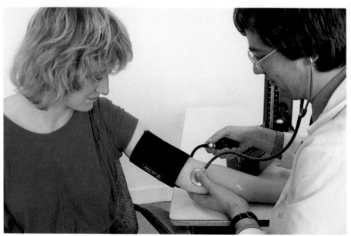

(iv) Use a stethoscope diaphragm to listen over the brachial artery.

The Random-Zero sphygmomanometer and the London School of Hygiene sphygmomanometer

These manometers, which are based on the conventional mercury manometer, are designed to reduce systematic error due to observer bias, terminal digit preference and observer error. They are not necessary in routine clinical practice, where a well-maintained conventional mercury sphygmomanometer is sufficient. However, in multicentre studies, epidemiological surveys and therapeutic trials, such error-reducing equipment is mandatory. The Hawksley Random-Zero sphygmomanometer is cheap and simpler than the London School of Hygiene manometer. Any clinician who is contemplating publishing data on blood pressure should obtain readings using the random-zero system.[4]

Automated manometers

A great many automatic electronic blood pressure measuring devices are now available. In general, the clinician armed with a well-maintained conventional mercury manometer has no need for other more expensive equipment. Many electronic devices are marketed, but with the exception of the Arteriosonde system and the Elag Koln apparatus many have been shown to be accurate; indeed some are very inaccurate. Unless there are data available on a particular manometer demonstrating that readings are closely matched to those of a conventional mercury manometer or a random-zero manometer, clinicians should avoid this type of equipment.

These systems can be made to measure blood pressure repeatedly at intervals of between thirty seconds and one hour, and provide a digital or graphical printout. They are therefore useful in clinical research as they provide bias-free readings. Automatic manometers can be used by patients to measure their own blood pressure at home.[5]

Intra-arterial blood pressure

This invasive technique for measuring blood pressure is mainly used in research units, and cannot be applied generally. It may be useful when the clinician is faced with a patient who is suspected of having a high blood pressure only when seeing a doctor, but may be normotensive between times. It is also useful for physiological and pharmacological studies. However, all the prognostic and therapeutic information available on high blood pressure and its treatment is based on the indirect cuff method of measuring pressure, and the prognostic significance of the lower ambulatory intra-arterial pressure is uncertain.

Non-invasive ambulatory and home blood pressure measurements

There is increasing interest in assessment of blood pressure away from the stressful environment of the clinic or hospital. In general, home blood pressures are lower than clinic readings. Automated non-invasive manometers are now coming into use and more information will soon become available. However, the fact remains that a casual pressure reading obtained by a doctor is a very reliable guide to prognosis, and the meaning of lower readings obtained at other times is uncertain.

Many patients are willing and able to measure their own blood pressure at home, and this can often provide useful information. It is difficult to know what action should be taken in patients who have pressures within the therapeutic range in the clinic, but would be considered normotensive if reliance were placed only on home readings.[6]

Technique of Blood Pressure Measurement

A poster to illustrate recommended techniques

Journal of Hypertension 1985, 3:293

BLOOD PRESSURE
MEASUREMENT
(Techniques recommended by the British Hypertension Society)

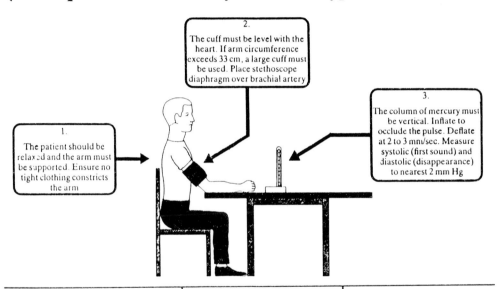

2.
The cuff must be level with the heart. If arm circumference exceeds 33 cm, a large cuff must be used. Place stethoscope diaphragm over brachial artery

3.
The column of mercury must be vertical. Inflate to occlude the pulse. Deflate at 2 to 3 mm/sec. Measure systolic (first sound) and diastolic (disappearance) to nearest 2 mm Hg

1.
The patient should be relaxed and the arm must be supported. Ensure no tight clothing constricts the arm

The rubber bladder should encircle at least 2/3rds and preferable the whole upper arm. The lower edge of the cuff should be 2cm above the cubital fossa to avoid contact with the stethoscope

	Cuff sizes Width	Length
Normal	12-13cm	23cm
Large adult	15-16cm	33cm
Thigh cuff	18cm	36cm
Neonates	2.5cm	encircle arm
1 – 4 yrs	5cm	"
4 – 8 yrs	9cm	"

Most large trials use seated blood pressures; lying or standing pressures may also be measured.

When the disappearance of sounds (phase 5) cannot be identified (eg in pregnancy, children and the elderly), diastolic pressures should be taken at muffling of sounds (phase 4).

Mercury manometers must be cleaned regularly and the meniscus should read zero when not in use.

Some manometers are designed to be tilted and have appropriate correction.

Aneroid manometers tend to deteriorate and need regular checking.

PRACTICAL POINTS

- Blood pressure measurement is the most important preventive check that can be made in clinical practice and should be routine for all patients.

- Phase 5 of the Korotkov sounds is considered the most reliable measurement of diastolic pressure.

- Seated blood pressure measurement is generally the most convenient for routine clinical practice.

- Clinicians should be aware of common errors due to faulty manometers, cuff size and fitting, and observation. These can be easily avoided.

- In mild hypertensives, blood pressure should usually be measured on several separate occasions to prevent an inaccurate assessment due to falsely raised pressure.

7
The assessment of a new patient

BACKGROUND

Most often a new hypertensive patient is detected during the course of a routine medical examination for employment or insurance or during some sort of case detection programme or screening survey. Many are diagnosed at a consultation for an unrelated condition, or when they sustain one of the vascular complications of hypertension, for example, a heart attack or a stroke. This is unfortunate, as early detection and management should prevent many of these vascular complications.

In women hypertension may be detected by obstetricians during pregnancy or whilst following-up patients receiving the oral contraceptive (the topic of hypertension in pregnancy is covered in Chapter 16). It is logical, however, to check the pressure of patients seeking any form of medical aid as this simple measure has such important preventive implications. All examinees whose diastolic pressure is between 90 and 100 mmHg should undergo a further assessment; those with diastolic pressures over 100 mmHg need extra attention in the manner suggested below, which takes up to about half an hour in most cases.

THE CLINICAL HISTORY

Patients from screening programmes or examined during routine consultation

In the absence of vascular complications these patients are usually symptomless, but once they have been diagnosed they sometimes develop symptoms owing to the anxiety created by the act of diagnosis. All patients should be asked whether they have ever had their blood pressure measured before and if they can remember the level.

Patients with symptoms

Headache This does occur in very severe hypertensives and those with malignant phase hypertension. Otherwise migraine and tension headaches, whilst troublesome, are not due to hypertension.[1]

Breathlessness Left ventricular failure with orthopnoea and paroxysmal nocturnal dyspnoea may occasionally be due to severe hypertension alone, but is more likely to be caused by associated coronary heart disease. Alternatively, rheumatic heart disease may coexist. Asthma and chronic obstructive airways disease are common but not associated with hypertension. When present, these diagnoses are important as they influence the choice of antihypertensive drugs. Patients with heart failure or asthma should not receive beta-adrenoceptor blockers but vasodilator drugs and diuretics may be favoured (see Chapter 14).

Precordial pain This may be due to angina or heart attack, both of which are complications of hypertension.

Palpitations A history of recurrent episodes of fast tachycardia raises the possibility of phaeochromocytoma, although it may be due to intrinsic cardiac disease, anxiety or thyrotoxicosis.

Intermittent claudication Aortic or femoral atheroma are complications of hypertension and when present, beta-adrenoceptor blockers are contra-indicated.[2]

Polyuria and nocturia These occur with intrinsic renal disease, which may cause hypertension, or may follow renal damage secondary to raised blood pressure. Nocturia also occurs more in men with advancing age owing to prostatic hypertrophy. Recurrent urinary infection may possibly cause raised blood pressure but, in the absence of structural damage to the kidneys, the association is controversial. Surprisingly there is little association between chronic retention due to prostatism and hypertension, unless there is concurrent renal failure.

Diabetes mellitus Patients with diabetes are more prone to hypertension and its vascular complications. The presence of diabetes substantially influences the management (see Chapter 14). In particular, diuretics should be avoided in type II diabetics as they may cause or aggravate glucose intolerance.

Visual symptoms Visual loss only occurs in hypertension if there are retinal haemorrhages or exudates due to malignant hypertension.

The relatively rare syndromes of central or branch retinal vein thrombosis and retinal artery occlusion are strongly associated with hypertension, as well as cigarette smoking.[3] Amaurosis fugax may result from embolus formation from carotid artery stenosis. There may also be visual disturbance due to transient cerebral ischaemia or strokes.

Neurological symptoms Transient or persistent hemiplegia may be due to cerebral haemorrhage or infarction, both of which are complications of hypertension. Hypertensive patients are also particularly prone to subarachnoid haemorrhages.

PAST HISTORY
It is important to take an accurate history particularly seeking for past renal disease, or evidence of previous vascular complications of raised pressure. In women a detailed obstetric history is necessary. Previous pre-eclampsia or pregnancy hypertension, or raised pressures whilst receiving the oral contraceptive, are important. There is an association between pregnancy, hypertension and raised blood pressures in later life.

THE FAMILY HISTORY
Frequently patients do not know whether their parents or siblings had hypertension, but useful indicators are family histories of premature death, heart attack or stroke.

- **Essential hypertension** This runs in families and the clinician should be influenced by a bad family history.

- **Polycystic kidneys** Adult polycystic disease is inherited as a mendelian dominant condition. If there is a very strong family history of hypertension, subarachnoid haemorrhage or renal failure, possibly requiring dialysis or transplantation, then polycystic disease should be considered.

  Relatives of patients with polycystic disease should undergo renal ultrasound examination to detect renal cysts, in addition to having a clinical assessment.

76

- **Familial diabetes mellitus** This raises the possibility that the patient may also be diabetic.

- **Relatives of hypertensive patients** Patients should be advised to tell their relatives to have their blood pressure measured.

THE SOCIAL HISTORY

The epidemiology of hypertension is discussed in Chapter 3. Some aspects are especially relevant to the individual case.

Occupation Hypertension is slightly more common in people of lower socioeconomic groups but is not associated with any particular occupational groups and is not necessarily associated with stressful jobs. The social class link may be explained by the higher prevalence of obesity, and alcohol and salt intake.

Some hypertensive patients show a very marked pressor response to stress at home or work, and detailed questioning may reveal this. The evidence that psychosocial stress causes chronic elevation of blood pressure is poor, and many reliable studies have demonstrated no association. However, relaxation therapy may be worth considering, as there is some evidence that it may reduce blood pressure.

High alcohol intake This is closely related to high blood pressure and its effect is independent of age, sex, personality and cigarette smoking or salt consumption. Alcoholics and heavy drinkers are frequently hypertensive and their blood pressures settle without drugs if they stop drinking. Detailed questioning on drinking habits is necessary in all hypertensive patients.

Salt intake Patients should be asked whether they consume much salt and particularly if they add it at the table or in cooking. Many processed foods and cooked meats have a high salt content.

Cigarette smoking This is an independent cardiovascular risk factor which is not related to high blood pressure. The only exception is in patients with the malignant phase of hypertension, who are more likely to be smokers than those with nonmalignant hypertension.

DRUG HISTORY

Antihypertensive drugs Often hypertensives are receiving unnecessarily complicated drug combinations. Many patients do not know what their tablets are or what they are for. At a clinical assessment where the previous drug history is not known, patients should be asked to bring all their tablets with them. There is often an alarming difference between the treatment the doctor thinks a patient is receiving and the tablets the patient actually takes. Patients should be given special cards or booklets which list drug names and doses as well as blood pressure measurements. These can be written in by any doctor or nurse who manages the patient, and improve liaison between family and hospital doctors.

Other medication Some drugs, notably the oral contraceptives and carbenoxolone, can cause hypertension. Some psychotropic drugs and nonsteroidal analgesics interreact with antihypertensive drugs (see Chapters 5 and 11).

EXAMINATION

The general appearance

Breathlessness, distress and anxiety may be present in hypertensive patients who are unwell. The following features suggest specific diagnoses relevant to raised blood pressure:

- **Plethoric appearance** This suggests polycythaemia, which is itself associated with raised blood pressure. It also occurs in patients with excessive alcohol intake and in Cushing's syndrome (see Figure 7.1). Diuretics also cause a rise in packed cell volume.

- **Cushingoid appearance** This suggests Cushing's syndrome, which does cause hypertension (see Chapter 8). More commonly, the alcoholic pseudo-Cushing's syndrome is present and the other stigmata of liver disease should be looked for.[4]

- **Sweating, tremor, restlessness and anxiety** These raise the possibility of hyperthyroidism, in which case the systolic blood pressure may be rasied. Phaeochromocytoma, or simply anxiety itself, can cause these symptoms.

- **Blanching and pallor** These features together with weight loss, sweating and tachycardia all raise the possibility of phaeochromocytoma. Most cases are persistently hypertensive, but with great fluctuations in pressure. Some are normotensive between attacks, and both hypotensive and hypertensive attacks may occur.

- **Obesity** This is associated with raised blood pressure, which is compounded by a tendency to overestimate the blood pressure in obese arms (see Chapter 6). Body weight should be checked at all consultations, and in obese patients it is useful to plot weight in relation to height to calculate by how many per cent they are overweight (see Figure 7.2).

- **Acromegaly** (see Figure 7.3) About 50 per cent of patients with this condition are hypertensive.

- **Von Recklinghausen's neurofibromatosis** Multiple neurofibromata and *café au lait* spots (see Figure 7.4) suggest this diagnosis, which is associated with phaeochromocytoma and renal artery stenosis.

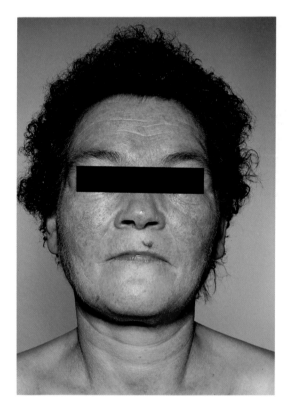

Figure 7.1 Patient with alcoholic pseudo-Cushing's syndrome.

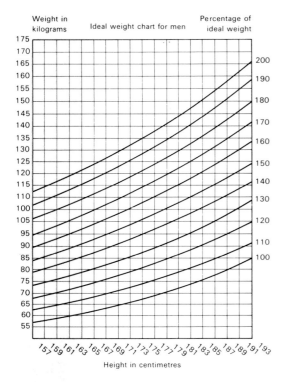

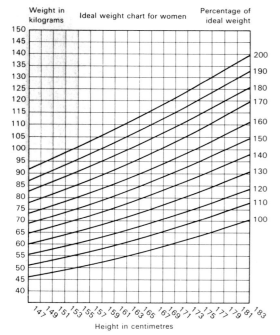

Figure 7.2 Ideal weight charts.

- **Marfanoid appearance** There is a very rare syndrome (Sipple syndrome) of a marfanoid habitus with arachnodactyly, phaeochromocytoma, parathyroid adenoma and medullary carcinoma of the thyroid.

The cardiovascular system

- **Blood pressure** The correct technique for measuring blood pressure is covered in Chapter 6. Pressures should be measured at least once in both arms. Seated blood pressures are best employed when assessing patients but pressures should also be

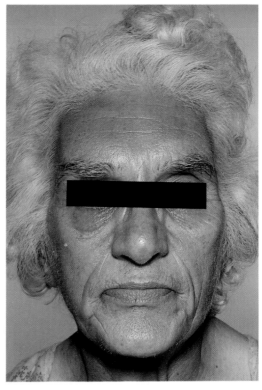

Figure 7.3 Patient with acromegaly and hypertension.

measured standing if the patient complains of postural dissiness. This may occur in the elderly and hypertensive patients with phaeochromocytoma and in those receiving adrenergic blocking drugs. Atrial fibrillation renders blood pressure measurement difficult and at least three readings should be taken. This may be due to coronary heart disease, alcoholic cardiomyopathy, thyroid disease or rheumatic heart disease.

- **The pulse** Classically in hypertension the pulse has a large volume but this is not a reliable physical sign. Tachycardia suggests anxiety, thyrotoxicosis and very rarely phaeochromocytoma. Bradycardia is most commonly due to beta-blockers. In untreated cases, bradycardia may be due to myxoedema or to heart block, and beta-blockers should be withheld until this has been excluded.

    All peripheral pulses should be checked, and the carotid and femoral pulses auscultated for bruits. The femoral pulse should always be checked once against the brachial or radial pulse to detect radio-femoral delay or a disparity in volume suggesting coarctation of the aorta or severe aortic atheroma.

- **The cardiac apex** The position of the cardiac apex should be measured and the presence of a left ventricular heave noted. The presence of left ventricular hypertrophy is a potent predictor of risk in a hypertensive patient and necessitates urgent drug therapy.

- **The heart sounds** In patients with raised blood pressure the aortic component of the second heart sound is loud. If there is clinical or subclinical left ventricular failure a third sound or even a combined third and fourth sound (summation gallop) may be heard.

    Cardiac murmurs are assessed in the conventional manner; hypertension can coexist with mitral valve disease and with aortic stenosis with or without regurgitation.

    Aortic systolic murmurs of no haemodynamic significance are common in hypertension. If, however, the aortic component of the second heart sound is quiet, aortic stenosis should be considered, particularly if there is evidence of disproportionate left ventricular hypertrophy.

    Coarctation of the aorta is usually associated with loud systolic murmurs over most of the left precordium and into the left scapular region.

The respiratory system

The presence of basal pulmonary crepitations suggestive of left ventricular failure, or of rhonchi suggesting obstructive airways disease, strongly influence the choice of antihypertensive drugs. With airways obstruction, beta-blockers are absolutely contraindicated (see Chapter 11).

The abdomen

The presence of hepatomegaly raises the possibility of liver disease caused by alcohol abuse, although in decompensated cirrhosis with jaundice or ascites, hypertension is rare. It is, however, seen in cases with compensated cirrhosis.

Bimanual palpation may reveal unilateral or bilateral renal enlargement so polycystic disease must be considered. Renal bruits suggestive of renal artery stenosis may be heard 4 in (10 cm) lateral and 2 in

(5 cm) above the umbilicus, although they are often better heard by listening in the back, 4 in (10 cm) lateral to the lower thoracic spine.

The central nervous system

Examination may reveal evidence of neurological defect due to cerebrovascular disease.

The optic fundi (see Figures 7.5, 7.6)

Ophthalmoscopy is an integral part of the assessment of every hypertensive patient.[5] A good view must be obtained, if necessary in a darkened room with dilatation of the pupils by homatropine or topicamide eye drops.

The features seen in hypertensives are:

- **Increased arterial tortuosity** This physical sign is as much related to the age of the patient as to the height of the blood pressure.

- **Silver wire changes** In the retinal arteries this suggests arterial wall thickening. It is seen in hypertension, but also with advancing age.

- **Arteriovenous nipping or nicking** This occurs when the retinal veins appear to be occluded as they pass under the thickened retinal arteries.

- **Retinal flame-shaped haemorrhages** These are related to severe hypertension.

- **Soft fluffy exudates or cotton wool spots** These are now known to be retinal infarcts.

- **Hard shiny exudates** These are lipid-laden retinal infarcts which frequently radiate from the macula (macula star).

- **Papilloedema** Swelling of the optic disc. This is usually associated with cerebral oedema.

To obtain an accurate record for future comparison retinal photography should be undertaken in all cases with haemorrhages, exudates or papilloedema. The Keith Wagener classification of hypertensive retinopathy may be misleading as it suggests degrees of seriousness. It is better to record features actually seen in both eyes. The classification is, however, very frequently referred to in medical journals:

—**Grade I** Minor vessel change only
—**Grade II** Silver wire vessel change, arterial tortuosity and arteriovenous nipping
—**Grade III** Retinal haemorrhages and/or cotton wool spots and/or shiny hard exudates
—**Grade IV** Retinal haemorrhages, exudates and papilloedema

Grades III and IV can be considered to represent accelerated or malignant phase hypertension. There is little point in differentiating between these two grades because the prognosis is much the same, and quite different from hypertension with grades I or II retinal features.

Other types of retinopathy Diabetic retinopathy may be present in hypertensive diabetics. It is particularly associated with poor control of blood pressure, inadequate control of blood sugar, long-standing diabetes and possibly cigarette smoking. Unilateral central retinal vein thrombosis or branch vein thrombosis with multiple haemorrhages occurs more

81

commonly in hypertensives. So florid are the haemorrhages that this has been called the sunset fundus.

Retinal artery occlusion with ischaemic pallor and empty arteries is also associated with hypertension.

Both conditions lead to later secondary optic atrophy, and blindness is usually permanent.

INVESTIGATIONS

Urinalysis The urine should be tested with dipsticks at least once in all newly diagnosed hypertensive patients and thereafter at least annually. Severe hypertensives with renal disease and patients receiving thiazide diuretics should have their urine tested at each visit to the outpatient clinic.

Proteinuria This can occur both in malignant hypertension, where it is due to fibrinoid necrosis, and in the nonmalignant phase, due to hypertensive nephrosclerosis. If proteinuria is heavy, however, it suggests intrinsic renal disease, for example, glomerulonephritis or the nephrotic syndrome. Dipstick tests for urinary protein are now very sensitive, so the occasional trace of proteinuria can usually be ignored.

Haematuria This occurs in many intrinsic renal conditions associated with hypertension, including cancer, glomerulonephritis or pyelonephritis, as well as in various urological conditions, all of which need investigating. Haematuria is common in malignant hypertension but also occurs in the nephrosclerosis due to nonmalignant hypertension.[6]

Glycosuria This suggests the diagnosis of diabetes mellitus (see Chapter 14). Furthermore, diuretics (particularly thiazides) used in treating hypertensives are diabetogenic.

Urine microscopy and culture This is not a useful routine investigation but should be reserved for patients who have urinary symptoms or in whom urine dipsticks have revealed an abnormality.

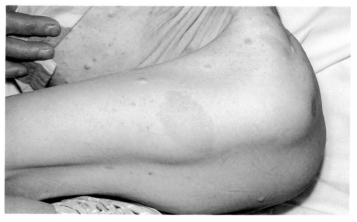

Figure 7.4 Patient with Von Recklinghausen's neurofibromatosis.

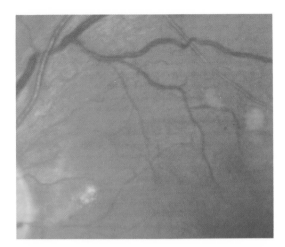

Figure 7.5 Optic changes in hypertension:
(i) Cotton wool spots and arteriovenous nipping
(ii) Cotton wool spots and flame-shaped haemorrhages
(iii) Retinal haemorrhages, exudates and papilloedema.

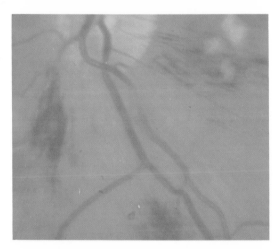

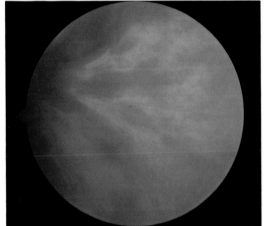

Figure 7.6 Central retinal vein thrombosis.

Reliable contaminant-free midstream specimens of urine are hard to obtain and are time-consuming for bacteriological laboratories. Bacterial growth without leucocytes is not an indicator of urinary infection. However, the presence of leucocytes in the urine without bacterial growth (sterile pyuria) is an important finding. It is most often due to partially treated urine infection but also occurs in renal tuberculosis or renal tumour.

All patients who are to receive antihypertensive drugs should also undergo routine biochemical and haematological profiling, although in most cases no abnormalities are found.

Haematology

- **Polycythaemia** Mild polycythaemia occurs commonly in essential hypertension. Frank polycythaemia occurs in some renal tumours. In population studies, haemoglobin levels and blood pressure are weakly positively correlated. A raised haemoglobin level should also raise the possibility of Cushing's syndrome, alcohol excess and chronic chest disease.

- **Anaemia** In the presence of chronic renal failure, there is usually a normochromic normocytic anaemia. This is due to deficient erythropoietin, mild marrow aplasia due to uraemia, mild haemolysis and sometimes intestinal blood loss.

- **Microangiopathic haemolytic anaemia** This is seen in some cases of glomerulonephritis and also in malignant hypertension.

- **Mean cell volume** A raised MCV is a moderately reliable indicator of alcohol intake. Hypertensive patients who have MCVs greater than 92 fl should be carefully questioned about their drinking habits (see Figure 7.7). Alcohol alters the composition of the lipid wall of red blood cells and also interferes with folate metabolism. This is a useful simple test for alcohol excess although it is not infallible. Its ready availability is a major advantage.[7]

- **The white cell count** Leucocytosis suggests infection. Leucopenia can occur very rarely after using diuretics (thiazides and frusemide), ACE inhibitors (captopril and enalapril), methyldopa and even the beta-blockers.

  Both hypertensive and normotensive black people have lower white cell counts than whites, and may even appear to have leucopenia by Caucasian standards.

- **Platelet counts** Thrombocytopenia may be due to many systemic diseases, or to drugs. It occurs in connective tissue diseases including systemic lupus erythematosus. SLE may cause hypertension due to renal damage and its treatment with corticosteroids may cause blood pressure to rise further. Hydralazine can cause a reversible drug-induced lupus syndrome. Platelet counting is a time-consuming procedure in some laboratories and should be performed only where there is a particular clinical suspicion, or during the monitoring of newly available antihypertensive drugs.

- **The ESR** This is a useful but non-specific test for infection and connective tissue disease.

Biochemistry

- **Serum sodium** This is high or high/normal in primary hyperaldosteronism (145 to 155 mmol/l) and returns to normal with treatment with spironolactone or with surgery.

  In renal or malignant hypertension, with or without chronic renal failure where there may be secondary hyperaldosteronism, serum sodium is low or low/normal (125 to 135 mmol/l). Rarely, diuretics, including Moduretic, can cause extreme hyponatraemia (110 mmol/l).[8]

- **Serum potassium** The commonest cause of hypokalaemia is diuretic therapy. In cases of suspected aldosterone excess it is therefore necessary to stop diuretics for at least four weeks to obtain a reliable measure of serum electrolytes. While normokalaemic primary hyperaldosteronism has been described, it is extremely rare, and even then serum potassium is usually in the lower part of the normal range. The presence of hypokalaemia with a serum potassium of 3.6 mmol/l or less is a strong indicator of either primary or secondary aldosterone excess and always requires further investigation.[9]

  Hyperkalaemia occurs in acute or chronic renal failure. It may also occur if the potassium-sparing diuretics, spironolactone, amiloride or triamterene, are given to patients with renal failure or with inappropriate potassium supplementation or with the ACE inhibitors (captopril or enalapril). Hyperkalaemia is also occasionally seen when ACE inhibitors are prescribed together with beta-blockers.

- **Serum bicarbonate** Hypokalaemia causes a metabolic alkalosis with a high serum bicarbonate. This occurs with aldosterone excess and with diuretic therapy. A metabolic acidosis with low serum bicarbonate in association with hypokalaemia suggests congenital or acquired renal tubular disease, particularly renal tubular acidosis in adults. It may also rarely occur in chronic pyelonephritis.

- **Serum urea or creatinine** Serum creatinine is a less labile index of renal function than serum urea. Patients should have their renal function monitored regularly, and at least once per year even if previous results are normal. In cases with chronic renal failure, the reciprocal of the serum creatinine when checked regularly may be a good index of deterioration of renal function, and can predict when future chronic dialysis may become necessary (see Figure 7.8). Estimations of creatinine clearance are not particularly useful in routine practice.

- **Serum calcium** Hypertension is present in up to 60 per cent of cases of primary hyperparathyroidism, so such cases are seen commonly in blood pressure clinics. Thiazide diuretics can also cause mild hypercalcaemia and may reveal covert primary hyperparathyroidism. If this diagnosis is suspected, diuretic therapy should be stopped for at least four weeks prior to rechecking calcium levels.

- **Serum phosphate** A raised serum phosphate may occur in chronic renal failure, and in primary hyperparathyroidism low levels are encountered.

HAEMATOLOGY DUDLEY ROAD HOSPITAL

Investigation Required

FBC, ESR please

Clinical Details

Hypertension

RESULTS	TEST	EXPECT RANGE		Date **6/7/86**	
~~75~~	WBC x10³/ul	4.8-10.8			
~~48.4~~	RBC x10⁶/ul	M 4.7-6.1 / F 4.2-5.4	ANISO		
17.1	HGB g/dl	M 14-18 / F 12-16	MICRO		
48.0	HCT %	M 42-52 / F 37-47	MACRO	**	
48	MCV fl	M 80-94 / F 81-99	VAR		
33.0	MCH pg	27-31	HYPO		
35.4	MCHC g/dl	33-37	HYPER		
	RDW %	11.5-14.5	LEFT SHIFT		
	PLT x10³/ul	130-400	ATYP		
DIFFERENTIAL ☐			BLASTS		
RESULT %	TEST	EXPECT RANGE	NRBC		
			OTHER		
	NEUT	40.0-74.0			
	LYMP	19.0-48.0	ESR (West) **6**		mm
	MONO	3.4-9.0	Retics		%
			P.T.T.		secs.
	EOS	0.0-7.0	Prothrombin		secs.
	BASO	0.0-1.5	Control		secs.

Surname OTHER	Ward OP	Unit No. 617819
First Names ANDREW	Consultant DGB	
Address 24 West Street Handsworth	Date of Birth 4/6/47	
	Date of Admission —	

Figure 7.7 A full haematological profile from a hypertensive patient, showing mild polycythaemia and macrocytosis, suggestive of a high alcohol intake.

- **Serum uric acid** Hyperuricaemia is found in about 40 per cent of untreated essential hypertensives, even when renal function is normal. It is more common in hypertension associated with renal damage. Hyperuricaemia is also common in people consuming excess alcohol. Diuretic therapy causes serum uric acid to be raised in 60 per cent of cases, even though clinical gout is seen only in about 2 per cent.

- **Serum lipids** Hyperlipidaemia is an important risk factor for coronary heart disease, independent of raised blood pressure.[10] There is also an association between hypercholesterolaemia and hypertension. Furthermore, both diuretics and beta-blockers cause a small rise in serum cholesterol (they lower HDL and raise LDL cholesterol) and cause a rise in serum triglycerides. If serum lipid levels are abnormal at routine screening, tests should be repeated after overnight fasting. Low cholesterol and animal fat diets may be recommended to control serum lipids and may help reduce blood pressure.

- **Serum glutamyl transpeptidase (GGT) or aspartate aminotransferase (AST)** These enzymes are useful indicators of alcohol excess, and GGT should be checked in hypertensive patients if they appear Cushingoid, have polycythaemia, macrocytosis or hyperuricaemia.

The chest x-ray

Radiological assessment of cardiac size is not very reliable as variations occur depending on the depth of inspiration. For this reason, a chest x-ray may be omitted unless specifically indicated. It is necessary if there is concurrent chest disease or left heart failure. The cardiothoracic ratio should be recorded each time a chest x-ray is taken.

The presence of fractured ribs should raise the possibility of alcohol excess.

In coarctation of the aorta there is notching of the inferior edge of the second to the sixth ribs owing to dilated intercostal arteries. Also there may be sharp indentation of the lateral border of the initial portion of the descending aorta, creating a figure 3 appearance (see Figure 7.9).

The electrocardiogram (see Figure 7.10)
All hypertensive patients requiring anti-hypertensive drugs should have an ECG taken. It is particularly useful as a reference if the patient subsequently develops symptoms of coronary heart disease. The ECG should also be checked annually in all severe hypertensives. It may reveal evidence of myocardial infarction or of left ventricular hypertrophy.[11] The presence of left ventricular hypertrophy should influence the clinician. If present it is an indication to take effective action to control blood pressure. If absent, the clinician may well opt to withhold therapy in mild cases. The ECG abnormalities in left ventricular hypertrophy are:

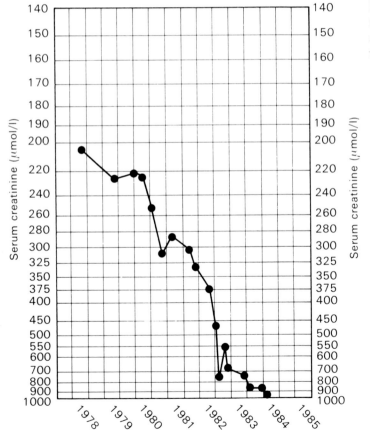

Figure 7.8 Example of a reciprocal creatinine chart in a patient with chronic renal failure.

- Biphasic p wave in leads V1 and V2 indicating left atrial dilatation. This is not a very specific ECG sign, but is seen before other features of hypertension.
- Tall R waves (more than 12 mmHg) in lead aVF.
- Chest lead criteria: R V5 or V6 plus SV1 more than 35 mm.
- ST depression and T wave inversion in leads V5 and V6, which indicate relative ischaemia due to a hypertrophied left ventricle (the strain pattern).

Atrial fibrillation which is otherwise unexplained, associated with cardiomegaly, strongly suggests alcohol excess.

Urinary sodium

With the increasing awareness of the value of sodium restriction in the treatment of mild hypertension, there is a good case for measuring twenty-four-hour urinary sodium output at the stage of first assessment and thereafter monitoring the reduction of salt in the diet. While this is a simple test, it cannot be conducted routinely unless local laboratories are geared up to estimate large numbers of samples. In the future this may become a normal routine, and dipsticks which provide a simple measure of urinary sodium concentration may become available.

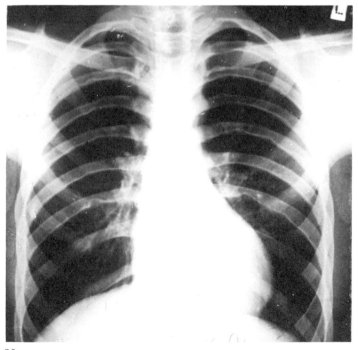

Figure 7.9 Chest x-ray of a patient with aortic coarctation showing notching of the inferior surfaces of the third to seventh rib.

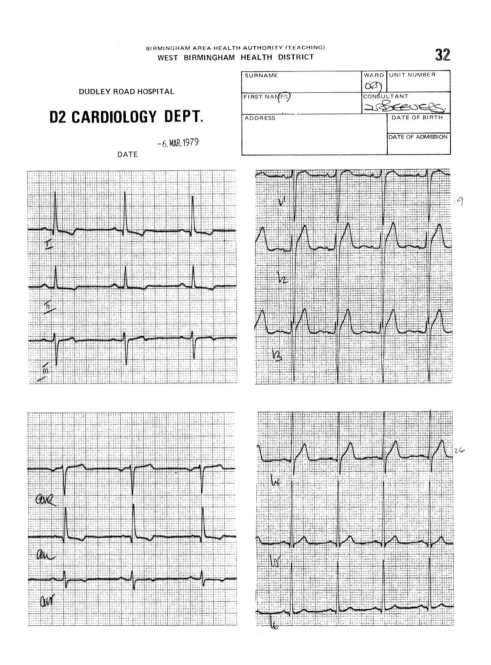

Figure 7.10 ECG from a patient with left ventricular hypertrophy.

INVESTIGATION OF HYPERTENSION IN PRIMARY CARE

This is discussed in Chapter 13. For the primary care practitioner, a reasonable rule is to investigate all patients in whom drug treatment is thought necessary. The investigations needed are a urine test, a full blood count, a biochemical profile and an ECG. In the majority of patients, however, no abnormalities will be found, but most of the abnormalities that are found are important.

More detailed investigation, possibly with referral to a hypertension clinic, should be reserved for those who fulfil the following criteria:

- Below the age of forty-five
- Blood pressure resistant to the combination of two drugs
- Severe hypertension (diastolic blood pressure 120 mmHg or more)
- Suspicion of a cause or complication of hypertension from clinical assessment or routine investigations.

FURTHER INVESTIGATION

The more detailed investigations to be conducted in these cases are discussed in Chapter 8. In a large primary health care group there may be one physician who specializes in hypertension, who may choose to investigate further without hospital referral. In resistant cases an intravenous urogram or a twenty-four-hour collection of urine for urinary catecholamine metabolites may be ordered. However, these require discussion with the local laboratories and radiology departments.

In hospital practice there are still too few blood pressure clinics so that patients are distributed between cardiologists, nephrologists and general physicians. Clinical care thus may be very unsystematic. There is a need for specialized hypertension clinics where, in close liaison with primary medical care, hypertensives can be managed efficiently.

PRACTICAL POINTS

- All new hypertensive patients in whom drug therapy is likely to be necessary should undergo the above tests when first seen.

- Any abnormalities should be monitored regularly.

- If diuretics are used, the biochemical profile should be rechecked after three months and thereafter annually.

- More detailed tests are unnecessary in most cases of uncomplicated essential hypertension, where the blood pressure can be controlled without difficulty.

8
Further investigation of hypertension

BACKGROUND

About 20 per cent of the general population have a diastolic blood pressure above 90 mmHg or a systolic pressure above 160 mmHg. However, studies based on hypertensives in the general population have shown that under 2 per cent of these people have an underlying cause for their raised blood pressure. Most other published series have been from hospital practice and here a larger number of patients have an underlying cause for their high blood pressure. In primary care probably less than one patient in fifty has an identifiable cause and the rest are classified as essential hypertension, which means that the cause is not understood (see Chapter 4). In the rare patient with secondary hypertension the condition may be curable, so detailed investigation is necessary.

How far to investigate Certain investigations such as routine haematological and biochemical profiles and urine tests should be done on all patients and may point to a renal or adrenal disease; these are discussed in Chapter 7. Investigating for rare causes of hypertension such as a phaeochromocytoma or renal artery stenosis is costly and complicated and may carry some risk. The dilemma is how far to investigate patients to be sure of not missing a rare but curable form of high blood pressure.

In general, patients whose blood pressures are very severe or who are resistant to conventional treatment should be investigated further. There is stronger chance of finding an underlying cause in younger patients. However, the majority of the investigations discussed in this chapter should be done only by doctors with a special interest in high blood pressure, as their interpretation is not always clear cut, and special experience is necessary.

NON-ROUTINE TESTS

Plain x-ray of the abdomen

This may sometimes be useful in revealing previously unsuspected renal or vascular calcification, renal stones or possibly a difference in kidney size, which is suggestive of unilateral disease. Phaeochromocytoma may occasionally be seen as a soft tissue shadow above one kidney.

Intravenous urography

This used to be done as a routine in patients referred to hospital with high blood pressure. Several studies have shown that this is not worthwhile as the yield of previously unsuspected abnormalities is small and the procedure itself may rarely cause life-threatening allergic reactions. The IVU should be done only in younger patients with severe hypertension or if there is some reason to suspect an underlying kidney disease, such as the presence of renal bruits, heavy proteinuria, red cells or casts in the urine, increased serum urea or creatinine concentrations, or clinical signs suggestive of polycystic disease.

Renal arteriogram

This test is done to exclude renal artery stenosis in selected cases.

CT scans

A CT scanner can play a vital role in localizing a phaeochromocytoma or an adrenal adenoma secreting aldosterone. However, the resolution and speed of most of the older scanners is such that some of the smaller tumours are missed.

Radioisotope imaging

Radioisotope renograms used to be used in diagnosis of renal artery stenosis, often with misleading results. They are not now widely used in the investigation of hypertension. Selenium cholesterol scans of the adrenal glands used to be done for primary aldosteronism, but these could also be misleading.

Nevertheless, while the investigation of hypertension by radioisotope imaging has been disappointing, there are certain centres where good results have been obtained. In particular, radioisotope methods have been employed successfully for localizing phaeochromocytomas.

Echocardiography

Echocardiography is a specialized test that is more accurate in assessing left ventricular size and wall thickness than the ECG. It may be a good indicator of the severity and duration of high blood pressure. However, at present it remains a research tool, outside the routine assessment of patients.

Twenty-four-hour urine specimens

Catecholamine excretions The routine measurement of the urinary metabolites of adrenaline (epinephrine) and noradrenaline (norepinephrine) should be done only in the younger, more severe

hypertensives, or those with symptoms suggestive of phaeochromocytoma.

Different laboratories measure different metabolites. Urinary metanephrines and vanillylmandelic acid (VMA) are most commonly assayed. The urine collection requires a preservative, usually hydrochloric acid.

Creatinine excretion The measurement of urinary creatinine concentration can be used to assess the completeness of a twenty-four-hour urine collection. Most people excrete just above 1g of creatinine daily. Creatinine excretion is higher in men and in people with larger muscle bulk. If serum creatinine is measured concurrently, creatinine clearance can be calculated. In patients with renal impairment repeated estimates of serum creatinine with plotting on a reciprocal creatinine chart are more useful.

Electrolytes A rough guide to the sodium and potassium intake can be obtained by measuring twenty-four-hour urinary electrolytes. This can help to assess the patient's compliance with advice on dietary sodium restriction.

Urinary protein If the dipsticks tests show more than a trace of proteinuria, a twenty-four-hour collection should be carried out to measure total urinary protein loss.

Accuracy Twenty-four-hour urine collections may be very inaccurate. However, if efforts are made to explain the correct procedure to the patient, reasonable collections can be achieved (see Table 8.1). One large enough bottle or three 1-l bottles should be provided, together with a nontransparent carrier bag.

Blood hormone measurements

These are all specialized tests, indicated only if there is good reason to suspect secondary hypertension.

The renin–angiotensin system Plasma renin concentration, plasma renin activity, plasma angiotensin II and plasma aldosterone levels can all be measured in specialized centres. The easiest measurement is plasma renin activity. These tests are indicated only in patients where there is suspected renal artery stenosis or renin-secreting tumour where renin levels are high, or in primary aldosteronism where plasma renin activity is low. In both primary and secondary hyperaldosteronism, plasma aldosterone concen-

For the Guidance of Patients

Table 8.1

24-HOUR URINE COLLECTION

1. It is *IMPORTANT* to collect all urine that your kidneys make during a 24 hour period.
2. The collection should start in the morning between 6.00 a.m. and 10.00 a.m. The exact time you start should be written down.
3. For example, if you start on Sunday at 6.00 a.m. then you should finish your collection at 6.00 a.m. on Monday.
4. When you start the collection, empty your bladder and discard the urine.
5. All urine produced for the next 24 hours should be put into the bottle provided.
6. Exactly 24 hours after starting a collection, empty bladder whether you need to or not, but this time into the bottle.

If you forget or spill some of your urine during this period the collection is no good. Discard the urine and collect a new bottle from the laboratory or the Out-Patients Department. The best times to commence and finish the urine collection are as follows:

	Sunday morning (date and time started)	to	Monday morning (date and time finished)
OR	Monday morning (date and time started)	to	Tuesday morning (date and time finished)
OR	Wednesday morning (date and time started)	to	Thursday morning (date and time finished)
OR	Thursday morning (date and time started)	to	Friday morning (date and time finished)

HINTS

1. Put the bottle in the toilet so that you do not forget to use it.
2. Ladies may find it easier to pass urine into a jug and then put it into a bottle.
3. When you find the need to open your bowels, make sure you pass urine into the bottle first.

IMPORTANT
The 24-hour specimen of urine must be brought into the hospital on the same day it is completed.

tration is high, whereas plasma renin activity is low in primary and high in secondary aldosteronism.

Plasma catecholamines Estimations of plasma adrenaline and noradrenaline levels are helpful in diagnosis of phaeochromocytoma. Unfortunately, they are not readily available and reliance has still to be put on twenty-four-hour urinary VMA or metanephrine excretions.

Plasma cortisol Routine estimation of plasma cortisol is indicated where Cushing's syndrome is suspected. It is of limited use because of the diurnal variability of plasma cortisol. If a random plasma cortisol level is normal, Cushing's syndrome is very unlikely, but plethoric obese hypertensive patients need further investigation. Raised plasma cortisol levels are also seen in the alcoholic-pseudo-Cushing's syndrome. Mild elevations of plasma cortisol can occur in response to stress but return to normal on rechecking. If raised random plasma cortisol levels persist, an overnight dexamethasone suppression test should be performed.

ENDOCRINE CAUSES OF HIGH BLOOD PRESSURE

Primary aldosteronism (Conn's syndrome)

A small (½-1 in, or 1–2 cm), usually benign unilateral tumour (adenoma) of the adrenal cortex may secrete large quantities of aldosterone and cause elevation of body sodium and water and raised blood pressure.[1] Removal of the tumour reverses these abnormalities. A similar clinical and biochemical picture is, however, seen in some patients who do not have adenoma but bilateral adrenal hyperplasia. Here surgery is not useful. Secondary aldosteronism due to stimulation of adrenal secretion by high levels of renin and angiotensin occurs in some forms of renal disease and in malignant hypertension. It

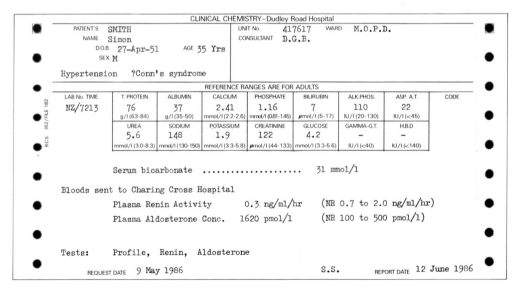

Figure 8.1 A clinical chemistry report in a patient with typical primary hyperaldosteronism, whose hypertension was corrected by removal of a right aldosterone-secreting adrenal adenoma.

is very important, therefore, to differentiate between these conditions.

Clinical features Most patients with primary aldosteronism have high blood pressure and low plasma potassium levels but no specific symptoms. Rarely, if they have very low potassium levels, they may have muscle weakness, tiredness and cardiac arrhythmias, which may be precipitated or worsened if thiazide diuretics are given. The blood pressure is sometimes severe and resistant to conventional treatment.

Biochemical features Plasma potassium is usually 1.5 to 2.5 mmol/l, although this level of hypokalaemia is not invariable and normokalaemic cases have been described. Plasma sodium is usually between 140 and 155 mmol/l. There is a metabolic alkalosis (high serum bicar-

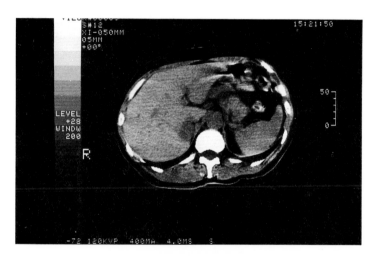

Figure 8.2 CT scan showing a large right adrenal tumour, which was an aldosterone secreting adenoma.

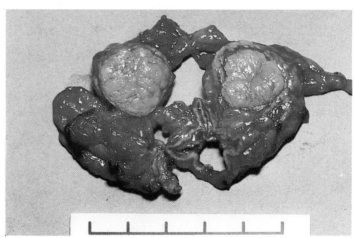

Figure 8.3 Typical adrenal adenoma causing primary aldosteronism.

bonate) in association with the hypo-kalaemia. Plasma aldosterone levels are high, but plasma renin activity is usually very low (see Figure 8.1).

Diagnostic procedures All patients with otherwise unexplained hypokalaemia should have plasma renin activity measured. If renin is low or low/normal further investigations including measurement of plasma aldosterone are necessary. If low-renin hyperaldosteronism is confirmed and surgical treatment of a possible adrenal tumour is contemplated, highly specialized further investigation is required.

Adrenal venography and adrenal vein sampling This highly specialized procedure may outline an adrenal tumour and provide proof that excess aldosterone secretion originates from one adrenal gland. It may be hazardous in inexperienced hands, leading to adrenal infarction, and is only rarely used.

CT scan (see Figure 8.2) While older CT scanners usually cannot detect the adrenal tumours of Conn's syndrome, the newer high-resolution scanners are more reliable, so this is now the most useful diagnostic and localizing procedure.

Diurnal variation In adenoma cases, there is loss of diurnal variation of plasma aldosterone secretion, and suppression does not occur after salt loading or treatment with fludrocortisone.

Treatment Once the adrenal adenoma has been localized, it is usual to remove it (see Figure 8.3). In cases where surgery is not feasible, the aldosterone antagonist spironolactone may be given in doses of between 100 and 300 mg daily, if necessary with the addition of nifedipine.

It is very rare for Conn's syndrome to be due to a malignant adrenal tumour, but it should be borne in mind and some recent reports of this suggest that adrenalectomy should be performed in all cases.

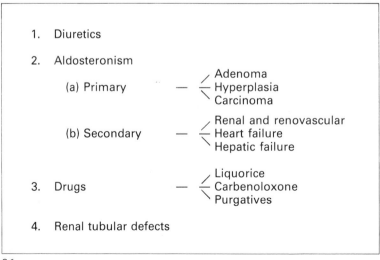

Table 8.2 Causes of hypokalaemia with high blood pressure.

1. Diuretics

2. Aldosteronism

    (a) Primary — Adenoma / Hyperplasia / Carcinoma

    (b) Secondary — Renal and renovascular / Heart failure / Hepatic failure

3. Drugs — Liquorice / Carbenoloxone / Purgatives

4. Renal tubular defects

Idiopathic aldosteronism

In this condition the biochemical features are similar to those of Conn's syndrome, but no tumour is found. Bilateral micronodular hyperplasia of the adrenal gland may be present. In general, patients without adrenal adenomas tend to have less marked hypokalaemia, less renin suppression, and only mildly raised plasma aldosterone levels. Rarely hyperaldosteronism may be controlled by dexamethasone.

Secondary aldosteronism

This occurs where aldosterone secretion is raised secondary to renin stimulation, in renal or renovascular disease. The prime abnormality is therefore not adrenal. This and other causes of hypokalaemia need to be excluded.

Other causes of hypokalaemia

The commonest cause of hypokalaemia is diuretic therapy, and the potassium levels may remain low for up to four weeks after treatment has been stopped. The aldosterone-like liquorice derivative carbenoxolone, used in the treatment of peptic ulcer, can cause hypertension with hypokalaemia (see Chapter 5).

Hypokalaemia occurs with intestinal potassium loss, particularly where there is overuse of purgatives and laxatives. Secondary aldosterone excess may also occur with cardiac failure and hepatic disease. Both increased renin release and decreased hepatic breakdown of aldosterone contribute to the raised aldosterone levels (see Table 8.2).

Cushing's syndrome

This results from excessive secretion of cortisol, which may be due either to autonomous oversecretion by the adrenal gland or to raised ACTH secretion from a pituitary tumour.[2] Cushing's syndrome is usually suspected on the basis of clinical appearance and estimation of plasma cortisol levels (see page 94). The diagnosis is confirmed either by the measurement of twenty-four-hour urinary free cortisol secretion or by an overnight dexamethasone suppression test and measurement of the diurnal rhythm of plasma cortisol levels.

Some ACTH tumours also cause excess aldosterone secretion and these may present with a low potassium/high blood pressure picture, not unlike primary aldosteronism. Further investigations to distinguish between ACTH–secreting tumours and excessive cortisol secretion by adrenal tumours or hyperplasia involve using a variety of highly specialized endocrine tests.

Adrenal enzyme deficiencies

Various congenital deficiencies of the enzymes responsible for the synthesis of adrenal steroid hormones from cholesterol have been described (11-beta-hydroxylase and 17-alpha-hydroxylase deficiencies). These are usually present in children or young adults who may present with high blood pressure, low serum potassium and failure to achieve sexual maturation or, sometimes, virilization.

Phaeochromocytoma

These are chromaffin cell tumours which produce the most dramatic form of hypertension.[3] They are not necessarily confined to the adrenal medulla but may occur in the sympathetic chain of ganglia down the retroperitoneal space. They have also been described in the thoracic sympathetic chain and in many other parts of the body. They are characterized by intermittent or continuous over-secretion of noradrenaline and adrenaline, with the expected symptoms of tachycardia, blanching, sweating and sudden rises in blood pressure. They may present at any age and are not uncommon in children.

Patients usually have very severe hypertension, often in the malignant phase. Some patients have only mild hypertension, but develop intermittent surges of very high blood pressure or episodes of postural hypotension (see Table 8.3).

Diagnosis Phaeochromocytomas are extremely rare, and routine investigation of all hypertensive patients either by measurement of plasma noradrenaline levels or the urinary metabolites is not practical. In view of this, clinical acumen has to be used in selecting patients for further investigation. The following symptoms suggest the need for measuring catecholamines in urine or blood:

- A story of intermittent high blood pressure, sweating attacks and palpitations
- Thin patients or those presenting with weight loss

- Patients with resistant hypertension or the malignant phase
- Congestive cardiac failure, which is not uncommon, due to a specific myocarditis secondary to high plasma catecholamine levels.

Investigation The simplest investigations are twenty-four-hour urine collections for catecholamines or catecholamine metabolites, for example, vanyllilmandelic acid (VMA) or metanephrines. However, some tumours do not cause excess VMA or metanephrines in the urine and will be missed.

The best test is to measure plasma noradrenaline levels. This is raised in the vast majority of tumours.

If plasma noradrenaline or urine VMA excretion is raised, the next step is to localize the tumour. Large adrenal tumours can be seen on a plain x-ray of the abdomen or during intravenous urog-

Site		Blood pressure		
Abdominal	98%	Hypertensive 98%	– intermittent	30%
– adrenal	70%		– sustained	50%
– extra-adrenal	10%		– paroxysmal	20%
– multiple	20%		– malignant	
– bilateral	10%		phase	40%
Thoracic	2%			
Neck	<1%	Normotensive 2%		
Familial	10%			
Malignant tumour	10%	**Symptoms**		

Symptoms	
Headache	80%
Sweating	70%
Palpitations	60%
Nervousness	40%
Nausea	40%
Weight loss	40%

Table 8.3 Phaeochromocytoma.

raphy. Abdominal ultrasound will locate tumours but CT scanning is the most accurate technique (see Figure 8.4). The majority are in the adrenal glands but they may be bilateral or extra-adrenal and are occasionally multiple. Some of the tumours are malignant and may metast-asize causing bone secondaries. It is often difficult to differentiate histo-logically between benign and malignant phaeochromocytomas.

Treatment Phaeochromocytomas should always be excised surgically (see Figure

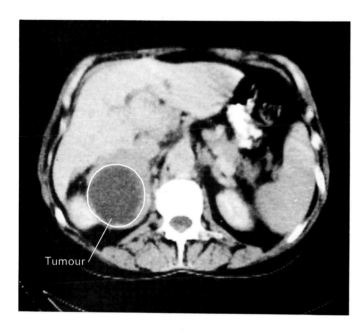

Figure 8.4 CT scan of a large right adrenal phaeochromocytoma.

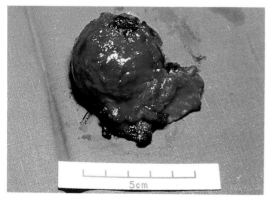
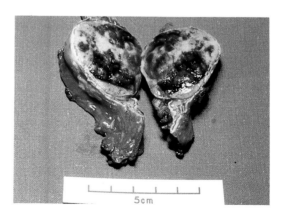

Figure 8.5 A typical phaeochromocytoma.

8.5). This is often not easy, as dramatic rises in blood pressure may occur owing to the release of noradrenaline during induction of anaesthesia and when the tumour is being mobilized. Patients must be carefully prepared preoperatively, and an expert anaesthetic and surgical team are needed.

Before operation all patients must be treated medically. Acute paroxysms of hypertension can be controlled with the alpha-blocker phentolamine, 2 to 5 mg being given intravenously. This is a short-acting alpha-blocker lasting for only a few minutes. However, phenoxybenzamine, a longer-acting alpha-blocker, can be given orally twice daily. The dose should be started at 10 mg twice daily and increased slowly until pressure is at the desired level. Occasionally, there may be postural hypotension. A beta-blocker such as propranolol should also be used in small doses to control heart rate but should not be started until after alpha-blockade has been established. Beta-blockade alone in a patient with phaeochromocytoma can sometimes cause dangerous rises in blood pressure. Other drugs such as prazosin and labetalol may be of use, but in our experience are not as good as a combination of phenoxybenzamine and a beta-blocker. It is important that all patients are adequately alpha-blocked to overcome the intense vasoconstriction prior to surgery, in order to avoid sudden profound hypotension after removal of the tumour.

Premedication prior to surgery can be hazardous, and diazepam alone is probably safest. During intubation blood pressure may rise to high levels. For this reason, intra-arterial blood pressure monitoring devices should be attached before the induction of anaesthesia. During the operation, blood pressures are best controlled by either sodium nitroprusside infusion or phen-

tolamine. Pulse rate can be controlled by an intravenous beta-blocker.

At the time of removal of the tumour it is frequently necessary to transfuse blood and saline quickly since blood pressure often falls to low levels, even with prior treatment with alpha-blockers.

Recurrences of phaeochromocytoma may occur, and all patients should be followed up carefully. This is commoner in children, and annual rechecking of urine catecholamine metabolites is sometimes necessary.

There are very rare familial varieties of phaeochromocytoma with other endocrine tumours, particularly hyperparathyroidism and medullary cell carcinoma of the thyroid (multiple endocrine neoplasia type II: the Sipple syndrome). Phaeochromocytomas are also associated with Von Recklinghausen's neurofibromatosis and carotid body tumours and are occasionally seen in association with renal artery stenosis.

Other neural crest tumours

Neuroblastomas and ganglioneuromas cause hypertension and abdominal tumours in children and occasionally in adults.

Parathyroid and thyroid

Many patients with primary hyperparathyroidism have hypertension. The mechanism of the high blood pressure is not known. Removal of the parathyroid adenoma does not usually correct the hypertension. There is no relationship between the height of the blood pressure and plasma levels of parathormone, calcium or creatinine. As serum calcium is often measured as routine biochemical profile, this is now a common clinical problem.

Hypertension itself is not necessarily an indication for parathyroidectomy unless there is renal damage, metabolic bone disease or other symptoms. Thiazide diuretics themselves cause an increase in plasma calcium in some people and this may be a diagnostic indicator of mild primary hyperparathyroidism.

Patients with hyperthyroidism often have an increase in systolic pressure. Patients with myxoedema may also have an increased blood pressure, but again the mechanisms are unknown.[2]

Acromegaly

Hypertension occurs commonly in cases of acromegaly, and cardiovascular complications are the commonest cause of death. Plasma renin levels are low, and the hypertension may be due to volume expansion. Cardiomegaly is also present. Diagnosis is made by measuring plasma growth hormone levels.

RENAL CAUSES OF HIGH BLOOD PRESSURE

High blood pressure secondary to kidney disease may be due to the underlying kidney damage causing sodium retention or an inappropriate release of renin, with consequent high circulating levels of angiotensin II.[4] Usually hypertension in parenchymal renal disease is due to a combination of both these factors, but it may involve other less well understood factors.

Renal artery stenosis

This, of all the causes of hypertension, has attracted the most attention because good animal models have been developed.[5]

Cause The arterial narrowing in patients below the age of forty may be due to fibromuscular hyperplasia of the renal or intrarenal arteries. In older cases, the stenosis is more likely to be due to atheroma.

Rarely there may be extra-arterial compression by retroperitoneal tumours. If there is a narrowing of the artery to one kidney, the reduced renal bloodflow causes increased release of renin, and plasma angiotensin II levels rise. This causes the high blood pressure. In reality, the situation is more complicated because often the other kidney is damaged and there may therefore be secondary sodium retention with some switching off of the renin system.

Diagnosis There are no particular clinical features of renal artery stenosis, although many patients have malignant hypertension. Renal bruits are audible in about 40 per cent of cases. All patients with malignant hypertension or blood pressure that is resistant to conventional treatment should be investigated for renal artery stenosis.

Investigations

- **Intravenous urography** Even in florid cases, the IVU may be normal. However, features suggestive of renal artery stenosis are:
  —One kidney smaller than the other, but with smooth outlines.
  —Delay in appearance of the radio-paque dye on the affected side; it is important when performing an IVU for hypertension to take an immediate film after the dye has been injected to detect this delay.
  —In films taken fifteen minutes or more after injection, there may be hyperconcentration with some dilatation of the renal pelvis on the affected side.

- **Isotope renography** This is not usually a reliable test for renovascular disease.

101

- **Renal arteriogram** This is the only reliable test for renal artery stenosis. It requires catheterization of a femoral artery, followed by a flush aortogram and selective renal artery catheterization (see Figure 8.6). It is not without hazard and should not be carried out if the blood pressure is very high, as bleeding from the site of arterial puncture may develop. It is only justified if there is a strong suspicion of renovascular disease, or occasionally if failure to control pressure means that the patient's outlook is so bad that, despite a normal IVU, special efforts are needed to exclude a treatable cause for the hypertension. Since the development of new techniques for balloon catheter dilatation of stenosed renal arteries, there has been a renewed interest in the diagnosis and treatment of this condition.

- **Digital subtraction angiography** Using special equipment it is now possible to visualize the renal arteries from an intravenous injection of radio-opaque contrast medium. This procedure is not yet fully assessed but is much less hazardous than arteriography and may be used as a screening test in suspected renal artery stenosis.

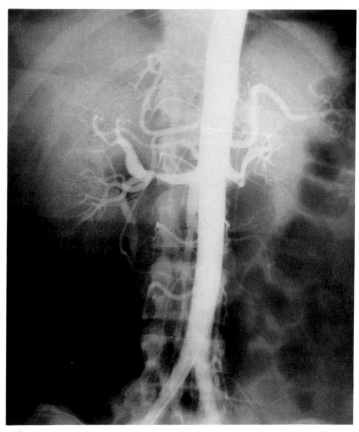

Figure 8.6 Bilateral renal artery stenosis in a young woman. Note the left kidney is smaller than the right.

- **Renin** Plasma renin activity levels are often high in renal artery stenosis, but unfortunately this is not a reliable indicator of the diagnosis. Renin levels may be normal even in cases where the renal arteries are markedly narrowed.

- **Renal vein catheterization** (see Figure 8.7) Measuring renal venous renin levels involves catheterizing both renal veins from the femoral vein. This is a relatively easy technique in specialized centres. The value of renal vein renin estimations is, however, controversial.

  Various criteria have been suggested to predict the outcome of surgery or balloon dilatation of the renal arteries.

Such treatment is said to be successful if the renal vein renin levels are at least 1.5 times higher on the affected side compared with the normal kidney. However, in severe renal artery stenosis, bloodflow to the affected kidney will be reduced and may be secreting very little renin but have a high renin concentration in venous blood owing to the low bloodflow. It is important therefore to compare the renal vein renin concentration with the renin levels above and below the kidneys in the inferior vena cava.

Treatment There remains some debate on the usefulness of surgical treatment for

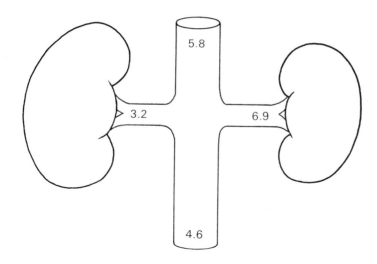

Figure 8.7 Plasma renin activity levels in renal artery stenosis. Renal venous renin ratio is 6.9:3.2, i.e., 2.2:1. Note the level above the kidneys is higher than on the unaffected left side.

renal artery stenosis, especially in older cases due to atheromatous narrowing. Often renal artery reconstruction is technically difficult and there has been doubt as to whether operation provides any advantage over good blood pressure control with drugs alone. With the recent advent of balloon catheter arterial dilatation, things may change (see Figure 8.8).

There are many reasons why more detailed investigation for renal artery stenosis is now justified:

- Surgery or balloon dilatation in reliable hands can produce excellent results, particularly in younger pati-

ents, thus avoiding lifelong drug therapy.

- Even if blood pressure is not normalized, control with drugs may be rendered easier.
- If the arterial supply to the kidney is seriously embarrassed, dilatation or operation may help to preserve renal function.
- Younger patients with severe hypertension should be operated on, particularly if they have fibromuscular hyperplasia of the renal arteries.
- Both fibromuscular hyperplasia and atheroma are progressive diseases and

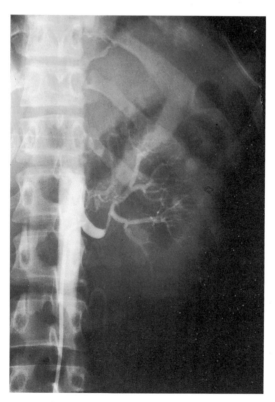 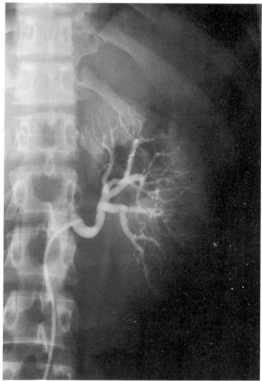

Figure 8.8 Balloon dilatation in a young woman with unilateral renal artery stenosis (*left*, before and, *right*, after dilatation).

they may recur either in the same renal artery or on the other side.

Other factors One of the most important aspects of the atheromatous group is that they are nearly always heavy cigarette smokers, and they should be persuaded to stop. Hyperlipidaemia is also an important risk factor for atheroma, so serum cholesterol levels should be measured and if it is raised, action should be taken.

Renin secreting tumours

There are very rare tumours of the renal juxtaglomerular cells (haemangiopericytomas) which directly cause high blood pressure by excessive renin secretion.[6] They usually occur in children or young adults who have malignant hypertension, with very high plasma renin and angiotensin II levels and hypokalaemia due to secondary hyperaldosteronism. Children may have retarded growth. Diagnosis involves differentiating these tumours from other causes of high renin secretion such as malignant hypertension itself or renal artery stenosis. Renal vein renin levels show excessive renin secretion from one side without renal artery stenosis, and these tumours, which are often small, may be seen on renal arteriography. They are a very rare cause of high blood pressure, but if the tumour can be localized and removed, the patient can be cured.

Hypertension may occur in association with renal carcinoma (Grawitz tumour) or juvenile renal tumours (Wilms' tumour).

Other causes of renal hypertension

Most forms of renal disease cause high blood pressure. The only renal diseases not complicated by raised blood pressure are those affecting the renal medulla alone, where there may be loss of sodium and therefore low blood pressure.[4]

Glomerulonephritis

Both acute and chronic glomerulonephritis are associated with high blood pressure. Particularly severe hypertension is found in patients with IgA nephropathy, very often with raised plasma renin activity. Many of these patients develop the malignant phase of hypertension with acute deterioration in renal function requiring dialysis and transplantation. Further investigation of renal disease is outside the scope of this book but involves microscopy of the urine, intravenous urography, exclusion of tuberculosis by early-morning urine cultures and, if indicated, renal biopsy. It is important to control the blood pressure before renal biopsy is performed.

Pyelonephritis

Features suggestive of radiological pyelonephritis with calyceal clubbing and areas of renal cortical thinning are sometimes seen in hypertensives. There remains some doubt as to whether this form of kidney damage causes hypertension, unless there is associated chronic renal failure. Similarly, there is controversy about associations between hypertension and chronic urinary infection even though renal function may be preserved.

Polycystic disease (see Figure 8.9)
This is a mendelian dominant condition causing bilateral renal cysts, berry aneurysms of the circle of Willis and sometimes hepatic and pancreatic cysts. Often it is not diagnosed until middle age. The presenting features are hypertension, subarachnoid haemorrhage, abdominal (renal) pain, haematuria and the insidious development of chronic renal failure. The accurate control of blood pressure can prevent or delay some of these complications.

It is important to screen symptomless

blood relatives of all patients for polycystic disease. Renal ultrasonography is the simplest noninvasive screening test. The urographic features are stretching and splaying of the renal calyces by the cysts with lobulated renal enlargement. Women of child-bearing potential discovered to have the condition should be advised that around 50 per cent of their children will have polycystic disease. However, with medical supervision, the prognosis is not sufficiently bad to recommend avoidance of pregnancy.

Diabetic nephrosclerosis

The topic of diabetic hypertension is discussed in Chapter 14. Hypertension is common in diabetics with renal involvement. Diabetics are prone to develop glomerular lesions, pyelonephritis and renal papillary necrosis.

Scleroderma (Progressive systemic sclerosis; see Figure 8.10)

Patients with scleroderma may develop malignant hypertension and acute renal failure. Treatment with the ACE inhibitor captopril may possibly help to preserve renal function, but usually longterm dialysis is inevitable.

Lupus

If systemic lupus erythematosus involves the kidney, hypertension and renal failure

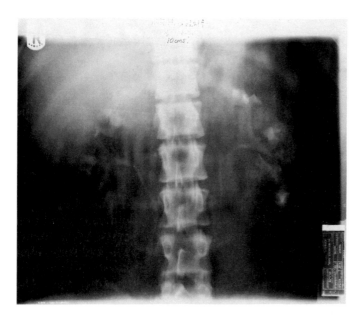

Figure 8.9 IVP showing splayed out renal calyces due to large cysts.

can follow rapidly. Corticosteroid therapy is usually mandatory as it may delay the progression of the renal lesion.

A reversible lupus syndrome can be caused by hydralazine therapy.

Unilateral renal parenchymatous disease

Occasionally hypertensive patients are found to have unilateral renal disease, either pyelonephritis or tuberculosis, and possibly renal agenesis. There must be some doubt as to whether other unilateral renal diseases cause hypertension or are just incidental findings.

Hypertension in chronic renal failure

Chronic renal failure of any cause is closely associated with hypertension. In most cases it is due to a combination of sodium and water retention and high plasma renin levels. Continued accurate control of blood pressure is important as it may delay further deterioration in renal function. Hypertensive patients with this condition should be referred to a nephrologist (see Chapter 14).

Retroperitoneal fibrosis

Fibrosis of the retroperitoneal tissues may occur after treatment with methysergide, or may be associated with retroperitoneal tumours. Most often, however, no cause is found. The ureters are pulled medially and may become obstructed, causing bilateral hydronephrosis. There has been some suspicion that beta-blockers other than practolol cause retroperitoneal fibrosis, but it is now felt that the association is apparent rather than real. The chain of events is that the fibrosis causes renal damage which causes hypertension, which is then treated with beta-blockers. Subsequent investigation reveals the retroperitoneal fibrosis on intravenous urography, and this is incorrectly blamed on the beta-blockers.

Obstructive uropathy

It is doubtful whether urinary outflow tract obstruction causes hypertension. If chronic renal failure ensues, then the blood pressure may rise. In older patients with prostatic enlargement and chronic urinary retention, hypertension would be expected to be common, but it appears to be no more so than in the general population of that age.

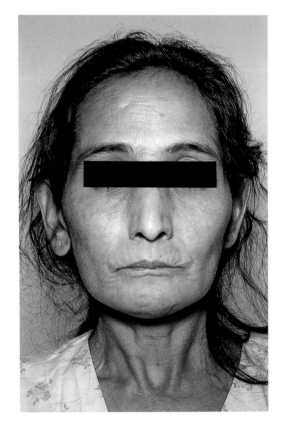

Figure 8.10 Woman with scleroderma showing the typical pinched mouth appearance.

PRACTICAL POINTS

- Under 2 per cent of hypertensives in the general population have a secondary cause.

- Primary hyperaldosteronism, phaeochromocytoma and renal artery stenosis, while rare, are potentially remediable causes of hypertension.

- Patients whose hypertension is very severe or resistant to conventional treatment should be referred for investigation by a specialist.

PART 3: MANAGEMENT

9
Who benefits from antihypertensive treatment?

BACKGROUND

Until about thirty years ago, hypertension was a most depressing disease; although a fair amount was known about the natural history, very little could be done to alleviate its consequences. Patients might be told to rest, to relax, or where relevant to lose weight—but otherwise there was little to offer. In very severe cases, particularly patients with malignant hypertension, heroic surgical procedures like adrenalectomy or sympathectomy were sometimes resorted to, with only limited short-term success.

The great event in the management of hypertensive patients was the development of antihypertensive drugs during the 1950s. Since that time, newer and better drugs have become available, and more and more people have benefited from treatment. There remain, however, some major unanswered questions on who and how to treat, and clinical trials are still under way to resolve some of these problems. The purpose of this chapter is to review the results of the trials available to date.

THE TREATMENT OF MALIGNANT HYPERTENSION

Malignant hypertension is a rare condition; if it is left untreated death occurs within one year from heart failure, renal failure, cerebral haemorrhage, and occasionally myocardial infarction (see Figure 9.1).

110

When the ganglion blocking drugs first became available, it rapidly became apparent that lives were being saved. The drugs used then—mecamylamine, pempidine, hexamethonium and pentolinium—were fairly intolerable with disabling side-effects but they saved lives dramatically. No placebo-controlled clinical trials were necessary or justified.[1]

BRIEF REVIEW OF THE CLINICAL TRIALS OF NON-MALIGNANT HYPERTENSION

The decision to institute antihypertensive drug therapy in a previously symptomless patient is a major one. The consequences to the patient, his job, his recreation and his general sense of well-being are obvious. Drug therapy should not be instituted unless the clinician is absolutely confident that therapy has been proven to be worthwhile. It has been suggested that hypertension could best be defined as that level of blood pressure where antihypertensive therapy does more good than harm. This pragmatic approach depends on a very careful scrutiny of the evidence that treatment prevents both fatal and nonfatal complications. The various published treatment trials need to be analysed critically, and clinicians must be aware not only of the proven benefits of treatment but also of the areas still to be investigated.

There have been only a limited number of trials of the drug treatment of hypertension in the prevention of vascular complications. These trials have to be large, with follow-up over many years. Statistically significant results can be achieved only by large multicentre studies, which are expensive and difficult to conduct. A review of these illustrates some of the problems and draws attention to the remaining unanswered questions.

The Chelmsford Study, 1964
The first controlled trial of antihypertensive treatment was conducted in Chelmsford, England in 1964. The control group patients did not, however, receive placebo therapy but were simply followed-up very carefully. Diastolic pressures all exceeded 110 mmHg before therapy.[2] Of the twenty-two men in the study, those treated clearly faired better than controls. In the thirty-nine women, there was little difference in morbidity between treated and controls, but this was partly because blood pressure was not reduced in some of the treated women. When the data for the women were re-analysed on the basis of blood pressure reduced versus not reduced, then clear-cut benefits were found in prevention of stroke and heart failure. Until 1979, this was the only published trial of the treatment of hypertension in women.

The First US Veterans' Administration Study, 1967
This study amongst 143 male armed services veterans largely confirmed the findings from Chelmsford.[3]

The Second US Veterans' Administration Study, 1970
This trial has received a great deal of attention and criticism and the points raised illustrate many of the problems of long-term treatment trials.[4] A total of 380 male

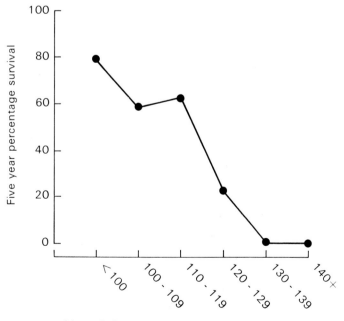

Figure 9.1 Five year survival rate in 200 cases of malignant hypertension, in relation to the accuracy of control of blood pressure at follow-up.

Five year percentage survival

Mean O P diastolic blood pressure (mmHg)

hypertensive patients with diastolic blood pressures ranging between 90 and 114 mmHg were randomly allocated to either an active or a placebo-treated group. Morbid events subsequently developed in thirty-five control group patients and nine actively treated patients. While the benefits of treating cases with blood pressures of 105 mmHg or more were impressive, detailed analysis of the milder cases provides suggestive evidence—but not proof—of the benefits of drug

therapy. Of the cases with diastolic pressures below 105 mmHg, 16 per cent of treated patients and 25 per cent of control patients developed morbid events. The greatest benefit was in the older patients who had vascular complications of hypertension before entry.

The frequency of vascular complication in the control group was surprisingly high, bearing in mind the relative mildness of their hypertension. There are several explanations for this. Firstly, all patients had been admitted to hospital prior to the study and only those whose diastolic blood pressures remained within the range 90 to 129 mmHg during the fourth to sixth day in the ward were entered into the trial. Even very high blood pressures may settle when patients are admitted to hospital. It can be argued that the data from this study do not reflect the results of treating mild hypertensives in the general population. The high proportion of black patients in the VA study (there were 157) may also explain the high frequency of vascular events. Black hypertensives do appear to differ from whites, with many more strokes, although they probably suffer fewer heart attacks (see Figure 9.2).

These early studies of antihypertensive treatment, whilst showing impressive reductions in stroke incidence, were disappointing in their apparent lack of coronary prevention. It is possible that this was because the process of deposition of coronary atheroma was so advanced in these relatively severe hypertensive patients that the introduction of therapy was too late to halt the process. It was argued that coronary prevention might be found if milder cases received treatment at an earlier stage of their disease. It was also considered possible that the use of thiazide diuretics, with their adverse

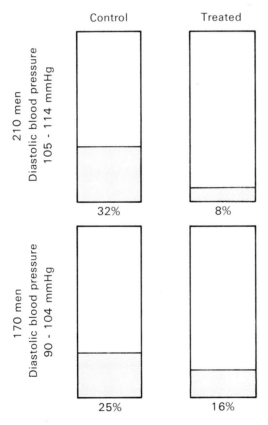

Figure 9.2 Results of the Veterans' Administration trial of the treatment of hypertension (the differences on the lower half of the figure did not reach statistical significance).

112

effects on potassium, glucose and lipids might have meant that the benefits of the reduction of blood pressure were partly offset by a harmful effect of other coronary risk factors.

After the 1970 VA study there was a surprising silence in the world literature and the much needed trials of treatment of mild hypertension did not appear until 1979 and after. There were in the meantime two interesting studies which do contribute to our knowledge of hypertension but do not provide definitive answers.

The Gothenburg Study, 1978

In 1978 a report from Sweden was published in which male hypertensives aged forty-seven to fifty-nine, derived from a single community, were studied.[5] Patients whose blood pressures exceeded 175/115 on two occasions were given active drug therapy. Those whose blood pressures were initially within this range, but which settled, constituted the untreated control group; they were regarded as having somewhat milder hypertension. The most important finding in this study was that the active treatment group suffered not only fewer strokes but also fewer heart attacks than the milder, untreated controls. This study is therefore the first to suggest that antihypertensive therapy might, after all, prevent coronary heart disease. As nearly all treated patients received beta-blocking agents, there was some speculation as to whether this coronary prevention was due to beta-blockers.

The United States Public Health Services Study, 1972

This was a small study of treatment of mild hypertension (diastolic blood pressure 90 to 114 mmHg) conducted in 389 men and women.[6] No significant differences were found in the frequency of strokes or heart attacks between the control and treated patients because there were too few participants to provide definite answers. However, the treated patients developed less radiographic and electrocardiographic evidence of left ventricular hypertrophy.

The Australian Therapeutic Trial of Mild Hypertension, 1979

This was a population-based multicentre trial of the treatment of hypertension in thirty to sixty-nine-year old men and women (see Figure 9.3).[7] Pretreatment diastolic pressures were between 95 and 109 mmHg. There were 3427 participants, half of whom received treatment with thiazide diuretics, with beta-blockers added where necessary, and half of whom received placebo therapy. Randomization and trial methodology were impeccable. After four years the results demonstrated a 30 per cent reduction in mortality in treated patients with a highly significant reduction in strokes. The data for myocardial ischaemia did not achieve statistical significance, although the results were encouraging. The continuation of the trial was considered ethically unjustifiable because strokes were being prevented; the thorny question of coronary prevention was only partially answered. The trial did, however, confirm beyond any doubt that drug treatment of mild hypertension is beneficial in those patients with diastolic pressures of 100 mmHg or more. Below this level the results were encouraging, but no more.

The Hypertension Detection and Follow-up Program (HDFP), 1979

This very large American study has been very controversial on both sides of the Atlantic, and its interpretation remains uncertain.[8] Eleven thousand hypertensive patients detected at screening surveys in fourteen centres were randomized to two different methods of managing hypertension. It was considered, on the basis of the 1970 VA study, to be unethical to withhold drug therapy from mild hypertensives, even though some sort of trial was considered necessary. So instead half the patients were randomized to attend special stepped care clinics (SC), which were established for the duration of the trial. Blood pressures were treated very aggressively, although therapy was withheld in 24 per cent of patients whose blood pressures fell spontaneously. Drugs were free. The control group (RC) were referred back to the usual medical services. Both groups were rescreened on four occasions during the study and this revealed that 60 per cent of the RC patients were given antihypertensive medication (see Figure 9.4).

There were significant differences in the average blood pressures of the SC and RC groups over the ensuing five years, and at the end of the trial a marked differences in the death rate of the SC and RC patients. SC patients had fewer strokes, fewer heart attacks and less cancer. The organizing committee did not consider it appropriate to apply statistical tests to these data.

The authors considered the trial proved that the drug therapy of hypertension had been validated in all cases where diastolic pressures exceeded 90 mmHg, but this interpretation has been challenged on many grounds. This was not a placebo-controlled trial of drug therapy and so the differences in outcome may have been due to variables other than the differences in frequency of use of antihypertensive drugs. The lower cancer mortality in SC patients suggests that some of the benefits of being in the SC group were due to better general medical care and earlier detection of disease. It is of interest, however, that by the end of the study there was no difference in the rates of cigarette smoking in the two groups.

The HDFP trial is of great interest, and it might be regarded as a validation of the benefits of a form of socialized medicine rather than the value of drug therapy for hypertension. Its results are relevant to the manner of delivering medical care in the United States and it is difficult to extrapolate the findings for other nations with different health care systems.

| Population study: | 3427 men and women aged 30-69 |
| Diastolic blood pressure : | 95 - 109 |

Figure 9.3 The Australian Study – Second report (1980).

No of entrants		No of events	
		Stroke	Coronary heart disease
1721	Treatment (thiazide)	12	70
1706	Placebo	25	88
	Significance (P)	< 0.025	NS

The Multiple Risk Factor Intervention Trial (MRFIT), 1982

This was a large community-based study in which 6428 high-coronary-risk patients were randomly allocated to an intensive multiple-risk-factor programme for blood pressure, smoking habits and plasma lipids.[9] The control group of 6438 people received no active intervention. At the end of the study there was no significant difference in coronary heart disease, strokes or mortality. These negative results are not easily explained, although it was suggested that the employment of thiazide diuretics in the antihypertensive regimes might have aggravated other coronary risk factors including hypokalaemia and hyperlipidaemia. Yet the coronary prevention seen in the Australian and HDFP studies was achieved even with the use of thiazides in the first-line choice of antihypertensive drugs. A more likely possibility is that the control group also received efficient medical care and so did not differ sufficiently from the intervention group.

The European Working Party on Hypertension in the Elderly (EWPHE), 1985 and the Hypertension in Elderly Patients Study (HEP), 1986

The topic of hypertension in the elderly is discussed separately in Chapter 15. The EWPHE study compared thiazide therapy with placebo in patients aged sixty years or more (average age seventy-two years). Significant reductions in stroke and in coronary events were reported in treated patients.[10] In the HEP study only stroke was reduced.[11]

The Medical Research Council Trial on Mild Hypertension, 1985

This was a British study of 18,000 men and women. Patients were included if after three visits the diastolic pressure remained between 90 and 109 mmHg.[12] Patients were randomized either to placebo therapy or to active treatment, with either propranolol or bendrofluazide. After 90,000 patient-years, the results were very disappointing. There was a small reduction in strokes, but no reduction in total death rates and no significant effect on coronary heart disease. Thiazides were quite as effective as beta-blockers in preventing complications, and appeared better at preventing strokes. There was some evidence that non-smoking patients receiving beta-blockers faired best in respect of coronary heart

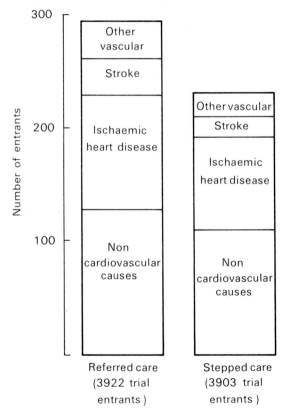

Figure 9.4 Results of the Hypertension Detection and Follow-up Program (Stratum 1) 90–104 mm Hg.

disease. The relatively unimpressive results from the MRC trial are likely to prove a source of controversy for years to come. Already some nihilists have claimed that the MRC results are a mandate to withhold therapy from patients with diastolic blood pressures of between 90 and 109 mmHg. This is a very dangerous interpretation of the trial, which is open to much criticism.

The main worry with the MRC trial is that blood pressures fell after entry into the trial to below 90 mmHg in between one third and one half of cases receiving placebo therapy. These cases might therefore be considered not to have hypertension at all. It is also important to note, however, that 14 per cent of placebo-treated patients sustained a rise in pressure, requiring withdrawal from the trial and the institution of antihypertensive therapy, as their cardiovascular risk would otherwise have been high.

The MRC trial raises many questions on the method of selecting patients for such trials. The act of screening potential entrants may well have caused a rise in blood pressure in a large number of people. The trial does demonstrate very convincingly that it is wrong to institute drug therapy in mild hypertensives on the basis of only three slightly raised blood pressure readings. Mild hypertensives require a longer period of assessment without therapy, and at this time non-pharmacological therapy can be attempted (see Chapter 10). We need more information on how to select out those mild hypertensives whose blood pressures will fall from those who will have sustained hypertension requiring therapy. The presence of minor ECG abnormalities (see Chapter 14) may be a useful indicator of more serious hypertension.

The MRC trial results must be considered in the light of the other

published studies of the treatment of mild hypertension, including the Australian trial and the EWPHE report. The benefits of treating mild hypertension over five years are not dramatic, as may be expected. The clinician must in the final analysis make his own judgment as to which mild hypertensives he will treat with drugs and whom he will simply counsel about associated coronary risk factors, particularly cigarette smoking. All patients do, however, need careful follow-up, as blood pressures tend to rise with age and many mild cases will develop severe hypertension if left untreated.

The United States Systolic Hypertension in the Elderly Program (SHEP)

This trial, initiated in the mid 1980s, has been designed to investigate the benefits of antihypertensive therapy in patients who have 'isolated systolic hypertension'.[13] This should provide useful information on the correct method of managing patients who have normal diastolic pressures but raised systolic pressures.

The Heart Attack Primary Prevention in Hypertensives (HAPPHY) Study and the International Projective Primary Prevention Study in Hypertension (IPPPSH)

These two international multicentre studies are designed to test whether patients randomized to receive a beta-receptor blocker develop fewer complications than those receiving a thiazide diuretic.[14,15] Preliminary results of the IPPPSH study suggest that beta-blockers are superior to thiazides only in coronary prevention in males who are nonsmokers. This confirms the findings of the MRC trial of an important cigarette smoking beta blockade interreaction. It is possible that in future these drugs will be considered to be first line therapy only in nonsmokers. More information is necessary on this point, particularly in relation to the effects of smoking on the metabolism of antihypertensive drugs.

GUIDELINES ON WHOM TO TREAT WITH ANTIHYPERTENSIVE DRUGS

Clinical trials provide information about the benefits or otherwise of treating groups of patients with various levels of hypertension. They cannot, however, provide all the answers about individuals. For the clinician the most useful data is on the extent to which the risk to the patient — both relative and absolute — may be altered. For example, the Australian National Blood Pressure Study demonstrated a 30 per cent reduction in mortality as a result of treatment. While this sounds impressive, the same data presented differently show that to prevent thirty-one heart attacks and strokes, 1721 patients need to receive drug therapy for up to five years. In that trial 1690 patients received treatment but derived no absolute benefit during the five years of the study. Similarly, the MRC trial reported that to prevent one cardiovascular event it is necessary to treat 625 patients for one year. It is likely, however, that more people would benefit over a longer period as blood pressures rise with age, and the development of more severe hypertension would be prevented. The pay-off of one complication prevented for 625 patients treated may seem very unimpressive. This statistic does not, however, take into account the many people whose blood pressure fell with placebo, and is also based on men and women combined. If men are examined alone, the number of patients who benefit over five to ten years becomes much higher.

The Australian study also showed the risk to a hypertensive patient, when his blood pressure is normalized by antihypertensive drugs, does not completely return to normal. His or her prognosis is still adverse when compared with that of a person whose blood pressure is normal without drugs. This is not particularly surprising; if hypertension and its sequelae take many years to develop, it would be unlikely that drug therapy delivered once blood pressures have reached 90 to 109 mmHg would totally abolish the excess risk.

THE PRESENT STATE OF KNOWLEDGE OF THE BENEFITS OF TREATING HYPERTENSION

From the above studies, a reasonable conclusion is that in patients under the age of seventy-five, if the diastolic blood pressure consistently exceeds 100 mmHg after three consecutive screening visits, blood pressure reduction is worthwhile. Strokes and heart failure are prevented, and there is some evidence now of coronary prevention as well. The WHO and the International Society of Hypertension have stated that this threshold should be at 95 mmHg rather than 100 mmHg.[16] It is also important to note that in treated hypertensive patients, the quality of control of the blood pressure is a better predictor of outcome than the severity of hypertension prior to therapy. This means that the efficient delivery of antihypertensive therapy remains a high priority.[17]

The information available for patients whose diastolic pressures are between 90 and 99 mmHg is still controversial. However, if after six visits, pressures remain within this range in spite of non-pharmacological measures, then antihypertensive drug therapy is justified. Those people whose blood pressures settle should not receive therapy but they must

117

be followed up as many will sustain a rise in pressure over the ensuing years, so that treatment becomes necessary.

It would be nice if more information were to become available to help the clinician decide whom he *must treat*, whom he *may treat* and from whom he may choose to *withhold treatment*. The following guidelines reflect our present knowledge.

Who must receive treatment

1. All patients below the age of seventy-five whose diastolic blood pressure is consistently more than 100 mmHg. In patients between the ages of 75 and 85, therapy is justified if the diastolic pressure exceeds 110 mmHg.
2. All pregnant women with diastolic pressures greater than 100 mmHg (see Chapter 16).
3. Patients whose diastolic pressures remain between 90 and 99 mmHg, but who have a high risk of death by virtue of other factors, for example, cigarette smoking and high blood cholesterol levels and possibly bad family history.
4. Patients with ECG or chest x-ray evidence of left ventricular hypertrophy, whose diastolic pressures exceed 90 mmHg or whose systolic pressures exceed 180 mmHg.

Who must not receive treatment

1. People with diastolic pressures below 90 mmHg.
2. Patients over the age of eighty-five unless they have diastolic pressures above 110 mmHg.
3. Patients who have suffered a stroke within the previous few weeks. After this period, however, antihypertensive therapy is worthwhile in presenting recurrences.
4. Stroke survivors with diastolic pressures below 100 mmHg.

Who may be left untreated – but with careful review

1. Patients with a diastolic blood pressure of 90 to 99 mmHg, who have low risk, i.e., nonsmokers with no abnormality of plasma lipids and a favourable family history, and whose pressures settle.
2. People who have intolerable drug side-effects despite all attempts to find a suitable regime and whose diastolic blood pressures are below 105 mmHg off therapy.
3. Very anxious patients in whom the clinician suspects or knows that blood pressure is usually normal when at home, and in whom there is no evidence of end-organ damage and no left ventricular hypertrophy on the ECG. In these people it may help to obtain some form of ambulatory home blood pressure recordings to confirm whether they do have a 'blood pressure clinic-induced hypertension'.

Men and women
While, for a given level of blood pressure, women have a lower risk of death than men, blood pressure levels remain a potent predictor of risk (see Chapter 3). The benefits of antihypertensive drug therapy in women are as important as in men, and the same therapeutic thresholds apply.

Black patients
Hypertension may be commoner in black people compared with whites in Britain as well as in the USA (see Chapter 3).

However, there is only unconvincing evidence that black patients, for a given level of blood pressure, have a higher risk of death than whites. Treatment trials have shown that blacks benefit as much as whites from antihypertensive therapy. Beta-receptor blockers and angiotensin-converting-enzyme inhibitors on their own may be slightly less effective. Thiazide diuretics and calcium-entry antagonists may, by contrast, be more effective in blacks than in whites.

The topics of hypertension in the elderly, in children and in pregnant women are dealt with elsewhere. Similarly, hypertension in the presence of established vascular complications is discussed in Chapter 14.

PRACTICAL POINTS

- In patients below the age seventy-five diastolic blood pressure above 100 mmHg should be reduced.

- The quality of care of hypertensive patients is critical.

- Controlled trials on the value of drug therapy have shown treatment has a beneficial effect in preventing stroke and possibly coronary heart disease.

- Efficient follow-up must be arranged for all cases to ensure that the therapeutic goals are achieved.

10
Non-drug control of blood pressure

BACKGROUND

When population screening surveys are conducted in Western countries 20 to 30 per cent of adults are found to have high blood pressure as defined by a diastolic pressure greater than 95 mmHg or a systolic pressure greater than 160 mmHg (see Chapter 1). An increased risk of cardiovascular disease is also present in those whose blood pressures are in the upper half of the normal distribution (i.e., around 50 per cent of the population), when compared with people in the lower part of the distribution. While many of these blood pressures tend to fall on rechecking, the prospect of 20 to 30 per cent of the population swallowing blood pressure lowering drugs must be viewed with alarm. Surely a new approach taking heed of the following issues is needed:

1. Can we prevent high blood pressure developing?
2. Can we lower pressures by altering our patients' lifestyles?

Since we are primarily concerned here with practical management, this chapter will be devoted to the second of these questions.

The immensity of the problem of treating hypertension on a population basis with drugs has forced a search for alternative ways of lowering blood pressure. There is now exciting evidence that blood pressure can be lowered by non-pharmacological means. However, many of the studies showing this are not well controlled and have small numbers of participants and a shorter duration than many drug-based trials. The subject of non-pharmacological blood pressure reduction is sometimes confused by enthusiasts who believe their particular method of lowering blood pressure is the most effective one. In general, there is an inverse relationship between evangelical zeal and real evidence. Results are often difficult to interpret because simple observation of the patient in the clinic over weeks or months may also cause a fall in pressure.

OBSERVATION

Repeated measurement during follow-up will cause a fall in blood pressure. This was best illustrated in the Medical Research Council Trial of Mild Hypertension (see Chapter 9). A group of patients on drug treatment were compared with a similar group on placebo and a similar group who were observed without even placebo tablets. All were seen at regular intervals during the trial.[1] There was a fall in blood pressure in all three groups. In the group receiving drug treatment it was only just significantly greater than in the other two. Placebo therapy did not have an additional effect compared with follow-up alone. The fall in blood pressure was therefore due simply to observation. Many other studies have shown similar results. The time that the blood pressure takes to fall in relation to the number of observations has not been established. However, three important conclusions can be drawn from these studies:

1. Patients with mild hypertension must always be observed for at least three months, and their blood pressure measured on three or more occasions, before any form of therapy is initiated.
2. If the initial three-month observation period is combined with some other manoeuvre such as weight reduction, salt restriction, correction of alcohol overuse or relaxation therapy, the blood pressure lowering may be falsely ascribed to that intervention.
3. In trials of non-pharmacological methods of lowering blood pressure an appropriate control group or a crossover with a placebo is necessary to ensure the effect is due to the intervention and not to the repeated measurement of blood pressure.

(a)	Minerals
	Sodium
	Potassium
	Calcium
	Magnesium
(b)	Saturated fat/polyunsaturated fat
(c)	Fibre intake
(d)	Calorie content/carbohydrate intake
(e)	Vegetarian diet
(f)	Alcohol
(g)	Caffeine

Table 10.1 Factors in diet that may influence blood pressure.

An important but unanswered question is whether the fall in blood pressure that occurs with observation alone is of benefit to the patient. Presumably the mechanism is that the patient becomes more familiar with the techniques of measurement and is therefore more relaxed. This also points to the possibility that at home some patients may have lower blood pressures than when seeing the doctor.

ALTERATION OF DIET
There is increasing evidence that altering the diet in Western countries may lower blood pressure. Table 10.1 summarizes the factors set out here.

Sodium restriction
We all eat very large amounts of salt, consuming ten to fifty times the amount eaten during man's evolution. There is overwhelming evidence in animals and good circumstantial evidence in man that a high sodium intake is an important initiating factor for high blood pressure, if not an underlying cause of essential hypertension.[2]

It is likely that the mechanism whereby sodium restriction lowers blood pressure in hypertensive patients is different from the longterm mechanism whereby a high salt diet may cause a rise in blood pressure in the population. The clinician is clearly more concerned with the possible benefits to his patients than with the implications of a high salt intake for the whole population.

Severe sodium restriction
Ambard and Beaujard, two French nephrologists of the early 1900s, were the first to point out that restriction of sodium chloride in the diet lowered blood pressure in patients with chronic renal failure and hypertension.[3] This early work was largely forgotten until Kempner in

the days before drugs were available had the idea of reducing protein intake in severe hypertension.[4] He developed a rice and fruit diet that was low in protein but also very low in sodium and rich in potassium. This was found to be effective in malignant hypertension and in patients with very high blood pressures. However, the diet, which consisted of plain boiled rice and fruit, was very monotonous so patients found it difficult to tolerate. With the development of the thiazide diuretics in the 1950s, this severe form of sodium restriction was largely abandoned.

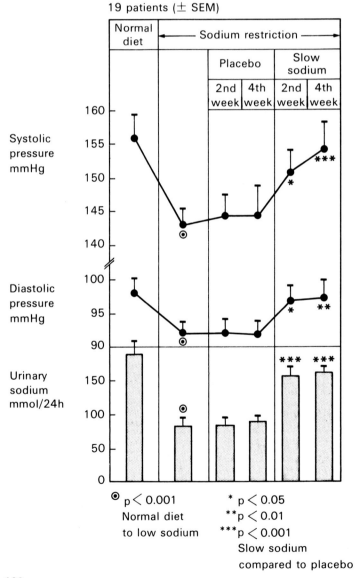

Figure 10.1 The effect of moderate sodium restriction on blood pressure and urinary sodium excretion in a double blind study using placebo and slow sodium tablets.[5]

Moderate sodium restriction

There is now increasing evidence that more modest restriction of sodium intake may lower the blood pressures of hypertensive patients (see Figure 10.1).[2,5] It may also be additive to antihypertensive drug therapy and limit the fall in plasma potassium caused by thiazide diuretics. In most studies sodium intake was reduced by about half and the fall in diastolic blood pressure was between 5 and 10 mmHg; an effect comparable to that of a diuretic or a beta-blocker.

Sodium restriction, in the short term, may be more effective in patients with high blood pressure when compared with normotensives (see Figure 10.2). When dietary sodium is restricted, there is a loss of body sodium resulting in a reduction in extracellular fluid and blood volume. This stimulates renin release and the formation of angiotensins II, which in normotensive subjects may largely prevent any fall in pressure. In hypertensives there is less rise in renin and therefore sodium restriction does cause a fall in blood pressure.[2] More studies are needed to look at the longterm effects of salt restriction and to identify which patients respond best.

Assessment of sodium intake

A dietary history does not give a very accurate estimate of sodium intake. This is because it is difficult to quantify the amount of salt added during cooking or at table. The best method is to measure the amount of sodium excreted in the urine as this represents about 90 per cent of dietary intake. Sodium consumption varies widely from day to day and urinary sodium excretion follows these changes. There is some confusion as to how many urine collections are necessary to reflect the average sodium intake of an individual patient. The collection of two consecutive twenty-four-hour urine samples gives a reasonable approximation as to whether a patient is eating large amounts of sodium (i.e., more than 200 mmol/day, equivalent to approximately 11 g sodium), an average sodium intake (around 150 mmol/day, approximately 9 g), or a low sodium intake (less than 100 mmol/day; approximately 6 g).

The collection of twenty-four-hour urine specimens requires some organization, but it is not as difficult as has been claimed if the patient is given clear written instructions (see Chapter 8).

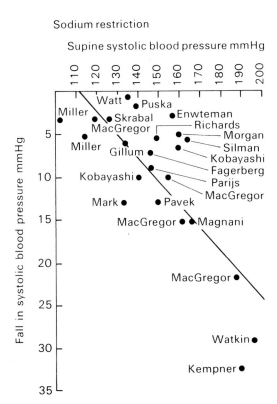

Figure 10.2 Fall in supine systolic blood pressure with sodium restriction plotted against pretreatment supine systolic blood pressure in different places.

How to cut sodium intake

At present all patients with high blood pressure should be told:

1. Not to add salt to the food at the table
2. To avoid or severely limit the addition of salt in the preparation of food; the person who cooks for the patient should be counselled
3. To avoid processed foods that have a very high sodium content, for example, ham, bacon, sausages, hamburgers and other processed foods
4. To avoid potato chips, salted peanuts and other sodium-rich snacks.

These four simple steps can halve sodium intake in most patients.[6] To reduce it further means cutting out many other processed foods and more detailed instructions are required, preferably from a dietitian. In some countries the labels on packaged and processed foods carry information about their sodium content.

It is especially difficult to restrict sodium intake if food is eaten regularly in a canteen or a restaurant. Fast foods and Chinese takeaway meals have a particularly high sodium content.

Increasing dietary potassium

Potassium was used as a diuretic in the early 1930s in patients with heart failure and it was suggested that an increase in potassium intake might lower blood pressure. These observations were not pursued until evidence from rats showed that increasing dietary potassium largely prevented the pressor effect of a high sodium intake. Very few studies have been done in man. So far they suggest that on a normal diet containing around 150 mmol of sodium per day, an increase in potassium intake does have a small but significant blood pressure lowering effect.[7] There is also some epidemiological evidence (see Chapter 3) suggesting that a low potassium intake is related to the prevalence of high blood pressure in a community. However, none of the evidence is as impressive as for sodium restriction and no longterm studies have been reported.

The antihypertensive effect of a high potassium diet may not be additive to the effects of sodium restriction but increasing potassium consumption through a higher intake of fresh fruit and vegetables makes patient compliance with sodium restriction easier. In addition, an increase in fruit and vegetable consumption may help reduce saturated fat intake and increase the fibre content of the diet. All these steps may be of benefit in the longterm prevention of atheroma.

An increase in potassium intake is, however, contraindicated in patients with hypertension with severe renal failure.

---

1. **Do not add salt** to cooking or at table
2. **Avoid very salty foods**, eg, bacon, ham, cheese and limit processed foods with high salt content
3. **Eat less fat** — if necessary substitute polyunsaturated for saturated fat
4. **Eat more fresh fruit and vegetables**

Table 10.2 Simple dietary guide for patients with high blood pressure.

Salt substitutes

The use of salt substitutes containing potassium rather than sodium chloride has been advocated both to help compliance with salt restriction and to increase potassium intake.

There are now many combinations on the market of sodium and potassium in so-called salt alternatives. These cannot be recommended in the treatment of high blood pressure as they contain appreciable amounts of sodium. Potassium salts should not be given to patients with renal failure.

Calcium

The epidemiological evidence relating calcium to blood pressure is discussed in Chapter 2. High blood pressure may be related to a low calcium intake and one clinical study has shown that increasing dietary calcium intake caused a surprisingly large fall in blood pressure.[2] Further well controlled double-blind studies are needed before any recommendations can be made, particularly as the main source of calcium in the diet is in dairy products, which are high in saturated fat, cholesterol and sodium.

Magnesium

Magnesium, like potassium, is an important regulator of the excitability of cell membranes and is found in many foods. Magnesium sulphate used to be given intravenously in pre-eclamptic toxaemia and was an effective blood pressure lowering agent. Magnesium supplements, when given to patients with high blood pressure who were already receiving a diuretic, appeared to cause a further fall in blood pressure. However, in a recent double blind study, magnesium supplements had no effect on blood pressure when compared with placebo.[8]

Saturated fat and polyunsaturated fat

There is some evidence from Scandinavia that substituting saturated fat intake with polyunsaturated fat may lower blood pressure in both hypertensive and normotensive subjects.[9] Further controlled studies are needed but there are other reasons for believing that reducing the saturated fat content of the diet may be beneficial. There is good evidence that high blood cholesterol levels and the low density lipoprotein (LDL) that carries cholesterol are important risk factors for arterial disease. High plasma cholesterol levels greatly increase the risk for a given level of blood pressure. The evidence that lowering saturated fat intake is beneficial is not yet conclusive. On the other hand, it is unlikely to be harmful and will reduce calorie intake, helping with weight reduction. Polyunsaturated fats are predominantly found in vegetable oils such as sunflower, soya bean and corn oil and many fish oils.

Dietary fibre

This consists of complicated carbohydrate substances that are not absorbed but decrease intestinal transit times and are useful in the prevention of constipation. They have also been claimed to reduce the incidence of colonic cancer as well as other gastrointestinal problems. One study from Southampton has shown that increasing the dietary fibre content did have the effect of lowering blood pressure.[10] It is not clear whether this was due to a direct effect of the increase in fibre in the diet or to a concomitant alteration in sodium intake or absorption. Increasing fibre in the diet with greater consumption of fruit, vegetables and wholemeal cereal products is probably beneficial. Hence the possible advantage of a vegetarian diet.

Weight reduction

There is no doubt from population studies that there is a close relationship between blood pressure and body mass index even after allowance for the tendency to over-estimate blood pressure in obese people. Patients with high blood pressure who are obese do sustain a fall in pressure when they reduce weight (see Figure 10.4).[11]

Studies of change in weight in relation to changes in blood pressure suggest that an eleven pound (five kilogram) fall in body weight is associated with a 5 mmHg fall in systolic blood pressure. This implies that many obese people with mild hypertension can normalize their blood pressure if they reduce weight, but that weight reduction alone is unlikely to be sufficient to normalize pressure in people with diastolic pressures above 110 mmHg. Some studies have reported that this fall in pressure is independent of the reduction in sodium intake that occurs with dieting.

It is important to encourage patients who are obese to try to reduce weight. This may be difficult to achieve and there is little point in encouraging patients with crash diets which result in dramatic falls in weight if, as soon as a normal diet is resumed, weight rises again. It is much

Figure 10.3 *(left)* Typical meal high in salt and fat, and *(right)* foods which should be encouraged in the diet. The meal on the right contains approximately twenty times less saturated fat and salt.

better to try to get patients used to eating less food over a longer period of time. A two pound (one kilogram) weight loss per week is all that should be aimed for, but the patient should be encouraged to carry on with this over many months. There is some evidence that professional dietitians are better than doctors at persuading their patients to lose weight.

Alcohol

There has recently been an increased awareness of the relationship between high alcohol intake and hypertension. Some of the epidemiological evidence is discussed in Chapter 3. Hypertensive patients have a higher frequency of alcohol abuse than normotensives. It is important to note that when alcoholics or heavy drinkers stop drinking, their blood pressures fall fairly rapidly.

While most mortality studies have shown an inverse relationship between alcohol intake and coronary heart disease, drinkers having lower cholesterol levels and less heart disease, they do show a strong positive relationship between alcohol and stroke. This relationship may be due to alcohol-induced hypertension, but it is also possible that acute strokes

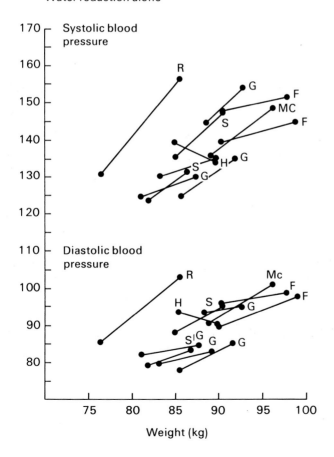

Figure 10.4 Published studies on the effect of weight reduction on blood pressure. Each line represents one study.

may occur after binge drinking, due to direct intracerebral vasoconstriction.

The mechanism of the relationship between alcohol intake and blood pressure is unknown.[12] But given in moderate quantities alcohol has multiple biochemical effects, on renin, aldosterone, cortisol, catecholamines, vasopressin and water output. One interesting phenomenon is that moderate drinkers who consume the equivalent of around seven pints (three litres) of beer per week (or the equivalent of 140 g of alcohol) have lower pressures than teetotallers. Above this level, however, there is a close relationship between alcohol consumption and the height of blood pressure. This is found in both beer drinkers and spirit drinkers.

Alcoholic patients may develop very high blood pressures while they are withdrawing from alcohol, and this pressor

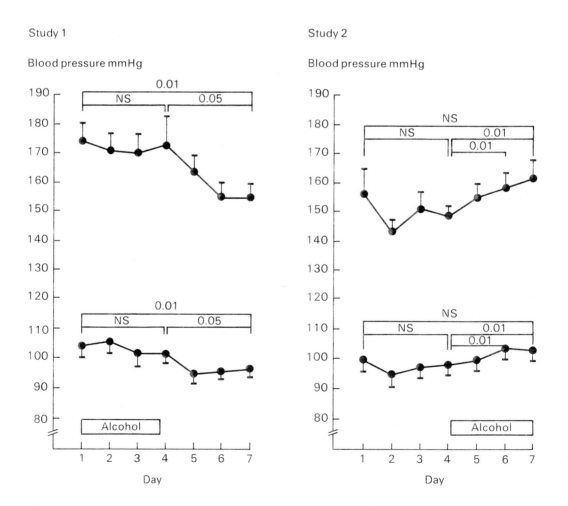

Figure 10.5 The effect on blood pressure of stopping and restarting drinking alcohol.[12]

response may be mediated by catecholamine release.[12] This mechanism probably does not explain the relationship between hypertension and more modest intake in non-alcoholics. However, hypertensive patients do have higher liver enzyme (gamma glutamyl transpeptidase) levels than normotensives. Even hypertensives who drink moderately sustain a fall in blood pressure when they stop taking alcohol (see Figure 10.5).

Alcohol intake is notoriously difficult to measure in both clinical and epidemiological practice. Detailed questionnaires are available, with separate questions about the consumption of beers, spirits and wines but answers cannot always be assumed to be reliable. Biochemical markers of high alcohol intake are a rasied mean red-cell volume (MCV) and raised GGT. Alcoholics and even people who simply consume a lot of alcohol also tend to have hyperuricaemia. Rib fractures on chest x-ray also suggest a high alcohol intake.

In both normal subjects and hypertensive patients, the rapid intake of about three pints (1.5 litres) of beer raises blood pressure, whereas the same quantity of alcohol-free beer has no effect.

In clinical practice, therefore, the following points are worth considering:

1. Clinical evidence of high alcohol intake should be looked for in hypertensive patients. Plethora and a Cushingoid appearance are two important clinical markers (see Chapter 7).
2. All patients should be screened with estimations of MCV (in the full blood count) and of liver enzymes, particularly gamma glutamyl transferase.
3. Patients who consume more than seven pints (three litres) of beer per

week should be advised to reduce their intake.
4. Patients can be advised that it is safe to consume some alcohol, but that they should not exceed seven pints (three litres) of beer, or a half bottle of spirits or three bottles of wine per week (see Table 10.3).

MEN	WOMEN
14 pints of beer	7 pints of beer
28 glasses of wine	14 glasses of wine
28 glasses of sherry	14 glasses of sherry
28 small glasses of spirits	14 small glasses of spirits
Permitted tobacco intake: Nil	

Table 10.3 Absolute maximum weekly consumption of alcohol for hypertensive patients.

Smoking

This is an independent risk factor for the premature development of arterial disease and particularly for heart attacks and sudden death. There is overwhelming evidence now that stopping smoking is of immense benefit. Indeed, a study of British general practitioners showed that after three months of stopping smoking the risk of a heart attack was reduced to about the same level as for non-smoking doctors.

The mechanism whereby smoking may cause an increased risk of arterial disease is controversial. It could be partly due to a direct effect of nicotine causing increased excitability of the heart and arrhythmias, or to a high level of carbon monoxide in the blood making the development of atheroma more likely.

Smoking is, after high blood pressure, the most preventable cause of death in the Western world. It is estimated that in the UK alone, over 200,000 persons per year die from smoking. Many people who are being treated for mild hypertension have not even been told to stop smoking. The risk in these patients from smoking is greater than the risks from their mild hypertension.

Smoking a cigarette causes an acute rise in blood pressure. Confusingly, however, epidemiological evidence suggests a slight negative effect on blood pressure, i.e., smokers have slightly lower blood pressures than non-smokers (see Chapter 3). The only exception to this negative smoking/blood pressure relationship is the strong positive association between cigarette smoking and the malignant phase of hypertension.

All patients who smoke should be told to stop. The risks of high blood pressure and of smoking in the same individual are not only additive but synergistic, i.e., the risk is greater than for the two factors added together. A careful explanation of this synergism may produce a far greater willingness in the patient to give up smoking.

Caffeine
Coffee drinking has been demonstrated to cause an acute rise in blood pressure. Epidemiological evidence does not, however, show any relationship between caffeine consumption and blood pressure and cutting back on coffee intake does not cause a fall in blood pressure. People who drink a lot of coffee may also smoke or drink heavily, and this does influence their cardiovascular risk.

130

RELAXATION
The most effective way of lowering blood pressure is to sleep. Indeed, if we spent the whole of our life asleep, very few of us would have high blood pressure. This fall in blood pressure during sleep is largely due to relaxation of the voluntary muscles. The reflex can be clearly demonstrated by relaxation of all muscles followed by measurement of the blood pressure. The thumb is then opposed against the index finger in isometric contraction. There will be a marked increase in diastolic pressure of approximately 10 to 20 mmHg.

All the relaxation therapies, for example, biofeedback, transcendental meditation, yoga, sleep therapy, behaviour therapy and psychotherapy use this simple but basic physiological reflex. There has been one well conducted randomized study which did show a fall in blood pressure of both nomotensives and hypertensives after relaxation therapy.[13] More studies are needed to confirm this.

It is sensible to review the lifestyle of patients with hypertension and ensure that they are not subjecting themselves to unnecessary stress, though there is little point in forcing people to relax who do not want to. Evangelists for fringe remedies should be treated with suspicion.

EXERCISE
During dynamic exercise such as running, swimming or bicycling systolic pressure rises, diastolic pressure falls and heart rate increases. In physically fit people, the rise in systolic pressure and heart rate are less and blood pressures may fall to lower levels after exercise. However, most positive studies claiming a relationship between blood pressure and exercise have not taken into account other alterations of lifestyle in fit people, including changes

in diet, reduction of alcohol consumption and stopping smoking.

People who are fit feel better. This in itself is sufficient reason for encouraging patients to take plenty of exercise, but adequate warnings must be given. Sudden strenuous exertion may be harmful, particularly in unfit patients. Isometric exercise, unlike dynamic exercise, causes a significant rise in both diastolic and systolic pressures, and could be dangerous in hypertensive patients. Carrying heavy suitcases may precipitate angina in patients with ischaemic heart disease and could precipitate cerebral haemorrhage in those with uncontrolled blood pressure.

REST

Putting patients to bed in hospital will have a marked blood pressure lowering effect, partly because of relaxation of voluntary muscles but also because there is a loss of sodium and water with decreased physical activity. There is no evidence that bedrest or admitting patients to hospital has any longterm effect on blood pressure. Patients with very severe or resistant hypertension may be admitted pending investigation and initiation of complex drug regimes. There is, however, not much point in controlling blood pressure only in hospital when patients' blood pressures usually rise and become uncontrolled when they are discharged.

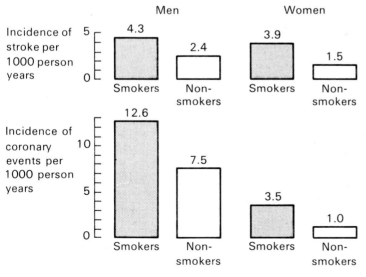

Figure 10.6 Incidence of stroke and coronary events in mild hypertensives who were smokers or non-smokers and who received placebo therapy in the MRC trial of mild hypertension (from MRC Trial Report, *Brit. Med. J. 291*, 1985, 97–104).

PRACTICAL POINTS

- All patients with high blood pressure, whether they are receiving anti-hypertensive drugs or not, should receive the following advice:

  1. Eat a more healthy diet
     —less salt
     —more fresh fruit and vegetables
     —less saturated fat and substitute with polyunsaturated fat
     —avoid being overweight
  2. Drink no more than one pint of beer (0.5 litre) or its equivalent per day
  3. Stop smoking.

- These forms of non-drug therapy can be effective in lowering blood pressure and are additive to drug treatment.

- They may prevent the progression of mild hypertension to more severe levels.

- Only with careful explanation and reinforcement will patients stick to their doctor's advice.

- Perhaps the best person to reinforce this advice is the clinic or practice nurse.

- The nursing profession has an increasing role to play, not only in the detection of hypertension, but also in its management. In particular nurses should be specially trained in the non-pharmacological treatment of high blood pressure.

- These measures would probably usefully be adopted by the whole population.

11
A review of antihypertensive drugs

BACKGROUND

In general, over the last thirty years drugs for lowering blood pressure have become more effective and, more important, they now have fewer side-effects. The improvement is likely to continue, and raises the questions of and when which new drug should be used. The best criterion is whether the new drug reduces the chances of stroke and heart attacks in addition to the blood pressure. In practice, we rarely know this. The choice therefore depends on:

- The experience of the doctor with a particular drug
- Its effectiveness in lowering blood pressure
- Side-effects
- Cost.

Ideally, each patient should undergo some sort of assessment to decide which of the appropriate drugs is the most tolerable and effective in his or her case. After all, the patient may receive this treatment for the rest of his or her life. Many drugs, while not having the serious side-effects of the older agents, have more subtle effects which may reduce the quality of life on a longer term basis. It is usually found that a combination of low doses of drugs has an additive effect on blood pressure, with fewer side-effects than high doses of one agent.

This chapter discusses the many drugs that are available, their mechanisms and their side-effects. In addition, information is provided on the current view of their role in the management of hypertensive patients (see Table 11.1).

DIURETICS

Thirty years after their introduction, there is increasing concern about potentially harmful metabolic effects of diuretics and speculation that they may possibly cause arrhythmias in some patients. In men, impotence has also emerged as a problem. Diuretics are additive to nearly all of the blood pressure lowering drugs, particularly the beta-blockers and converting-enzyme inhibitors. Many of the arterial vasodilators like hydralazine and minox-

---

Diuretics

Beta adrenoceptor blockers

Calcium-entry antagonists

Angiotensin-converting enzyme inhibitors

Others
Alpha adrenoceptor blockers

Peripheral vasodilators

Central acting agents

Adrenergic neurone blockers

Table 11.1 Drugs that lower blood pressure.

idil cause sodium retention which may offset their the blood pressure lowering effect. In this situation diuretics must be used, and some patients may become oedematous without them.

Prostaglandin-inhibiting drugs, particularly indomethacin, may interfere with the effects of diuretics, and when introduced in a previously well-controlled patient may cause an unexpected rise in blood pressure.

Thiazide diuretics

There are slight differences in the duration of action and major differences in dosage between the different thiazides but they

	Normal daily dose for hypertension
Thiazides	
*Bendrofluazide	2.5 mg
*Hydrochlorothiazide	12.5 to 25 mg
Cyclopenthiazide	0.25 mg
Chlorothiazide	500 mg
Hydroflumethiazide	50 mg
Thiazide related compounds	
Chlorthalidone	12.5–25 mg
Indapamide	2.5 mg
Mefruside	25 mg
Xipamide	20 mg
Metolazone	5 mg
Polythiazide	1 mg
Loop diuretics	
Frusemide	40 mg (more in renal failure)
Bumetanide	1 mg (more in renal failure)
Piretanide	6 mg
Potassium sparing diuretics	
Amiloride	5–10 mg
Triamterene	50 mg
Spironolactone	25–100 mg
*Recommended for routine treatment	

Table 11.2 Dosage for diuretics.

can all be given once daily. Related sulphonamide compounds such as chlorthalidone and metolazone are longer acting and more powerful.

All the thiazide diuretics have a fairly flat dose–response curve, so that increasing the dose has little further effect on blood pressure but does increase the metabolic consequences on potassium, glucose, lipids and uric acid.[1] It is best to use the minimum dose necessary, as nothing is gained by giving larger doses.

Mode of action The thiazide diuretics act on the renal tubules to block sodium and chloride reabsorption. After a degree of sodium and water loss has occurred, compensatory mechanisms block the effect on the kidney so that within a few days no additional loss of sodium occurs but total body sodium is maintained at a slightly lower level as long as the diuretic is taken. This causes a fall in the extracellular fluid volume and a small decrease in plasma and blood volume. With the loss of sodium and water there is a rise in renin release from the kidney leading to the formation of the powerful vasoconstrictor angiotensin II. The fall in blood pressure with a diuretic is largely determined by the fall in extracellular volume and the compensatory rise in angiotensin II levels. This may explain why diuretics are more effective in black patients and in older white hypertensive patients, both of whom tend to have lower plasma renin levels and a smaller rise in plasma angiotensin II with diuretic therapy.

Beta-blockers partially inhibit the renin release caused by diuretics, and the converting-enzyme inhibitors enalapril and captopril almost totally abolish the compensatory rise in plasma angiotensin II levels. For this reason beta-blockers or converting-enzyme inhibitors are very effective when used in combination with diuretics. However, there is a flat dose response to diuretics in the presence of a beta-blocker, whereas with the converting-enzyme inhibitors increasing the dose of diuretic does cause a further fall in blood pressure.

Side-effects Thiazide diuretics are well tolerated, particularly at lower doses. Very rarely, severe reactions do occur causing skin rashes, thrombocytopenia and leucopenia. There was therefore some surprise when the MRC Trial on Mild Hypertension, using large doses of bendrofluazide (10 mg daily) reported a higher incidence of impotence with thiazides compared with beta-blocker or placebo therapy (see Figure 11.1). Whether this adverse effect occurs at lower doses of thiazides remains to be seen. Nevertheless, patients on thiazides should be questioned about this as it may be an important but previously unrecognized problem.

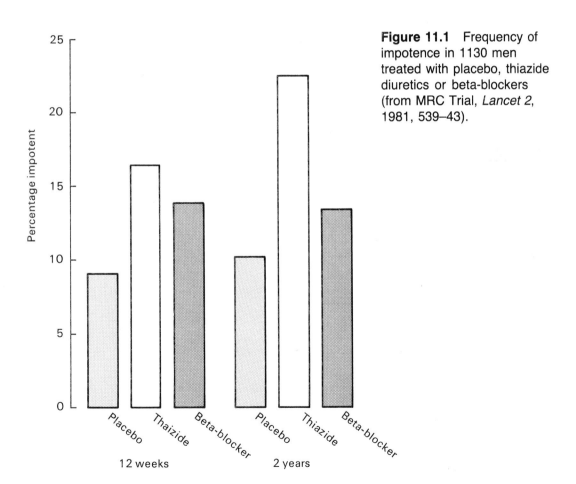

Figure 11.1 Frequency of impotence in 1130 men treated with placebo, thiazide diuretics or beta-blockers (from MRC Trial, *Lancet 2*, 1981, 539–43).

The metabolic problems of thiazide diuretics

Hypokalaemia Almost all patients treated with a thiazide sustain a fall in plasma potassium. This fall varies with the dose but averages between 0.3 and 1.0 mmol/l. A high salt diet increases the fall in plasma potassium, whereas in those patients who restrict their salt intake the fall is smaller. The dangers of hypokalaemia are many. The MRC trial demonstrated that in patients receiving 10 mg of bendrofluazide daily there was a higher incidence of multifocal ventricular ectopic beats in thiazide-treated patients compared with those receiving either a beta-blocker or placebo therapy.[2] This effect may be increased by exercise (see Figure 11.2). There is also evidence that patients who have suffered a heart attack have a worse prognosis if they have a low plasma potassium. As hypertensives are especially prone to heart attacks, and the commonest cause of hypokalaemia is diuretic therapy, this finding is worrying although the MRC trial demonstrated no excess mortality in the thiazide-alone group.

The plasma potassium level should be measured in all patients before starting diuretic therapy. If it is already low further tests should be instituted. After a few months of treatment it is worth rechecking plasma levels, but there is some doubt as to whether the fall in plasma potassium is accompanied by a fall in total body potassium. It is possible that it is due to redistribution rather than loss

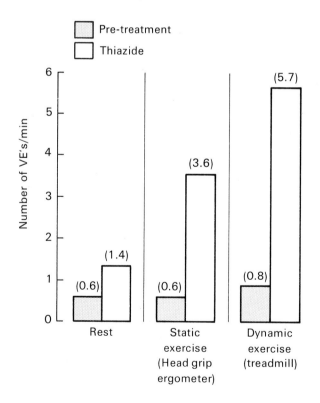

Figure legend: Pre-treatment / Thiazide

Figure 11.2 The frequency of ventricular ectopic beats in patients on thiazide diuretics (from J. W. Hollifield, *RSM International Congress Series 44*, 1981).

of potassium from the body. In general, clinicians have neglected to watch plasma potassium levels. This is because hypokalaemia rarely causes obvious clinical side-effects. It is the longterm effects that are worrying, and this is one of the main reasons why beta-blockers are preferred as the first-line antihypertensive agents.

Potassium supplements should be used only when plasma potassium falls to below 3.5 mmol/l, or if there is concurrent heart failure. Potassium supplements themselves have side-effects and are not always effective and are therefore only rarely indicated. Most of the combined diuretic and potassium chloride tablets contain trivial amounts of potassium and are of no benefit.

Small doses of thiazides (for example, bendrofluazide 2.5 mg daily or hydrochlorothiazide 12.5-25 mg daily) cause a smaller fall in plasma potassium and when combined with beta-blockers usually cause no fall. This is because beta-blockers themselves cause a slight rise in plasma potassium by virtue of their suppression of renin and aldosterone levels. This also occurs with ACE inhibitors.

Profound hypokalaemia If serum potassium falls to very low levels, the possibility of another underlying cause of hypokalaemia—particularly primary aldosteronism—should be considered.

Hyperuricaemia All of the thiazide diuretics cause an increase in plasma uric acid levels and may occasionally precipitate acute gout. It is uncertain whether a symptomless longterm rise in serum uric acid level is important. Hyperuricaemia is common in hypertensive patients even without thiazides, but it is doubtful whether serum uric acid is an independent cardiovascular risk factor. Lower doses of diuretics have less effect on uric acid levels.

Glucose tolerance Many patients treated with thiazide diuretics on a longterm basis develop a deterioration in glucose tolerance (see Figure 11.3). Some develop elevated fasting blood glucose levels and, more rarely, frank diabetes may be precipitated. In patients who already have diabetes there may be a slight worsening of diabetic control. Thiazides should not

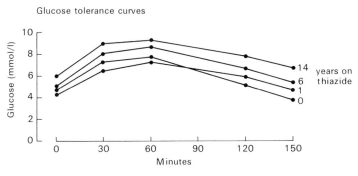

Glucose tolerance curves

Figure 11.3 The longterm effect of thiazide diuretics on glucose tolerance (from M. B. Murphy, *Lancet 2*, 1982, 1293–5).

therefore be used in people who have borderline glucose intolerance. It is not uncommon in the diabetic clinic to see patients who can normalize their blood glucose levels simply by changing from a thiazide diuretic to another agent.

Blood lipids There is general agreement that a small rise in plasma cholesterol and triglyceride levels results from longterm treatment with thiazide diuretics. This may hasten the development of vascular disease and partly offset the benefits of reducing the blood pressure.

Calcium Thiazides sometimes elevate plasma calcium levels to the range where a diagnosis of hyperparathyroidism should be considered.

Other problems In those patients who are already salt depleted, diuretics may cause further volume depletion. Patients with chronic renal disease may show a deterioration in renal function. Rarely thiazides cause large falls in plasma sodium with frank hyponatraemia (serum sodium 110 to 125 mmol/l). Usually there is some intercurrent illness, but the hyponatraemia may cause confusion, dehydration, vomiting and muscle weakness.

A small rise in packed cell volume and haemoglobin level is common with diuretics. Both are potential risk factors for strokes. Thiazides also increase platelet aggregation, which may cause thrombotic disease.

Pregnancy Thiazides should not be used for hypertension in pregnancy as they may reduce placental bloodflow (see Chapter 16).

Loop diuretics

Frusemide and bumetanide act on the

ascending limb of the loop of Henle and block sodium reabsorption. They are much faster-acting diuretics than the thiazides, with a shorter duration of action. They have not therefore been widely used in the first-line treatment of hypertension, neither is this use advised. They are used in resistant hypertension, in combination with other drugs, and also in patients with renal impairment where high doses may be necessary. The loop diuretics have the same sort of complications as the thiazides although frusemide at low doses may cause fewer effects. They are useful in patients receiving vasodilators who develop fluid retention, and they are almost always needed when minoxidil is used in very resistant hypertension. They are also useful in combination with ACE inhibitors. Slow-release forms of frusemide and bumetanide are now becoming available and may be useful.

Potassium-sparing diuretics

These drugs act on the distal renal tubule and reduce potassium excretion at the same time as increasing sodium and water loss. There are three potassium-sparing diuretics currently available: spironolactone, triamterene and amiloride.

Spironolactone is an aldosterone antagonist which may also have a direct effect on the distal renal tubule. Given alone in large doses it can control the blood pressure in patients with primary aldosteronism prior to surgery, or in cases where surgery is contraindicated. It is as effective as a thiazide diuretic, although it has a slower onset of action. It has fewer metabolic consequences than the thiazides but may cause a slight elevation in plasma potassium. Patients with renal failure should not therefore be given spironolactone unless plasma potassium is carefully monitored, as dangerous hyperkalaemia may result.

Spironolactone unfortunately has endocrine side-effects including gynaecomastia and loss of libido in men, and intermenstrual bleeding in premenopausal women.

Combined with other diuretics it is useful in preventing a fall in plasma potassium. Spironolactone is also marketed combined with a thiazide diuretic but these preparations usually contain an unnecessarily large amount of thiazide and are therefore not recommended.

Triamterene This drug is less effective in lowering blood pressure than spironolactone but it does partially block the potassium lowering effect of thiazide diuretics. It has therefore been combined with thiazide diuretics to prevent the fall in plasma potassium.

Amiloride Although structurally different to triamterene, amiloride has a similar action on the distal tubule. It has therefore been marketed combined with a thiazide diuretic. This combined preparation can cause hypokalaemia, and, rarely, profound hyponatraemia.

Both triamterene and amiloride have been reported to cause nausea, flatulence and skin rashes. Both drugs, like spironolactone, can cause hyperkalaemia in patients with renal failure.

Indapamide
This diuretic is similar to the thiazides but it is claimed to have additional blood pressure lowering effects independent of the loss of sodium.

BETA-BLOCKERS[3]
Potentially beta-blockers have advantages independent of their blood pressure lowering effect; they may also reduce the incidence of coronary disease. However, recent trials in hypertension have shown only a marginal effect in non-smokers and no effect at all in smokers.

Mode of action
The beta-blockers compete with the endogenous catecholamines for adrenergic beta-receptors. Beta-receptors can be divided into two classes: beta-1 and beta-2 receptors. Blocking the beta-1 receptors reduces the heart rate and the contractility of the heart with a concomitant reduction in cardiac output. This may be part of the mechanism of the blood pressure lowering effect. Blockade of the beta-2 receptors causes vasodilatation in voluntary muscle but can cause bronchoconstriction, particularly in asthmatic subjects.

Beta-blockers inhibit renin release, leading to falls in plasma angiotensin II levels which may explain some of the blood pressure lowering action. Beta-blockers are less effective in patients with low plasma renin levels, particularly in blacks and older white hypertensives.

Classification
All beta-blockers are effective in reducing blood pressure. There are, though, some important differences between them, which are shown in Figure 11.4.

Cardioselectivity Some beta-blockers are not cardioselective (for example, propranolol and oxprenolol) as they block both beta-1 and beta-2 receptors equally. The cardioselective beta-blockers (acebutolol, atenolol, metoprolol) have a greater effect on cardiac beta-1 receptors. There is no difference in the blood pressure lowering effect of selective and nonselective beta-blockers.

Intrinsic sympathomimetic activity Like many competitive inhibitors, some beta-blockers stimulate the beta-receptors as well as block them, particularly when endogenous levels of catecholamines are low. This intrinsic sympathomimetic activity (ISA) or partial agonist activity (PAA) is seen particularly with pindolol, oxprenolol and, to a lesser extent, acebutolol.

Membrane-stabilizing activity Some beta-blockers also have a quinidine-like membrane-stabilizing effect (for example, propranolol) but this is not of any clinical significance.

Lipophilicity Some beta-blockers are more lipid-soluble that others. Lipid-soluble (lipophilic) drugs are more likely to enter the brain and cause central side-effects. The less lipid-soluble (more hydrophilic) drugs such as atenolol, acebutolol, sotalol and nadolol may cause fewer central effects.

Lipid-soluble drugs are mainly metabolized by the liver, and water-soluble agents are excreted by the kidney. This is significant if there is either hepatic or renal impairment, and may influence the choice of beta-blocker.

Duration of action All beta-blockers reduce blood pressure by about the same amount. This response starts within one to two hours of a single oral dose. Most beta-blockers can be given once a day.

There are wide variations in the total daily dose of each individual drug. It is probable that in many patients lower doses are needed than those recommended by the manufacturers (see Table 11.3).

Side-effects of beta-blockers (Table 11.4)

Heart failure When these drugs were first introduced there was some concern that they might precipitate heart failure, particularly in patients with angina who may already have damaged heart muscle. In patients with high blood pressure where the left ventricle is performing well beta-blockers are unlikely to precipitate heart failure. Nevertheless, patients with high blood pressure and heart failure should not be given beta-blockers except under very carefully supervised conditions (see Chapter 14).

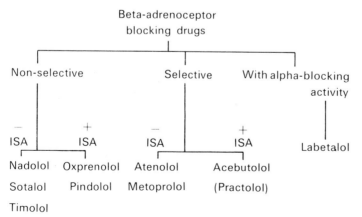

Figure 11.4 A classification of beta-adrenoceptor blockers based on cardioselectivity and intrinsic sympathomimetic activity.

Reduction in peripheral bloodflow
Because of the reduction in cardiac output and a reflex increase in peripheral resistance, all beta-blockers tend to reduce peripheral bloodflow and cause cold hands and feet, particularly in colder climates. They may worsen symptoms in patients with Raynaud's disease or intermittent claudication. If symptoms are mild advice about keeping hands warm and wearing gloves may suffice, particularly if the clinician does not want to alter the antihypertensive regime. In severe peripheral vascular disease, gangrene has been precipitated by the use of beta-blockers. It is possible that beta-blockers with partial agonist activity, for example, pindolol and oxprenolol, are less likely to do this, but beta-blockers are best avoided and calcium-entry antagonists or converting-enzyme inhibitors should be used instead.

Bronchospasm All beta-blockers may precipitate bronchospasm, especially if there is a preceding history of asthma. The more cardioselective beta-blockers atenolol, metoprolol and acebutolol are less likely to have this effect. They are still contraindicated in asthmatics, although they may be safer in patients with chronic obstructive airways disease. If there is any possibility of precipitating bronchospasm with beta-blockers it is probably better to use other types of antihypertensive drugs.

Reduction in exercise tolerance All beta-blockers cause a reduction in exercise tolerance and this can be a major problem for active young patients who notice, for example, that they feel tired when climbing stairs, particularly with a feeling of heaviness in the legs. Either a calcium-entry antagonist or a converting-enzyme inhibitor should be used instead.

Cardioselective blockers	
Atenolol	25 – 100 mg
Metoprolol	50 – 400 mg
Acebutolol	200 mg – 800 mg
Non-selective beta-blockers	
Propranolol	80 – 360 mg
Betaxolol	10 – 40 mg
Nadolol	20 – 80 mg
Penbutolol	(available only in combined preparations)
Sotalol	80 – 160 mg
Timolol	5 – 10 mg
Beta-blockers with partial agonist activity	
Oxprenolol	80 – 320 mg
Pindolol	5 – 15 mg

Table 11.3 Dosage for beta-adrenoceptor blockers.

Sleep disturbance	Heart failure
Nightmares	Reduction of exercise tolerance
Lethargy	
Bronchospasm	Raynaud's syndrome
Bradycardia	Claudication
Impotence	

Table 11.4 Some side-effects of beta-blockers.

141

Central nervous problems Beta-blockers may cause sleep disturbance, vivid dreams and nightmares. These may be more common with the lipid-soluble beta-blockers such as propranolol and oxprenolol. The hydrophilic blockers atenolol, nadolol or sotalol should be tried, but if sleep disturbance persists a calcium-entry antagonist or converting-enzyme inhibitor should be used instead. More commonly beta-blockers may cause a subtle loss of intellectual function or drive, or energy, and if this occurs other forms of therapy should be considered.

Diabetes mellitus Theoretically, beta-blockers could interfere with insulin secretion. More importantly, they may interfere with the symptoms and metabolic responses to hypoglycaemia, in insulin-dependent diabetics, although this may be less likely with the cardioselective beta-blockers. Diabetics should nevertheless be warned that the symptoms of hypoglycaemia may be masked by the therapy they are taking. Beta-blockers are probably best avoided in very brittle diabetics on insulin, but in most other cases they can be used with safety.

CALCIUM-ENTRY ANTAGONISTS

These were known to lower blood pressure some years ago, but this potential was not exploited until the 1980s. They are very effective blood pressure lowering agents in all grades of hypertension. However, their exact mode of action on the arteriolar smooth muscle cell has yet to be elucidated. It is thought that they reduce the concentration of free ionized calcium within the cell, thereby relaxing smooth muscle and causing arteriolar vasodilatation. Indeed, it has been suggested that this class of compounds may at least in part be attacking the mechanism whereby blood pressure is raised. In view of their effectiveness in lowering blood pressure large numbers of calcium-entry antagonists are now being developed, although they may not differ from each other significantly. All are vasodilators, but some, such as verapamil, have a greater negative ionotropic and chronotropic effect on the heart. Their major advantage is that unlike the older vasodilators they do not cause tachycardia or fluid retention.

Verapamil, nifedipine and diltiazem have been shown, at least acutely, to be natriuretic, and probably chronically they have a mild diuretic action, which may further reduce blood pressure. Most patients notice that they can exercise normally whilst receiving calcium-entry antagonists and there is no interference with cerebral function.

Verapamil[4]

Verapamil was originally introduced in the 1960s as a beta-blocker and used intravenously as an anti-arrhythmic agent, but it was subsequently realized to be a calcium-entry antagonist. When used in

	Normal daily dose
Nifedipine	10 to 40 mg twice daily
Verapamil	160 – 320 mg twice daily
Sustained release preparation	240 mg once daily
Diltiazem	60 – 120 mg twice daily
Nicardipine	20 – 30 mg three times daily

Table 11.5 Dosage for calcium-entry antagonists.

patients already receiving a beta-blocker it may rarely cause sinus arrest. In view of this, there has been a reluctance to combine oral verapamil with a beta-blocker.

On its own verapamil has been shown to be an effective blood pressure lowering drug.

Dosage Verapamil is usually started at 80 mg twice daily and can be built up to 160 mg twice daily, with increased effect. A once-daily 240 mg tablet has recently become available

Side-effects Its major side-effect is constipation, which occurs particularly with higher doses. It can cause facial flushing and redness of the hands and feet. In most patients, however, it is well tolerated.

Nifedipine[5]

Like verapamil, nifedipine is a calcium-entry antagonist which was initially used in the treatment of angina pectoris. It has less effect on cardiac conduction, and possibly a greater peripheral vasodilating effect.

Dosage The 10 mg capsules are very rapidly absorbed. Recently, 20 mg tablets of nifedipine have been developed, which are less rapidly absorbed and are slightly longer-acting than the capsules, so in longterm therapy these should be used in preference to the capsules.

The 20 mg tablets of nifedipine can be given twice daily. There is good evidence of an increasing dose response, and 40 to 60 mg twice daily may be prescribed safely. Blood pressure falls within one to two hours of the first dose being taken. For this reason, nifedipine tablets are very useful when managing severe or malignant hypertension.

Side-effects Nifedipine commonly causes facial flushing and tingling of the extremities, and a sensation of warm hands and feet and occasionally headaches. These symptoms usually occur with the first dose, particularly with the 10 mg capsules, and are less frequent with the 20 mg tablets.

A few patients develop oedema of the legs. This occurs particularly in middle-aged women. Unlike the direct arteriolar vasodilators, it seems that this is not

1 Nifedipine and nicardipine	2 Verapamil
(a) Facial flushing	(a) Constipation
(b) Headaches	(b) Facial flushing
(c) Ankle oedema	(c) Nausea
(d) Lethargy	(d) Vomiting
(e) Gum hyperplasia	(e) Brady-arrhythmias
(f) Nocturia	(when used with beta-blockers)

Table 11.6 Side-effects of calcium-entry antagonists.

related to renal sodium and water retention but may be due to local tissue factors encouraging the formation of oedema. This side-effect is sometimes abolished by reduction of the total daily dose. Altogether about 10 to 15 per cent of patients are unable to tolerate nifedipine, but the remainder encounter no problems.

Indications for nifedipine Nifedipine has been given in severe hypertension resistant to other therapy and has been found effective. It is additive to a beta-blocker but there is some controversy as to whether diuretics are additive to it. Recent reports have shown that the converting-enzyme inhibitor captopril is additive to nifedipine and this can be an effective combination in very resistant hypertension. As nifedipine has been widely used in angina for many years without any longterm adverse effects, it is likely that the same will apply to hypertension. It is particularly useful in patients where there is a contraindication to beta-blockers or there are side-effects. Nifedipine has probably replaced hydralazine as the most effective third-line agent in resistant hypertension, and is now being increasingly used as a first-line agent (see also Chapter 12).

Nicardipine

This newer calcium blocker has virtually no cardiac side-effects.

Diltiazem[6]

This calcium-entry antagonist has similar vasodilating properties to nifedipine and fewer chronotropic and inotropic effects than verapamil. It is used fairly widely in the USA but little-known in the UK.

Many more calcium-entry antagonists will become available over the next few years but it remains to be seen whether they will have any special advantages.

144

ANGIOTENSIN CONVERTING-ENZYME INHIBITORS (ACE INHIBITORS)[7]

These drugs were designed to block the enzyme that is responsible for converting angiotensin I to angiotensin II. The first inhibitor was found in snake venom, and from this an injectable peptide was developed. Subsequently compounds that could be taken orally were synthesized. Captopril, the first of this class of compounds, was originally introduced for resistant hypertension but has been found to be effective in mild to moderate essential hypertension as well. More recently enalapril has become available and it is likely that there will soon be several more ACE inhibitors on the market.

ACE inhibitors also prevent the breakdown of bradykinin to inactive kinins, thus increasing circulating levels of this vasodilator hormone, and they influence prostaglandin metabolism. It is uncertain whether these biochemical effects also contribute to the antihypertensive response.

Captopril

This is rapidly absorbed and starts to lower blood pressure within about fifteen to thirty minutes of the first dose. Two hours after a single oral dose, there is virtually no circulating angiotensin II present. The drug is partially metabolized by the liver and is excreted in the urine along with its metabolites. Therefore, both may accumulate in renal failure.

Captopril causes a fall in blood pressure, dependent on the initial plasma level of angiotensin II. Patients with very high levels of angiotensin II, as may be seen in malignant hypertension or renal artery stenosis, may sustain a larger fall in pressure. Care should also be taken when giving captopril or enalapril to patients already on large doses of diuretics. Patients with low levels of renin have a smaller response. In them, almost invariably, a diuretic has to be added which raises plasma renin levels and removes some fluid, thus rendering the ACE inhibitors more effective.

Dosage In most patients, captopril is started on a dose of 12.5 to 25 mg twice daily. The total daily dose should never exceed 100 mg. In severe renal failure as little as 6.25 mg twice daily may control the blood pressure.

Side-effects Patients often volunteer that they feel remarkably well on captopril. Indeed, a recent double-blind study has confirmed that captopril has fewer side-effects and less effect on the quality of life than propanolol or methyldopa.[8] Because the drug is acting peripherally it does not interfere with intellectual function or cause drowsiness or deterioration in exercise tolerance. Although the drug was well tolerated in the original trials, where it was given in large doses, particularly to people with renal failure, occasional serious side-effects (proteinuria and leucopenia) were encountered. When captopril is used in lower doses (12.5 or 25 mg twice daily) in patients with normal renal function serious adverse reactions are very rare. Occasionally patients may develop a skin rash, characteristically morbilliform, and more rarely loss of taste.

Hyperkalaemia Owing to the fall in aldosterone secretion there is a slight rise in plasma potassium with captopril. This is usually of benefit, particularly when captopril is combined with small doses of diuretics. However, in patients with severe renal failure, particularly those being treated with potassium-sparing diuretics such as spironolactone, there may be a marked rise in plasma potassium.

Patients with severe renal failure should have plasma potassium monitored carefully during the first few weeks.

Other converting-enzyme inhibitors
Some rare but serious side-effects of high dose captopril, proteinuria and agranulocytosis, were thought to be due to one of its constitutents, the sulphydryl group. Several converting-enzyme inhibitors have now been developed without a sulphydryl group.

Enalapril This is a nonsulphydryl ACE inhibitor, which has a similar action to captopril. The other differences are that it is a pro-drug that is converted in the liver to its active form, and it is longer-acting than captopril, so that it can be given once daily. Experience with this drug so far is more limited than with captopril and as it has not been given in high dosage to patients with renal failure or connective tissue disorders it is not possible to say whether it shares the very rare adverse reactions

	Normal daily dose
Captopril	12.5 – 50 mg twice daily
Enalapril	2.5 – 20 mg once or twice daily

Table 11.7 Dosage for angiotensin-converting enzyme inhibitors.

reported with high doses of captopril. Both captopril and enalapril at the low doses now used are remarkably well tolerated by patients.

When should ACE inhibitors be used?
The major indication for captopril or enalapril is in patients who do not respond to a beta-blocker with a diuretic or in patients in whom beta-blockers are contraindicated, or in those who have developed side-effects. In severe hypertension not controlled by conventional therapy—for example, beta-blocker, diuretic and direct arteriolar vasodilator–converting-enzyme inhibitors may also be very effective combined with either a diuretic or a calcium-entry antagonist. They may also be used in malignant hypertension. As more experience is gained they are now being increasingly used as first-line drugs in mild to moderate hypertension.

Heart failure with high blood pressure Patients with these two conditions may do particularly well with captopril, often showing a remarkable improvement in symptoms. They should be administered cautiously in patients with severe heart failure who are already receiving diuretic therapy, as the initial fall in blood pressure may be rapid.

Scleroderma Patients with scleroderma and malignant hypertension develop rapidly progressive renal failure. Recent reports suggest that captopril may reverse or halt the deterioration in renal function.

Renal artery stenosis The converting-enzyme inhibitors will be effective in lowering blood pressure in renal artery stenosis, but in some patients with bilateral renal artery stenosis or unilateral renal artery stenosis with only one functioning kidney the drugs may cause a deterioration in renal function: indeed, this has been suggested as a diagnostic test. They should be used in this situation with caution, although the deterioration in renal function is usually reversible when the drug is stopped.

1 Skin rash
2 Taste disturbances (very rare with lower doses)
3 Large fall in blood pressure if patient is grossly volume depleted or in some patients with renal artery stenosis
4 Irritating cough

Table 11.8 Side-effects of angiotensin-converting enzyme inhibitors.

	Normal daily dose
Methyldopa	250 – 750 mg twice daily
Clonidine	50 – 500 µg twice daily
Reserpine	100 µg once daily

Table 11.9 Dosage for central acting agents.

146

Combination therapy

Both captopril and enalapril can be used alone, and if necessary with diuretics. There is some controversy about whether these agents are additive to beta-blockers. Beta-blockers inhibit renin release and ACE inhibitors block the formation of angiotensin II. Beta-blockers may prolong the action of captopril. In patients with angina there is no contraindication to the use of captopril or enalapril.

CENTRAL ALPHA-RECEPTOR STIMULATORS

During the 1960s methyldopa became the most commonly used antihypertensive drug after the diuretics. It was thought that by inhibiting the enzyme that converted dopa to dopamine it would also inhibit the synthesis of noradrenaline, so reducing sympathetic activity and blood pressure. Recent research has shown that both methyldopa and clonidine probably lower blood pressure by central alpha-receptor stimulation. They are effective in lowering blood pressure and are additive to diuretics and arterial vasodilators.

Methyldopa

There are still large numbers of patients who were started on methyldopa in the 1960s and 1970s and have learned to live with the side-effects described below, or may not have even noticed them. Our view is that all patients receiving methyldopa should be offered a trial of alternative therapy. Where beta-blockers or thiazides were contraindicated, for example, for patients with bronchospasm, methyldopa was an alternative drug. If the total daily dose is kept below 1000 mg, side-effects are less common. However, the calcium-entry antagonists and converting-enzyme inhibitors should be used in patients where there are contraindications to beta-blockers and diuretics.

Side-effects Nearly all patients notice that they feel sleepy, particularly during the first few weeks of therapy, and many feel somewhat debilitated. This is likely to become apparent to patients who have been on longterm methyldopa therapy when they stop the drug and suddenly feel much better. The drug may also cause erectile impotence.

There are several serious drug reactions that can occur with methyldopa. These include severe liver dysfunction, a positive direct Coombs' test (although haemolytic anaemia occurs only in fewer than 1 per cent) and drug fever.

Pregnancy Methyldopa is effective in patients with pregnancy-related hypertension and appears to be safe to the fetus. As it is only given for a short time and the side-effects are not severe it remains useful in the treatment of blood pressure associated with pregnancy, although beta-blockers may be preferable (see Chapter 16).

Clonidine

This is very similar to methyldopa. It is an effective drug in lowering blood pressure, but it too causes sedation. Unlike methyldopa it does not cause hepatic and haematological problems. Much more worrying, however, is the rebound hypertension that occurs when clonidine is withdrawn. This is particularly dangerous if patients are also receiving a beta-blocker, when the omission of one dose of clonidine may result in a hypertensive crisis. Because of this and because of the side-effect profile, which is similar to that of methyldopa, clonidine is now hardly used in the UK.

In patients in whom clonidine is being stopped it is important to withdraw the beta-blocker first. It is best to substitute a thiazide diuretic or a vasodilator. Then the dose of clonidine should be reduced

147

over about seven days before final discontinuation.

ALPHA-RECEPTOR BLOCKERS

Phenoxybenzamine

Phenoxybenzamine is almost exclusively used in patients with phaeochromocytoma, where it can be extremely effective. The usual dose is 10 mg twice daily. In patients with phaeochromocytoma this has to be titrated until control of the blood pressure is obtained, and sometimes larger amounts may be needed; usually a beta-blocker is given concomitantly to control the pulse rate. Phenoxybenzamine has been used as a fourth-line agent in resistant hypertension.

The most prominent side-effects are postural hypotension and problems with ejaculation.

Phentolamine

This is a shorter acting alpha-blocker that is available only by intravenous injection. It is sometimes used to control hypertensive crises in, for example:

- Phaeochromocytoma
- Rebound hypertension following clonidine withdrawal
- Reactions of monoamine-oxidase inhibitors with pressor amines contained in food.

Prazosin

Prazosin was originally thought to be a direct vasodilator but has now been shown to work through its peripheral alpha-adrenergic blocking properties and may be relatively selective for post-synaptic alpha-1 adrenoreceptors. Unfortunately, although it results in peripheral arteriolar vasodilatation there is also some venous dilatation, and postural hypotension may be encountered. This may be

responsible for the first-dose hypotension and collapse that is occasionally seen. This can be avoided by giving a low starting dose (0.5 mg) at night. Once the first dose is tolerated, there are few further problems with hypotension. As expected with an alpha-blocker, other side-effects are not uncommon.

Generally prazosin should be reserved as a third- or fourth-line drug for patients not responding to a beta-blocker and/or a diuretic.

Indoramin

This is similar to prazosin but appears to have more side-effects, including a high incidence of failure of ejaculation. Indoramin has no particular advantages over prazosin and should not be used unless there are special indications.

ALPHA- AND BETA-RECEPTOR ANTAGONISTS

Alpha-receptor antagonists and beta-blockers have been used together to treat hypertension. While this combination does lower blood pressure, the side-effects of the alpha-antagonists have often been unacceptable. More recently labetalol, which is both a beta-blocker and a weak alpha-blocker when taken orally, has been introduced. When given intravenously it has greater alpha-blocking properties. Its longterm effect on blood pressure is similar to the beta-blockers although at higher doses the alpha-blocking properties cause postural hypotension. Apart from this, labetalol appears to have no more side-effects than beta-blockers, and is probably no more effective. Some clinicians find it a useful agent, and it has been used to good effect in pregnancy hypertension.

VASODILATORS

The direct arteriolar vasodilators, the first of which was hydralazine, have been used for many years in the treatment of high blood pressure. They all cause a decrease in peripheral vascular tone, with a reflex activation of the sympathetic nervous system leading to an increase in heart rate. They also cause a rise in cardiac output, increased release of renin and higher angiotensin II and aldosterone levels. However, when they are used in combination with a beta-blocker and a diuretic these side-effects are minimized.

Hydralazine

Hydralazine has a direct effect on smooth muscle cells in the peripheral arterioles and only a very small effect on veins. It is largely metabolized in the liver. On its own, it was found not to be very effective in lowering blood pressure because of the reflex sympathetic stimulation and the high doses needed.

Hydralazine has been extensively used as a third-line drug in patients with more severe hypertension who do not respond to a beta-blocker in combination with a diuretic. It is also used in patients with renal failure. While hydralazine has, until recently, been the most commonly used third-line drug, nifedipine and captopril are now becoming more popular. It is likely that the use of hydralazine will decline now that nifedipine, enalapril and captopril are being more widely used.

Dosage As with many other older blood pressure drugs, hydralazine was initially given in excessively high doses. It is best to start with 25 mg twice daily, increased to 50 mg twice daily. Above this level there is a greater risk of side-effects. Patients who do not respond or who require higher doses of hydralazine may be fast hepatic acetylators who metabolize the hydralazine more quickly. Slow acetylators develop a greater antihypertensive response, but suffer more side-effects.

Alpha-adrenoceptor blockers	Normal daily dose
Phenoxybenzamine	10 – 50 mg once or twice daily
Prazosin	0.5 – 5 mg three times daily
Indoramine	25 – 100 mg twice daily
Alpha and beta-receptor antagonists	
Labetalol	200 – 2000 mg twice daily

Table 11.10 Dosage for alpha-adrenoceptor blockers and alpha and beta-receptor antagonists.

	Normal daily dose
Hydralazine	25 – 100 mg twice daily
Minoxidil	2.5 – 20 mg twice daily
Diazoxide	injection only 100–300 mg

Table 11.11 Dosage for peripheral vasodilators.

Side-effects Many patients, particularly the younger ones, develop symptoms of peripheral vasodilatation including headaches, flushing and palpitations. These may be overcome by combining hydralazine with a beta-blocker. Some patients develop a lupus-like syndrome with arthritis, pyrexia and general malaise. This usually occurs at higher doses or in patients who are slow acetylators. It is usually fully reversible by withdrawal of the drug. If the dose of hydralazine is kept below 100 mg daily, the lupus syndrome is rare. It may also be under-recognized if the arthritic symptoms are mild.

Minoxidil

This is one of the most potent vasodilators known. Its mode of action is similar to that of hydralazine, and it similarly causes tachycardia owing to reflex sympathetic stimulation. It also always causes sodium and water retention, leading to oedema. In view of the side-effects it has largely been reserved for men with uncontrolled hypertension. With the increasing use of captopril and the calcium-entry antagonists the use of minoxidil has diminished.

Sodium and water retention can be prevented by the use of diuretics. Frusemide is almost always needed, often in large doses. The tachycardia means that beta-blockers are also always needed. The other serious side-effect is a generalized increase in hair growth, particularly on the forehead and temples. This hirsutism virtually precludes its use in women (see Chapter 12).

Dosage The usual starting dose is 2.5 mg twice daily. It may be necessary to increase the dose to 15 mg twice daily. There is some doubt as to whether it is possible to give minoxidil in a single dose once daily, but in combination it may be long-acting.

Diazoxide

Oral diazoxide is now hardly used, although it is still available in Britain. It is a potent vasodilator that has similar side-effects to minoxidil. It may also induce acute diabetes mellitus and a Parkinsonian syndrome. This drug is no longer needed, since the introduction of minoxidil, nifedipine and captopril.

OTHER HYPERTENSIVE DRUGS

Rauwolfia alkaloids

These drugs have both central and peripheral effects on noradrenaline release. They are not much used now in Britain because of their side-effects.

Reserpine

Reserpine was once widely prescribed and found to be effective both when used alone and when combined with a diuretic. When given in a low dose (0.1 to 0.2 mg) at night, side-effects are not serious. However, at higher doses it causes sedation and depression, even leading to suicide. Consequently it has been largely abandoned in Western countries, particularly since the introduction of methyldopa. Nevertheless, worldwide, it is still commonly used in combination with a diuretic and hydralazine. It remains the treatment of choice in many Third World countries, because of its low cost.

Postadrenergic blockers (guanethidine, bethanidine and debrisoquine)

These drugs can be considered together as they have similar effects. Although they are effective in lowering blood pressure, they have serious side-effects:

- Severe exercise-induced and postural hypotension
- Failure of ejaculation, sometimes impotence and rarely severe diarrhoea.

These drugs should therefore no longer be used and patients already on them should be changed to more modern treatment.

PRACTICAL POINT

- Thiazides, beta-blockers, calcium blockers and ACE blockers are all acceptable first-line antihypertensive therapy.

12
Schemes for reducing blood pressure

BACKGROUND

There are well over one hundred different drugs that lower blood pressure with approximately twenty different mechanisms of action. New types of drugs and new formulations or combinations of existing agents are continually being developed.[1] It is not surprising, therefore, that there is some disagreement even between experts about which drugs or combinations of drugs are best for individual patients. Often, by the time definitive evidence of the usefulness of one particular group of drugs has become available, new products have been developed that may have advantages or fewer side-effects.

Some drugs may have added beneficial effects or fewer harmful effects which are independent of their blood pressure lowering action. For example, whilst the thiazide diuretics have few clinical side-effects, their metabolic effects on potassium, glucose and lipids continue to cause concern. Conversely, the beta-receptor blockers despite their side-effects may have some protective effect against cardiac disease in selected cases. However, despite the many important differences between the various types of antihypertensive agents it is probably true that it does not really matter how blood pressure is reduced, but it must be reduced, and with the minimum of side-effects. Unfortunately about one half of all patients receiving antihypertensive drugs have inadequate control of their blood pressure.

During the last decade the treatment of most forms of hypertension was relatively simple; patients were started on either a beta-blocker or a thiazide diuretic, and if one drug was insufficient the two were used in combination, and further drugs were then added in sequentially. This so-called 'step-care' approach has recently been overtaken by the advent of the angiotensin-converting (ACE) inhibitors and the calcium-entry antagonists, which are now being used as second or first-line drugs. As further experience is gained it is becoming clear that individual patients respond to different drugs in different ways so that rigid schemes for blood pressure reduction are not appropriate. In this chapter we outline our current practice in treating hypertensive patients.

The goal of antihypertensive therapy

The clinician's objective in drug therapy should be to reduce the blood pressure to the normal range (below 90 mmHg diastolic pressure), at the same time leaving the patient feeling completely well. The better the control of the pressure the lower is the risk of premature death or illness from cardiovascular, cerebrovascular and renal disease. The more severe the hypertension the greater is the risk of death, but greater too are the benefits of treatment.

In general the same drugs are used whatever the level of blood pressure, but in more severe cases there is a greater urgency for reduction of the pressure so there may be little time initially to establish the best approach for the individual patient. However, the urgency of treatment is commonly over-stressed and, apart from cases with encephalopathy, gross left ventricular failure or aortic dissection, there is no need to reduce blood pressure over minutes or hours. Even in malignant hypertensives, blood pressure should be lowered only over twenty-four to forty-eight hours, and in that period it should not be reduced to normal. In such cases pressure should be normalized over a few days. Over-rapid blood pressure reduction can be as dangerous as a very high blood pressure left untreated.

BLOOD PRESSURE LOWERING REGIMES

Non-pharmacological blood pressure reduction All patients should be instructed on non-pharmacological ways in which blood pressure may be lowered (see Chapter 10). Paradoxically, non-pharmacological treatment is most often stressed to patients with only mild hypertension where these measures are less effective. Patients with more severe hypertension should also be instructed on how they can help to lower their blood pressure by salt restriction, and where relevant by weight loss and moderation of alcohol intake. Salt restriction is known to have a useful additive effect to many antihypertensive drugs.

First-line antihypertensive drug therapy There are now at least four possible first-line antihypertensive drug groups. These are the thiazide diuretics, the beta-blockers, the calcium-entry antagonists and the ACE inhibitors. If any one of these causes side-effects or is ineffective another type should be substituted or added. If the blood pressure is still not satisfactorily controlled, different combi-nations of antihypertensive agents are added in until the optimum blood pressure is achieved.

THE FIRST STEP

Diuretics

There are no basic differences between the many thiazide diuretics. If this group of drugs is to be used then the best option is to prescribe the cheapest, and at the lowest possible dose. It is our practice to use either bendrofluazide in a single daily dose of 2.5 mg or hydrochlorothiazide (12.5 mg–25 mg daily) as this minimizes the clinical and metabolic side-effects.[2]

Thiazide diuretics are most useful in:

- Older patients
- Black patients
- Patients with mild or incipient heart failure

They are best avoided in:

- Maturity onset diabetics
- Patients with hyperlipidaemia
- Pregnancy
- Patients with gout

They should be discontinued in:

- Men complaining of impotence
- Patients developing hypergly-caemia or hyperlipidaemia.

Patients receiving diuretics of any type should have their serum electrolytes checked after about two months and thereafter at least annually. It is not our practice to prescribe potassium supplements. Combined diuretic and potassium chloride tablets should not be used as they contain small amounts of potassium. If the serum potassium falls then the potassium sparing diuretics (amiloride, triamterene or spironolactone) may be added. The addition of a beta-blocker or an ACE inhibitor to a low dose of a thiazide diuretic also blunts the fall in serum potassium. Patients on longterm thiazide therapy should have occasional checks of their urine or blood for glucose and their serum lipid levels should be checked. If marked hypokalaemia develops with the use of thiazide diuretics, a diagnosis of primary hyperaldosteronism should be considered.

Beta-blockers

The differences between many beta-blockers are not great.[3] The main advantages of this group of drugs are that they can usually be given in a single once-daily dose, there are no major problems with toxicity and most of the contraindications are well recognized. As with the thiazide diuretics it is generally advisable to use the lowest dose. Only rarely does increasing the dose lead to improved blood pressure control.

Beta-blockers are most useful in:

- Younger patients
- Anxious patients
- Non-smokers
- Patients with renal insufficiency
- Pregnancy
- Angina pectoris
- Patients who have had a myocardial infarction

Beta-blockers should be avoided in:

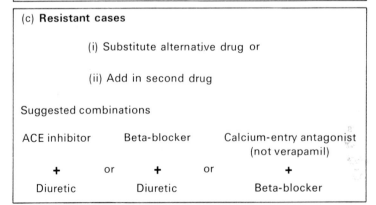
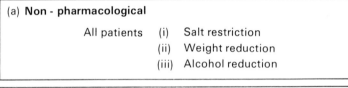
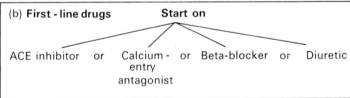

Figure 12.1 A guide to blood pressure treatment.

(a) **Non - pharmacological**

All patients	(i)	Salt restriction
	(ii)	Weight reduction
	(iii)	Alcohol reduction

(b) **First - line drugs** **Start on**

ACE inhibitor or Calcium-entry antagonist or Beta-blocker or Diuretic

(c) **Resistant cases**

(i) Substitute alternative drug or

(ii) Add in second drug

Suggested combinations

ACE inhibitor		Beta-blocker		Calcium-entry antagonist (not verapamil)
+	or	+	or	+
Diuretic		Diuretic		Beta-blocker

- Asthmatics
- 'Brittle' insulin-requiring diabetic patients
- Intermittent claudication
- Raynaud's syndrome
- Second and third degree heart block
- Patients with heart failure

Beta-blockers should be discontinued in:

- Patients developing heart failure
- Patients developing asthma
- If the pulse rate falls to below 48 beats per minute.

The minor differences between the beta-blockers mean that the clinician may favour one particular drug in an individual case. However, if major problems develop with one beta-blocker, it is likely that they will also be encountered with other members of the group.

Hydrophilic beta-blockers (atenolol, nadolol and sotalol)
- May cause less tiredness and loss of exercise tolerance
- Should be given in lower dose in patients with renal failure

Cardioselective beta-blockers (atenolol, acebutolol, metoprolol)
- May have fewer effects on airways resistance
- May cause less interference with the autonomic and metabolic responses to hypoglycaemia in insulin-dependent diabetic patients

Intrinsic sympathomimetic activity beta-blockers (oxprenolol, pindolol, acebutolol)
- May cause less reduction of peripheral bloodflow.

As discussed elsewhere (see Chapter 11), there was at one stage considerable optimism that the beta-blockers would have special advantages over other agents by having a 'cardioprotective' effect. Recent evidence has proved disappointing except in non-smokers, where a beneficial effect has been found. This advantage is still, therefore, to be gained by hypertensive patients who do not smoke and this evidence further emphasizes the importance of persuading patients to stop smoking.

Calcium-entry antagonists
There are two distinct types of calcium-entry antagonists: those that are principally arterial vasodilators (such as nifedipine and diltiazem) with little effect on the heart and those (such as verapamil) that also slow the heart rate.[4] While these are not new drugs their use as first-line therapy in hypertension is a relatively novel approach. Nifedipine should be used in the 20 mg tablet 'retard' formulation, given twice daily.

Nifedipine is most useful in:

- Older patients
- Black patients
- Patients with peripheral vascular disease
- Patients with cerebrovascular disease
- Patients with angina pectoris

Verapamil is most useful in:

- Patients with concurrent tachyarrhythmias
- Angina pectoris

Verapamil should be avoided in:

- Patients with cardiac failure
- Any degree of heart block.

155

A disadvantage of nifedipine and nicardipine is that they cannot, at least in the present formulations, be used in a once daily dosage. While nifedipine is a very effective drug, approximately 10 to 15 per cent of patients prescribed it are unable to tolerate it owing to the side-effects of flushing, headache and occasionally diuretic-resistant ankle oedema. Several new calcium-entry antagonists will soon become available. It is not yet clear whether they will have any special advantages.

Angiotensin-converting enzyme (ACE) inhibitors

This group has the fewest side-effects of all the blood pressure lowering drugs.[5] Apart from the once daily prescription of enalapril it is doubtful whether there are any major differences between enalapril and captopril when used in the correct dosage.[6,7]

ACE inhibitors are particularly useful in:

- Younger patients
- Patients with incipient or mild heart failure
- Patients who develop side-effects from other drugs

ACE inhibitors should be used with care in:

- Renal artery stenosis
- Severely fluid-depleted patients, especially those already receiving a loop diuretic such as frusemide, unless the diuretic is stopped.
- Avoid in pregnancy.

The lowest possible dose should be used to initiate therapy, e.g., 12.5 or 25 mg captopril, 2.5 or 5 mg enalapril. The maximum with captopril should not exceed 100 mg and enalapril 40 mg daily.

Centrally acting antihypertensive drugs

This group is at present out of favour. While clonidine certainly should never be used, both methyldopa and reserpine do have a role in selected cases. The major side-effects of sedation and depression can be minimized if these drugs are used in low doses. However, both should be used as last-resort first-line drugs.

Other antihypertensive agents

It is not our practice to use alpha-blocking drugs (indoramin, phenoxybenzamine and prazosin), adrenergic blockers (guanethidine, bethanidine and debrisoquine), direct vasodilators (hydralazine, minoxidil and diazoxide) or non-thiazide diuretics (loop diuretics or potassium retaining agents) as first-line therapy. Occasionally patients are encountered taking drugs such as reserpine, methyldopa or prazosin who are entirely well, with good blood pressure control. It is then justifiable to continue these drugs' use.

THE SECOND STEP

If optimum control of blood pressure is not achieved with the first-line drugs used appropriately and in the correct dose, then it is usual to add in another type of antihypertensive agent. Most can be used together but there are some combinations which are not particularly effective or are potentially harmful.

Commonly used drug combinations

1. Thiazide diuretic with added:
   beta-blocker

2. Beta-blocker with added:
   thiazide diuretic
   nifedipine or diltiazem

3. Nifedipine or diltiazem with added:

beta-blocker
ACE inhibitor

4. ACE inhibitor with added:
   thiazide diuretic
   calcium-entry blocker
   beta-blocker

Drug combinations which may be hazardous or pointless

1. Beta-blocker with verapamil
2. Two drugs of the same class used together.

THE THIRD STEP

Patients whose blood pressure is resistant to double therapy in the combinations suggested above have a high risk of the cardiovascular complications of hypertension. It is advisable for such cases to be referred to specialist blood pressure clinics, particularly as it is important to exclude an underlying cause for the hypertension. The policy in resistant hypertensive patients is to:

Check compliance

Enquire whether the patient is taking the prescribed drugs and whether he finds the tablet regime difficult to remember. Lack of compliance is suggested where there is no fall in pulse rate in patients taking beta-blockers, or no fall in serum potassium in those receiving thiazides alone.

Simplify the antihypertensive regime

Complex regimes can lead to poor compliance. It is reasonable to convert patients to once daily regimes and single tablet diuretic/beta-blocker combinations are justified. No regime for any patient need be more frequent than twice daily.

Give advice on salt restriction

A rough guide to a patient's usual sodium intake can be obtained from a twenty-four hour urine collection for electrolytes. Specific advice from a dietitian may be helpful.

Weight reduction Where relevant give advice on weight reduction and moderation in alcohol intake.

Check for underlying remediable causes of hypertension (see Chapter 8).

Triple-therapy drug regimes

The therapeutic principles of managing resistant hypertension are the same as for milder grades; it is usual to add in a third drug of a different class.

Regimes used in resistant hypertension

1. ACE inhibitor plus nifedipine, diltiazem or verapamil, plus frusemide
2. Beta-blocker plus nifedipine or diltiazem plus a thiazide diuretic
3. ACE inhibitor plus frusemide plus beta-blocker
4. Beta-blocker, diuretic, nifedipine or diltiazem and ACE inhibitor
5. Beta-blocker plus frusemide plus minoxidil
6. Beta-blocker plus diuretic plus alpha-blocker (e.g., prazosin).

Minoxidil is a very powerful vasodilator but its side-effects necessitate the concurrent use of both a beta-blocker and a loop diuretic. Increased facial hair growth precludes this drug in women.

Hydralazine is a less powerful vasodilator, and if the total daily dose is kept below 100 mg there are fewer side-effects. It may be usefully added to a beta-blocker/thiazide combination.

157

In patients receiving a beta-blocker with a vasodilator, the substitution of frusemide for a thiazide diuretic may be helpful, especially if there is evidence of undue weight gain after treatment has been started.

Patients receiving an ACE *inhibitor* can, with care, be given increasing doses of frusemide. At very high doses of frusemide, postural hypotension may be a problem. The combination of an ACE inhibitor with a calcium-entry antagonist may be as effective.

It is sometimes helpful to add in the aldosterone antagonist spironolactone to triple-therapy regimes that include a thiazide or loop diuretic.

Most of the regimes described above are complex and it is important that they are built up gradually.[8] In some cases it is

helpful for the patient to be admitted to the hospital so that changes can be made every few days, but it should be remembered that in-patient blood pressure readings obtained with the patient resting may be very misleading, and out-patient blood pressure readings may still be uncontrolled.

Occasionally a patient is encountered whose blood pressure, while never dangerously high, appears to be resistant to all treatment. It is worth checking whether the patient has only transient elevations of pressure in response to attending the clinic. If he or she is rested in a quiet room for half an hour and the blood pressure is checked by a reliably trained nurse, lower readings may be obtained. If such patients have absolutely no evidence of cardiac, renal or cerebral damage, and particularly if the ECG shows no evidence of left ventricular hypertrophy (RV5 + SV1 less than 35 mm) or left atrial dilatation (biphasic P wave in lead V1), then it may be reasonable to accept less-than-optimal control of blood pressure in the clinic. In such cases, home blood pressure monitoring, possibly with an automatic sphygmomanometer, may confirm that pressures are low when the patient is away from the potentially threatening clinical environment.

MALIGNANT HYPERTENSION

All patients with the malignant phase of hypertension (i.e., those with retinal haemorrhages or exudates, with or without papilloedema) should be admitted to the hospital as soon as possible for controlled blood pressure reduction as well as detailed investigation of their hypertension. If blood pressure is not adequately reduced, the disease progresses rapidly to end-stage chronic renal failure requiring dialysis or to death from cardiac failure or stroke. As with other grades of

---

(a) **Check compliance with lifestyle changes**
   (i) salt restriction
   (ii) weight reduction
   (iii) alcohol restraint

(b) **Check therapeutic compliance**
   (i) tablet counts
   (ii) monitor drug levels in blood if possible
   (iii) simplify therapeutic regime

(c) **Investigate further for underlying cause of hypertension**
   (i) Renal arteriogram (even if IVP is normal)
   (ii) Urinary catecholamines

Figure 12.2 A guide to resistant blood pressure control (i.e., not controlled by two drugs).

158

hypertension, the outlook is closely related to the quality of care during the weeks and months following diagnosis. The five-year survival rate for malignant hypertension should now be around 80 per cent.

Perfect control of blood pressure should be achieved over a period of a few weeks as more rapid treatment can lead to acute reductions of bloodflow to the brain and kidneys, causing cerebral infarction or deterioration of renal function. The aim should be to lower the diastolic pressure with the use of oral therapy only[9] to around 110 mmHg over a period of twenty-four to forty-eight hours, and to lower it to below 90 mmHg only after a week or two, often after the patient has been discharged from hospital.

Regimes for malignant hypertension

1. Atenolol 50 or 100 mg in a single oral dose, and thereafter 100 mg daily (see Figure 12.3)
2. Captopril—initially 6.25 mg followed by 25 mg twice daily
3. Nifedipine 10 or 20 mg in a single oral dose and thereafter 20 mg twice daily.

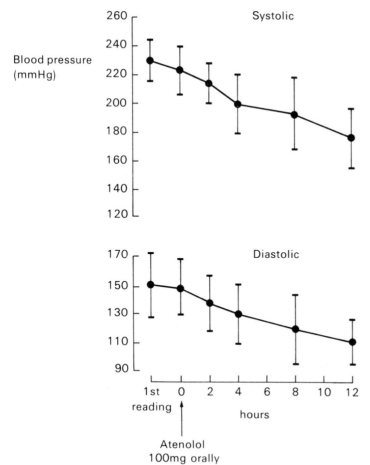

Figure 12.3 The effect of a single dose of oral atenolol (100 mg) on systolic and diastolic pressure in ten patients (from *Brit. Med. J.* *282*, 1981, 1757–8).

These are suitable for most cases of malignant hypertension. Parenteral antihypertensive drugs are never justified unless the patient has severe heart failure or hypertensive encephalopathy.

After the first few days the principles of managing malignant hypertension are the same as for more routine cases, although triple therapy is almost always necessary. These patients are best supervised on a

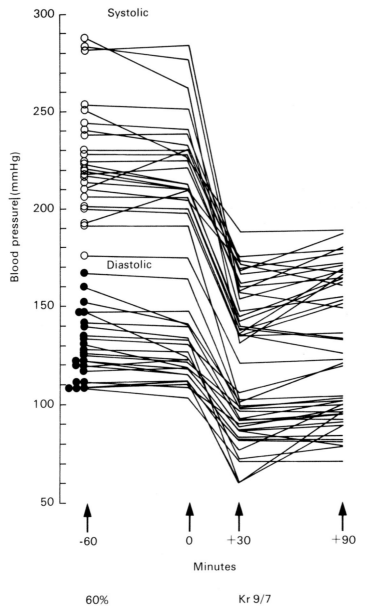

Figure 12.4 The effect of a single 10 or 20 mg capsule of nifedipine on systolic and diastolic blood pressure (from *Brit. Med. J. 286*, 1981, 19–21).

60%   Kr 9/7

longterm basis by physicians with a special interest in hypertension.

HYPERTENSIVE EMERGENCIES

Many blood pressure lowering drugs can be given intravenously or intramuscularly and they lower blood pressure very rapidly. Their only indication is in the treatment of hypertensive encephalopathy or gross ventricular failure directly due to raised blood pressure or dissecting aortic aneurysm.[10]

Diazoxide

This drug has been widely used as a parenteral agent. Some years ago it was recommended to be given rapidly as an intravenous bolus of 300 mg. This produces an immediate fall in blood pressure

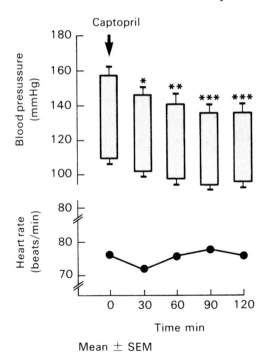

Figure 12.5 The effect of a single dose of captopril (25 mg) on systolic and diastolic blood pressure in twenty-two patients (from *Brit. J. Clin. Pharm. 14*, 1982, 1215–65).

of 30 to 40 per cent within two or three minutes and serious complications have been described. A much better way of giving diazoxide is either by infusion or in 50 mg intravenous boluses every ten minutes, the dose being increased as necessary until adequate blood pressure control is reached. Using this method the blood pressure may be reduced over thirty minutes to two hours to the desired level avoiding precipitous falls.

Labetalol

When given by intravenous infusion, labetalol has a predominant alpha-blocking effect and lowers blood pressure rapidly but can cause severe postural hypotension. It is not therefore to be recommended for parenteral therapy. Intravenous boluses of labetalol have an even more unpredictable effect.

Nitroprusside

This is a potent vasodilator that invariably lowers blood pressure when given by intravenous infusion. The fall in blood pressure is controlled by the rate of infusion. It must be given under very close supervision as severe hypotension can occur. As well as causing the expected side-effects of any arteriolar vasodilator, including flushing and postural hypotension, nitroprusside is metabolized to cyanide and thiacyanate. This is not important during short-term infusion but toxicity can develop if the drug is given over several days, particularly if there is renal failure.

New solutions need to be made up to every four hours and must be covered by light-proof paper to prevent photo-deactivation. The starting dose is 0.5 μg/kilogram/minute. For a 70 kg (150 pound) patient this means starting at 3.5 μg/minute but the dose can gradually be increased to 200 μg/minute. Blood pressure should be measured frequently, preferably using an automatic manometer, and great care must be taken to avoid precipitous falls in pressure.

Hydralazine

Hydralazine can be given either intravenously or intramuscularly and is widely used, particularly in obstetrics. The normal dose is 10 to 40 mg injected slowly. In most situations where it is used, oral hydralazine would be just as effective.

Oral therapy

For patients able to take drugs by mouth, most blood pressure lowering drugs given orally act rapidly. For instance, nifedipine given in a 10 mg capsule, either bitten and held under the tongue or even swallowed, will cause blood pressure to fall within ten to fifteen minutes (see Figure 12.4). The ACE inhibitor captopril when taken orally lowers blood pressure within thirty minutes (see Figure 12.5), although enalapril has a slower effect on blood pressure since it must be converted by the liver to an active metabolite. Oral beta-blockers with or without hydralazine reduce blood pressure over a period of two to three hours.

PRACTICAL POINTS

- Antihypertensive regimes are now more complex than they used to be, mainly because of the wide choice of agents. It is, however, now usually possible to control blood pressure with relatively few side-effects and regimes can be tailored for patients with specific problems. (The problem of blood pressure reduction in patients who have concomitant diseases is discussed in Chapter 14.)

- The goal of therapy in all patients up to the age of about seventy-five years is to reduce the diastolic blood pressure to below 90 mmHg.

- The outlook depends on the quality of patients' blood pressure control rather than on the initial severity of their hypertension.

- If optimum control of pressure is not obtained, patients should be referred for further treatment to physicians who have a special interest in hypertension.

13
Hypertension in primary medical care

BACKGROUND

Other chapters in this book have dealt with the value of the investigation and reduction of high blood pressure. The next question is, who should actually deliver this potentially life-saving treatment? There is evidence that the quality and efficiency of blood pressure reduction is a more potent predictor of a patient's life expectancy than the severity of the hypertension in the first place. Regrettably, practically every population survey in the UK, the USA and elsewhere has reported a depressing and woeful state of underdiagnosis, undertreatment and inadequate follow-up of hypertensive patients. The 'rule of halves' described in Chapter 1 means that less than 15 per cent of all hypertensives are receiving adequate clinical care. The need for improvement in detection and management of hypertension ranks with the abolition of cigarette smoking as a major public health concern in developed countries. In developing countries this new epidemic is just around the corner.

The responsibility for the organization of case detection, treatment and follow-up of hypertensive patients must rest with the primary health care team, in the context of good general or family practice. This chapter contains the justification for this view and suggestions for its organization.[1]

SCREENING FOR HYPERTENSION

As outlined in Chapter 1, hypertension is an eminently suitable disease for some form of screening programme. The exact method employed depends on the health care facilities available in individual countries.

Selective screening

A very strong case has been made for selective screening of people who are at particular risk.

Family history It should be the responsibility of patients and doctors alike to seek out symptomless relatives of patients with hypertension or its complications, particularly heart attack and stroke, who may benefit from antihypertensive treatment.

Pregnancy Another high-risk group are pregnant women; here the efficient detection and management of high blood pressure is already an integral part of good obstetric care (see Chapter 16). The rest of the medical profession have a lot to learn from this.

Previous complications Patients who have already suffered a vascular complication of hypertension have a very high risk of recurrence. Second strokes can be prevented if blood pressure is controlled on a longterm basis.

The routine selective screening of survivors of heart attacks or strokes once they have gone home must be regarded as an integral part of good clinical care.

Mass screening

The so-called 'well population screening' of fit populations is an emotive issue. Screening alone is not enough; there must also be efficient follow-up of abnormalities detected. This means that the establishment of screening programmes is expensive. Mass screening using mobile screening buses is an efficient means of recruiting patients for clinical trials, but obviously this one-off exercise cannot solve a longterm problem.

Occupational screening

Screening of employees clearly has its place but this is available only to a minority of the population, mainly men who are employed in large firms or industries. There are also problems of confidentiality of clinical information, and usually industrial medical officers do not organize follow-up or drug treatment.

Casual screening

The provision of blood pressure measurement equipment and staff in supermarkets, department stores and public places can make only a small impact without follow-up and treatment. There is evidence that casual screening programmes such as these tend to attract hypertensive patients who are already diagnosed; people whose pressures have never been measured tend to ignore them. Increased public health education may alter this tendency, but the system is certainly not ideal at present.

Screening by the primary health care team

In an ideal world every person from childhood upwards would have his or her blood pressure measured. Screening people below the age of about thirty would, however, yield relatively few hypertensive cases. Furthermore, the benefits of intervention in very mild hypertension in childhood and adolescence are unknown. People examined over the age of seventy-five would produce a very large number of abnormalities, but this would be in a group of patients in whom the benefits of therapy of mild hypertension are less certain.

A reasonable compromise is for case detection programmes to be instituted for everyone between the ages of thirty-five and seventy. This represents about 980 examinees in an average general practice in Britain, which has about 2300 people on each practitioner's list. Of those examinees about 20 to 25 per cent (190 to 240 people) will have diastolic pressures at first screening of 90 mmHg or more. As many blood pressures settle on rechecking, after three visits between 100 and 120 patients are likely to have blood pressures within the range requiring antihypertensive treatment.

In developed countries, more than 75 per cent of the adult population see a doctor for some reason over a period of three years and initial screening can be carried out at these visits.[2] The organization of family medicine varies from place to place and from country to country, but there are several ways in which individual doctors or groups of family doctors may organize their case detection programmes.

Case detection of patients as they present

All this requires is for the doctor, or the practice nurse or receptionist, to check that there is a recent blood pressure reading in the records of all attenders. The system is simple and continuous and, most important, feasible for every family doctor's practice.

Appointments for eligible examinees

A faster way is to arrange appointments for all patients considered at risk to have a routine blood pressure check. This will require extra paperwork and time spent on screening clinics. However, it can achieve a complete screen over a period of a few months. The primary care team should therefore consider sending appointments to all men and women for blood pressure checks. At the same time, 'well woman' and 'well man' health checks can be made including examination for breast lumps, cervical cytology, urine testing and possibly screening for hypercholesterolaemia.

Screening of newly eligible patients

Once the backlog of previously unscreened patients has been examined it is important to continue the programme to include individuals who become eligible for screening over the ensuing years. For this purpose, the doctor should ideally have an age/sex register of the patients on the practice list. Patients reaching the age of thirty-five can thus be summoned for screening. One general practitioner in England sends his patients a birthday card together with an appointment for a blood pressure and health check.

In addition, when a new patient joins the list an appointment should be arranged for a medical check.

Medical records

Any attempt to establish a systematic case detection programme requires good medical records. In the UK the general practitioner medical records system is adequate, but certain additions are recommended.[3]

Flags Any type of sticker, or protruding section of an inserted card, renders individual patients' records readily identifiable. These can be used to draw attention to important diagnoses, not only of hypertension, and to identify patients due for blood pressure checking.

The system has been used in many practices and it is simple, cheap and effective. With a few hours' work per week a doctor or his secretary or receptionist can in about six weeks go through the medical records and insert flags as needed.

Screening record cards Inside the record folder a separate screening card is useful. Information on smoking habits, weight and other relevant diseases should be included. The card can also be designed to act as a follow-up record sheet, with spaces for subsequent appointments, names of drugs and dosages, general comments and possibly a graphical blood pressure chart. Many such screening and follow-up record cards have been devised by individual doctors and by pharmaceutical companies, and their use is strongly recommended (see Figures 13.1 and 13.2).

Age/sex register A register of patients by age and sex is invaluable as an aid in all preventive medicine. Many groups of family doctors have created their own, to good effect. In the UK, where well over 90 per cent of the population are registered with a National Health Service practitioner, perhaps the most useful assistance given by community health doctors would be to provide general practitioners with an up-to-date computer printout of all patients registered with them. A list of known hypertensives and of patients due for screening would also be useful.

Diagnostic lists Some doctors have found it convenient to keep an updated

165

card-index of patients diagnosed as hypertensive so that they can easily check, for example, who has been seen, who is receiving drug therapy or how many patients still have inadequate blood pressure control.

Computerization Computerized records are time and space-saving. Microcomputers are now relatively cheap and they can be programmed to store information such as patient lists, appointments, follow-up records, repeat prescriptions and blood pressures. There is an increasing need for manageable commercially produced software for the detection and follow-up of hypertensive patients.

Patient-held records Pilot surveys have demonstrated that patients can be relied upon to carry their own medical records in a single wallet-sized folder. Alternatively, a blood pressure personal record card may be used. These are particularly useful as shared-care record cards for patients who are attending a hospital clinic as well as seeing their family doctor. They aid communication and obviate the need for a great many letters. These cards can display blood pressure readings in tables or graph form together with a list of drugs and dosages. Other relevant information including investigation results and weight can also be included. An additional advantage is their educational role; the patient

HYPERTENSION		
SURNAME	FORENAMES	DATE OF BIRTH
ADDRESS		
SUMMARY OF HISTORY		
....		
FAMILY HISTORY	OBSTETRIC HISTORY	
SMOKING	AVERAGE WEEKLY ALCOHOL INTAKE	
ANTIDEPRESSIVES	STEROIDS	CONTRACEPTIVE

Figure 13.1 A blood pressure screening card suitable for use in primary medical care. This can also be used as a patient-held record system.

knows his or her blood pressure and the names of the drugs being used, and can see the effect of the treatment.[4]

Who measures blood pressure?
The techniques for blood pressure measurement are covered in Chapter 6. An ordinary well-maintained mercury manometer is all that is needed, and there should be two cuffs: one of normal size and a larger one for obese patients.

In group practices, nurses or receptionists can be trained to measure pressures and to maintain good medical records. This is probably the ideal; paramedical staff, suitably briefed, seem to be more reliable than doctors.[5]

Within a group practice it is best for a single doctor to undertake responsibility for the detection and management of hypertension. He or she should be able to collaborate with local hospital-based specialists in cardiovascular and renal diseases.

LEVELS OF BLOOD PRESSURE REQUIRING ACTION
The present state of knowledge is that antihypertensive drug therapy is justified if a patient's diastolic blood pressure persistently exceeds 95 to 100 mmHg. There is now evidence that therapy is justified in patients up to the age of about eighty (see Chapter 15). However, pati-

DATE	4/6/84	18/6/84	20/7/84	22/8/84	7/9/84	2/10/84	7/12/84
B.P. Sitting/Lying	174/102	172/104	160/92	158/84	162/92	150/86	48/84
PULSE	96	92	68	64	76	72	76
WEIGHT kg st lbs	84.0	83.5	83.0	83.5	84.0	84.5	82.5
DRUG (Dose/Day) 1 PROPRANOLOL		START 40mg x2	40mg x2	STOP			
DRUG (Dose/Day) 2 ENALAPRIL				START 5mg daily	10mg/day	10mg	10mg
DRUG (Dose/Day) 3							
DRUG (Dose/Day) 4							
SERUM UREA	3.6			4.1			
SERUM POTASSIUM	4.1			4.8			
OTHER INVESTIGATION	LIPIDS NORMAL				IVP NORMAL		
TIME TO NEXT VISIT	2/52	4/52	4/52	2/52	5/52	2/12	3/12
COMMENTS	Advice only	must lose weight	tired	very tired	better	must lose wt!	
DOCTOR's SIGNATURE	DW	DW	DW	DW	DW	DW	DW

Figure 13.2 A blood pressure follow-up card suitable for use in hospital and general practice.

ents whose pressures are only just below this dividing line, or whose pressures, having been raised, have settled, also require general advice and, of course, regular rechecking.

Figure 13.3 provides recommendations on procedures at the time of screening. These take into account the increasing prevalence of hypertension with age and the current data on the benefits of treatment. The recommendations in patients below the age of thirty-five and above the age of eighty are included for completeness, although at the moment screening programmes are not recommended.

The recommendations are related to an otherwise symptomless patient attending a screening programme. Clearly they cannot cover every eventuality. It could be argued that all patients should be given good general health advice on weight control, salt reduction, alcohol moderation and, of course, cigarette smoking. If patients' blood pressures are raised, it is only rarely necessary to institute drug therapy on the basis of a single reading, and patients with such very high blood pressures should probably be admitted to hospital anyway.

In most cases blood pressures should be rechecked at a second and even a third visit. In the moderate grades of hypertension, the second visit should be within a few days, but in mild hypertension it should be within a month or two. If blood pressures are settling a further rechecking visit may be considered worth while. Most of the published clinical trials of the management of hypertension with diastolic pressures of around 100 mmHg have instituted therapy only on the basis of the average of blood pressure readings taken on three separate visits. There is evidence that in many mild hypertensives pressures continue to settle even after this so patients should be monitored for about six

months and only if pressures remain raised should drug therapy be introduced.

INVESTIGATIONS IN GENERAL PRACTICE

The investigations recommended and their interpretation are discussed in Chapter 7. Briefly, we suggest that all patients should have their urine tested by a dipstick method. Biochemical and haematological profiles and an ECG should be performed only in patients who are to receive antihypertensive drug therapy, or if there are specific reasons to suspect some associated disease or complication.

BLOOD PRESSURE REDUCTION REGIMES IN GENERAL PRACTICE

The possible schemes for the reduction of blood pressure are discussed in Chapters 10 and 11. There is no basic difference between the drug regimes recommended in primary care and in hospital practice.

- Step 1 Non-pharmacological therapy
- Step 2 Thiazide beta-blocker, calcium-entry antagonist or converting-enzyme inhibitor
- Step 3 Combination of two drugs
- Step 4 Combination of above three drugs.

It is recommended that family doctors should where necessary proceed as far as triple therapy, and this should provide adequate blood pressure control in up to about 80 per cent of cases. Patients whose pressures remain uncontrolled should be referred for specialist consultation and detailed investigation.

HOSPITAL REFERRAL

Each family doctor probably has on his list about ten to fifteen hypertensive patients with clinical problems requiring

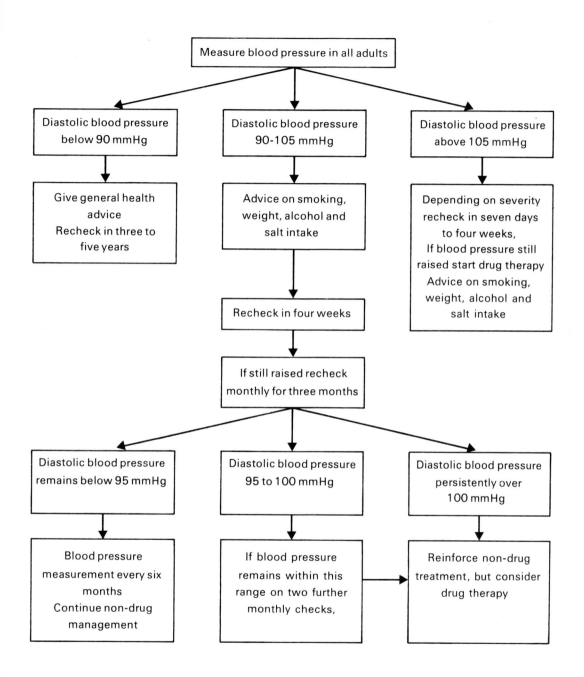

Figure 13.3 Guidelines for the protection and management of mild hypertension: the recommendations of WHO and the International Society for Hypertension (from *J. Hypertension 4*, 1986, 383–6).

referral to a specialist clinic (see Chapter 8). Sometimes a discussion by telephone with the consultant in charge of the local blood pressure clinic may prove sufficient.

The main disadvantage of hospital clinic referral is that it can lead to fragmentation of the patient's care, confusion about changes in drug regimes and an excessive proliferation of paperwork. Furthermore, the family doctor frequently 'loses' his patient to the hospital and feels inhibited from involving himself in clinical care. This can be minimized if the concept of shared care is followed.

SHARED CARE

It is important that the family doctor continues to contribute to the management of the patient throughout treatment for hypertension. If patients are provided with a patient-held record card (see above) the doctor can continue to provide the clinic with blood pressure readings taken at the time of each repeat prescription.

Thus the specialist can see that the family doctor is still taking an active interest, and will be encouraged to discontinue clinic attendance if blood pressure control is satisfactory.

A further development of the shared-care principle is that the hospital clinic arranges to discharge the patient but, by six monthly or annual postal questionnaire to the family doctor (usually with the aid of a computer), checks that medical care continues and that the blood pressure is satisfactory. If no information is available or blood pressure control is inadequate, then an appointment is sent to the patient automatically. Thus the hospital continues to receive information on the patient, who may not actually attend for years, and a high quality of continuous clinical care is ensured.[6] It is to be hoped that developments along this line will continue and the efficiency of longterm control of blood pressure will thus be improved.

PRACTICAL POINTS

- Better longterm control of blood pressure is now increasingly common in the US and in some centres in Britain.[7]

- The family doctor, perhaps in collaboration with a local specialist, should attempt to improve efficiency in case detection and follow-up.

- Clinical trials have demonstrated the effectiveness of these manoeuvres in preventing premature heart attacks and strokes.

- The management of hypertension in the community is primarily the responsibility of the practitioner.

- Case detection and follow-up should now be regarded as an integral and routine part of good clinical care.

PART 4: HYPERTENSION IN SPECIAL CIRCUMSTANCES

14
Hypertension in the presence of other diseases

BACKGROUND

Most of the formal clinical trials discussed in Chapter 9 were confined to previously uncomplicated hypertensive patients, who had no other medical condition affecting their survival. While in middle-aged patients hypertension may be the only clinical problem, with advancing age an increasing number of patients have more than one diagnosis. Very often the second disease seriously influences the management and outcome of the first, and the method of managing these patients requires detailed consideration.

HYPERTENSION AND HEART DISEASE

High blood pressure is a prime risk factor for the development of coronary heart disease. Many hypertensive patients have subclinical or clinical evidence of myocardial ischaemia or heart failure or may have suffered a previous heart attack. Alternatively many patients may have concurrent heart disease which is due to other causes; for example, rheumatic heart disease, cor pulmonale or congenital heart disease. High alcohol intake causes a specific form of alcoholic cardiomyopathy, and also causes hypertension. It is uncertain whether alcoholic cardiomyopathy and hypertension occur commonly together.

Hypertension and angina pectoris

Raised blood pressure is itself an important cause of angina. Myocardial ischaemia due to atheromatous narrowing of the coronary arteries will be made worse if there is concurrent left ventricular hypertrophy where the already compromised vascular supply has to oxygenate a larger, thicker ventricular wall.

In hypertensive patients with left ventricular hypertrophy, the ECG, in addition to showing voltage changes, may also show ST wave depression in the lateral chest leads. This pattern used to be called left ventricular 'strain' but is now known to be due to relative ischaemia.

In hypertensive patients with angina, blood pressure reduction alone can reduce or even abolish symptoms. This is true for all antihypertensive drugs. However, as beta-blockers are specifically effective in angina pectoris, it is logical to use them unless there are contraindications. The calcium-entry antagonists, nifedipine, diltiazem and verapamil, are also effective in angina and reduce blood pressure, so these may be employed alternatively. Long and short-acting nitrate drugs can be given safely. Other risk factors, including cigarette smoking, obesity and hyperlipidaemia should also receive attention.

If patients continue to have pain due to angina pectoris after the blood pressure is controlled with beta-blockers and calcium blockers, then a full cardiological assessment, with exercise ECG and possible coronary arteriography, should be considered.

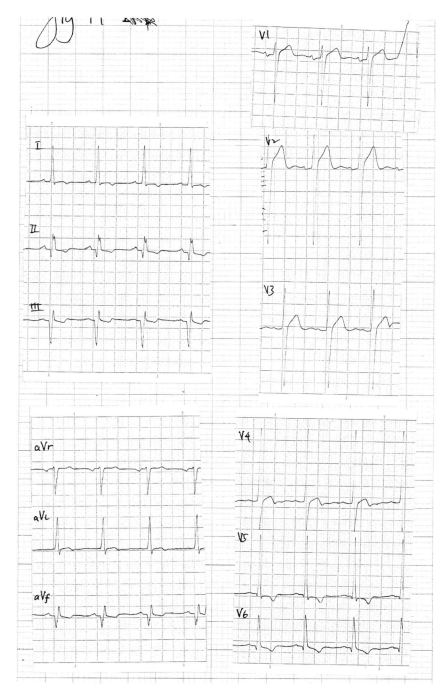

Figure 14.1 An ECG taken from a hypertensive patient with uncontrolled severe hypertension, showing gross left ventricular hypertrophy on an old inferior myocardial infarction.

Hypertension after a heart attack

Hypertensive patients are prone to heart attacks. In those who have sustained a major myocardial infarction, blood pressures frequently fall and sometimes remain low thereafter. The degree and duration of hypotension is an important prognostic sign; hypertensives who cease to have high blood pressure after their heart attack may have a poor outlook, and antihypertensive drugs are no longer indicated.

After a heart attack diuretic drugs, which are also antihypertensive, may be necessary. Beta-blockers or calcium-entry antagonists may be indicated to control angina, but beta-blockers must not be used if there is clinical evidence of cardiac failure. Thiazide diuretics cause hypokalaemia in a large proportion of patients, and this may be particularly hazardous in patients immediately after a myocardial infarct. Serum potassium levels should be checked regularly.

Figure 14.2 ECG showing (i) grade I heartblock (ii) complete heartblock (iii) atrial fibrillation.

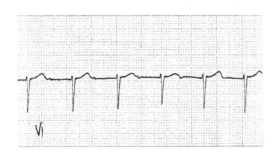

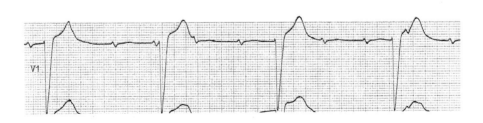

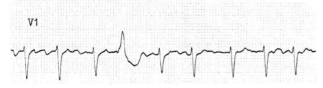

There is good evidence that beta-blockers can induce up to a 30 per cent reduction in re-infarction rates over the subsequent two years, and in the absence of specific contraindications such as heart block, asthma, heart failure or hypotension beta-blockers should probably be prescribed for all heart attack survivors, whether hypertensive or not.[1] Patients should be rechecked for hypertension after discharge from hospital as blood pressures that may have settled can rise again.

Even at this late stage the benefits of stopping smoking are well documented and the dietary correction of hyperlipidaemia is probably worth while.

Hypertension and heart block (see Figure 14.2)

Patients with third-degree heart block may have high systolic and low diastolic blood pressures. Both second- and third-degree heart block are absolute contraindications to the use of beta-blockers. In stable first-degree heart block (PR interval exceeds 0.21 sec), beta-blockers may be used unless there are other contraindications. In all degrees of heart block, diuretics, calcium-entry antagonists (excluding verapamil) and the converting-enzyme inhibitors can be used and centrally acting antihypertensive drugs are also safe.

---

1 Verapamil

2 Beta-blockers

NB Care when adding ACE inhibitors to a regime already including a diuretic

---

Table 14.1 Drugs to avoid in heart failure

Hypertension and the tachyarrhythmias

In chronic or intermittent supraventricular tachycardia in a hypertensive patient, beta-blockers or the calcium-entry antagonist verapamil are logical first-line drugs. The addition of verapamil to to a beta-blocker may, however, induce heart failure or complete heart block and should be used only in exceptional circumstances.

Beta-blockers are suitable agents for use in patients with frequent ventricular premature beats.

Atrial fibrillation

This may be due to ischaemic, rheumatic, thyrotoxic, hypertensive or alcoholic heart disease. The underlying cause must be investigated and treated. Digoxin therapy is usually indicated. If the heart rate is not controlled with digoxin, then thyrotoxicosis and alcoholic cardiomyopathy should be suspected. Beta-blockers may be coprescribed with digoxin, both to control blood pressure and to reduce the ventricular rate.

Hypertension and heart failure

Heart failure may be due to severe uncontrolled hypertension alone. This syndrome is now quite rare, owing to the treatment of severe hypertension and more often there is concurrent coronary heart disease or some other cardiomyopathy. Lone hypertensive heart failure should never occur if hypertensive patients are detected and managed properly.

In a new patient with even mild left ventricular failure, beta-blocking drugs are absolutely contraindicated (see Table 14.1). The ACE inhibitors captopril and enalapril are very useful in treating cardiac failure, and also lower blood pressure effectively. There is some evidence that ACE inhibitors are more effective than

175

Percentage incidence
of complications

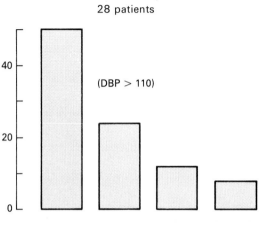

Poor blood pressure control
28 patients

(DBP > 110)

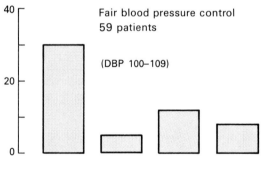

Fair blood pressure control
59 patients

(DBP 100–109)

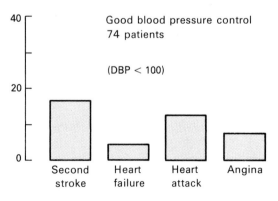

Good blood pressure control
74 patients

(DBP < 100)

Figure 14.3 The relationship between accuracy in control of blood pressure and the incidence of stroke recurrence.

other vasodilators in improving the symptoms and signs of heart failure. If not effective, a diuretic should be added.

Acute and very severe left ventricular failure may very rarely be caused by high blood pressure alone. If blood pressure is lowered, heart failure should regress. Parenteral drugs such as sodium nitroprusside by infusion (0.02 to 0.5 mg per minute) or diazoxide (50 mg by intravenous injection) repeated in larger doses as necessary are sometimes required. Frusemide, and diamorphine by slow intravenous injection may also be required in severe cases. Precipitate drops of blood pressure by parenteral therapy are very dangerous as they may provoke cerebral infarction.

HYPERTENSION AND STROKE

First stroke
Raised blood pressure is the most important predictor of the development of stroke. This may be haemorrhagic, due to rupture of the microaneurysms of Charcot and Bouchard, or thrombotic, due to cerebral atheroma. Good control of hypertension can greatly reduce the incidence of both these types of strokes (see Figure 14.3). However, very rapid reduction of blood pressure can cause a fall in cerebral perfusion, resulting in cerebral infarction.

Second stroke
In a hypertensive patient who has suffered from a stroke, immediate antihypertensive therapy is hazardous. In both normotensive and hypertensive patients a system of cerebral autoregulation ensures that, despite fluctuations in blood pressure, cerebral bloodflow remains constant. This breaks down at extremely high blood pressures, when encephalopathy occurs, and at extremely low blood pressures,

when cerebral ischaemia develops. In addition, immediately after a stroke the cerebral autoregulatory mechanism is impaired for up to six weeks and blood pressure reduction can cause a fall in cerebral bloodflow. It is now known for how long antihypertensive medication is contraindicated. Admission to hospital alone may reduce blood pressure but if the patient remains severely hypertensive and his or her neurological condition is stable or improving, gentle antihypertensive medication may be instituted after about a week.

There is ample evidence that ambulant survivors of stroke attending the blood pressure clinic do benefit from antihypertensive therapy. Those whose blood pressure are controlled (diastolic blood pressure reduced to below 100 mmHg) have fewer second strokes than those whose blood pressures are not controlled.[2] The choice of drugs is the same as for ordinary cases.

HYPERTENSION AND SUBARACHNOID HAEMORRHAGE

Subarachnoid haemorrhage is an important complication of hypertension. It may be due to rupture of a berry aneurysm of the circle of Willis, but in a large number of cases no aneurysm is found. Hypertensive patients with polycystic disease are particularly prone to intracranial aneurysms and subarachnoid haemorrhage.

In the acute phase there may be marked spasm of the cerebral arteries and, as with ordinary strokes, rapid blood pressure reduction can be dangerous. However, as up to 50 per cent of patients with subarachnoid haemorrhage have a second haemorrhage within the first ten days, accurate control of blood pressure is necessary. There is some recent evidence which suggests that subarachnoid haemor-

rhage survivors who are treated with beta-blockers fare better than untreated cases.[3] Surgical management may be indicated if berry aneurysms are found.

On a longterm basis, it is vital that blood pressure is well controlled along conventional therapeutic lines, to prevent further haemorrhage.

HYPERTENSION AND AORTIC ANEURYSM

Aortic aneurysms are frequently associated with hypertension. Thoracic aneurysms are rarely amenable to surgical treatment, and the only manoeuvre that may favourably influence survival is control of the blood pressure. Once the aneurysm has started to dissect, the prognosis is terrible. It is still important to control the pressure, and in specialized centres surgical repair may be feasible.

Abdominal aneurysms, once detected, should normally be treated surgically, as the prognosis once the aneurysm has ruptured is very poor. Good control of blood pressure is mandatory both before and after surgery.

HYPERTENSION AND INTERMITTENT CLAUDICATION

High blood pressure is a major cause of peripheral vascular disease, although claudication is also common in people with normal blood pressure. Although there is no information on whether treating hypertension prevents or ameliorates this problem, treatment may be necessary to prevent other complications.

Claudication may be induced or worsened by the treatment of hypertension with beta-blockers. This occurs in patients with pre-existing atheroma of the iliac, popliteal or femoral arteries. Beta-blockers reduce cardiac output and therefore reduce peripheral bloodflow. Blood pressure should therefore be controlled with other drugs. The best choice is to use the calcium-entry antagonists or ACE inhibitors, with a diuretic added if needed. The centrally acting drugs are also safe in this situation. It is possible that beta-blockers with intrinsic sympathomimectic activity (ISA), such as pindolol or oxprenolol, cause less claudication than other beta-blockers but they should be used only if blood pressure cannot be controlled with other drugs.

RAYNAUD'S SYNDROME
Although Raynaud's syndrome is not associated with hypertension, it commonly occurs when patients are treated with beta-blockers. Patients who complain of cold hands and feet whilst taking beta-blockers should be advised according to the severity of their symptoms. If symptoms are mild, in the winter months only, then advice about keeping hands warm and wearing gloves may suffice, particularly if the clinician does not wish to alter the antihypertensive regimen. Alternatively beta-blockers with ISA can be tried, although even these drugs can induce Raynaud's phenomenon. In such patients it is better to use either a calcium-entry antagonist or a converting-enzyme inhibitor rather than a beta-blocker.

In patients who have Raynaud's syndrome associated with scleroderma and hypertension the prognosis is poor, as renal function deteriorates rapidly. In this situation ACE inhibitors have been claimed to give encouraging results.

RENAL FAILURE (see Figure 14.4)

Intrinsic renal disease
If hypertensive patients have persistent haematuria or proteinuria then they need investigation, usually with a renal biopsy

178

to exclude glomerulonephritis, which may be the cause of the raised blood pressure. In particular, IgA nephropathy is an important cause of hypertension. Pyelonephritis and polycystic disease may also cause hypertension, which in turn can cause further renal damage. It is important to break the vicious cycle of renal damage and further elevation of blood pressure. The choice of drugs is similar to that for essential hypertension. However, excessive or rapid blood pressure reduction can embarrass renal bloodflow and cause further renal damage.

Chronic renal failure
Many beta-blockers have been reported to reduce renal bloodflow, even without excessive falls in pressure, and there are a few reports in the literature of a reversible renal failure induced by beta-blocking drugs.[4] In patients with established chronic renal failure, it is important to

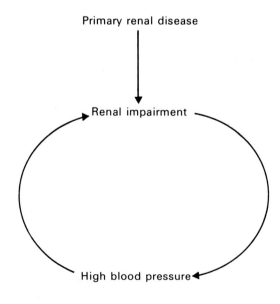

Figure 14.4 The vicious cycle of renal hypertension.

control blood pressure accurately. The otherwise inevitable deterioration in renal function can be delayed, and some improvement may be achieved. High doses of loop diuretics may be necessary to control fluid retention and to help control the pressure, particularly when arteriolar vasodilators such as hydralazine or minoxidil are used. Excessive use of diuretics may cause a deterioration of renal function if there is a marked reduction in blood volume and renal bloodflow.

Beta-receptor blockers are favoured in chronic renal failure as their effects on blocking renin release may be useful. When using the water-soluble beta-blockers atenolol, nadolol or sotalol, excretion may be reduced in chronic renal failure. The dose of these drugs often has to be halved or given on alternate days.

The use of calcium-entry antagonists may be very effective in renal failure and it appears that no adjustment in dose is necessary. There is also evidence that ACE inhibitors are useful in patients with renal failure. However, if patients are dehydrated, or already receiving large doses of diuretics, over-rapid falls in pressure may occur with deterioration of renal function. It is best to start with the smallest possible dose of captopril (6.25 mg orally) or enalapril (2.5 mg) and gradually to increase the dose.

Care should be taken to monitor serum creatinine levels. Special charts in the medical records, with the reciprocal of the serum creatinine levels plotted on the vertical axis, help to achieve accurate monitoring of renal function. All hypertensive patients should have their serum creatinine levels checked annually.

Hypertension and chronic dialysis

A large proportion of patients on chronic dialysis programmes have hypertension, and therefore have an increased risk of strokes and heart attacks. Furthermore, a tiny remaining amount of renal function may be of use to the patient and efforts should be made to preserve it by controlling blood pressure.

In most patients on both haemodialysis and chronic ambulatory peritoneal dialysis, blood pressure can be controlled by removing sodium and water during the dialysis. Between dialyses, even with oral fluid restriction, sodium and water accumulate, thus raising the blood pressure. Occasionally blood pressure lowering drugs are necessary.

In a small minority of patients with chronic renal failure who still have their severely damaged kidneys *in situ*, blood pressure cannot be controlled by dialysis and antihypertensive drugs. In these patients there is evidence that as sodium and water are removed during dialysis, the juxtaglomerular apparatus of the damaged kidneys is supersensitive and responds by secreting large quantities of renin, which by generating large amounts of angiotensin II causes a rise in blood pressure. Further fluid restriction aggravates this situation.[5] Such cases develop anorexia, muscle wasting and hypertensive crises, and may develop focal myocardial necrosis. Drugs which block the secretion of renin (for example, beta-blockers), or block the generation of angiotensin II (for example, captopril or enalapril) help to control blood pressure, but care must be taken as in the presence of fluid depletion they may cause profound hypotension.

Hypertension after renal transplantation

Hypertension is common after renal transplantation, and may be due to many factors, including the immunosuppressive doses of corticosteroids, fluid retention, renal impairment and occasionally stenosis of the transplanted renal artery. It is important to control blood pressure, along similar lines as in cases which chronic renal failure.

DIABETES MELLITUS

Association with hypertension

The relationship between hypertension and diabetes mellitus is complex.[6] Epidemiologically there is a slight tendency for blood pressure and blood sugar to be positively related, with body mass index as an important associated variable. Diabetic clinic attenders have an excess of hypertension, particularly amongst non-insulin-requiring (type 2) diabetics, but this may be accounted for by a tendency for selective referral or investigation of patients with either known hypertension or diabetes, rather than a true association.

Risk

Diabetics are prone to develop coronary heart disease, strokes and intermittent claudication. So are hypertensives; but there remains some doubt as to whether diabetics who are also hypertensive have a prognosis consistent with the two diagnoses or whether their prognosis is even worse with a synergistic rather than an additive effect. Hypertensive patients who are also diabetic have a greater risk than those without glucose intolerance.

In the general population there are differences in the relationships between the cardiovascular risk in relation to the height of the blood pressure and the risk related to the height of the blood glucose. Whereas there is a smooth gradient of blood pressure versus risk—the higher the pressure the worse the prognosis—this is not so for blood glucose. Blood glucose levels do not accurately predict mortality or morbidity until they reach levels of about 8 mmol/l (120 mg/100 ml). The

blood sugar mortality curve has a distinctly 'dog leg' appearance.

Mechanisms

It is possible that the increased blood pressure of diabetic patients can be accounted for simply by their higher body mass index. However, there are some biochemical factors which may also play a part. Maturity onset diabetics tend to have more suppression of renin secretion and some expansion of body fluid volume. After correction for body mass index, total exchangeable sodium is about 10 per cent higher than normal. In addition diabetics are prone to diabetic nephrosclerosis, urinary infections, papillary necrosis and renal tuberculosis, which may cause raised blood pressure.

Diagnosis

Diabetologists have in the past tended to neglect the blood pressure of their patients, and frequently the medical records of diabetic clinic attenders contain no record of blood pressure. This has been to the peril of the patients. Recent increased awareness has improved the situation, and much more information should become available over the next few years.

Non-pharmacological therapy

It has recently been shown that intensive dietary treatment with a diet low in sodium and high in fibre and potassium, and a reduction of fat intake, can reduce blood pressure and help control the diabetes. This effect was of similar magnitude to the effects of either beta-blockers or thiazides. As diabetics are seen by dietitians regularly anyway, this approach is both feasible and worthwhile.[7]

Diuretics

Thiazide diuretics are mildly diabetogenic and best avoided in non-insulin dependent

DIABETIC CLINIC

Initial Acceptance and Annual Review

SURNAME:

HOSP. NO.

FIRST NAME:

DATE OF BIRTH:

ADDRESS:

CONSULTANT:

WEIGHT	URINE GLUCOSE	URINE BLOOD	URINE PROTEIN	URINE KETONES	BP	BP

BLOOD GLUCOSE   mmol/L

DATE   / / 19

DATE OF DIAGNOSIS OF DIABETES: / / 19

DATE OF DIAGNOSIS OF HYPERTENSION: (IF PRESENT)   / / 19

GLYCOS Hb   %

DATE   / / 19

HISTORY:

OTHER ILLNESSES:

. . . .

. . . .

Hb   g/dl
WBC $\times 10^3/\mu l$
MCV   fl
PLAT $\times 10^3/\mu l$
ESR   mm

DATE   / / 19

FAMILY HISTORY:

CIGARETTES: per day

ALCOHOL   drinks per week

Na   mmol/L
K   mmol/L
Ca   mmol/L
PO4   mmol/L

HEART:

CHEST:

ABDO:

ALK P   IU/L
ASP   IU/L
ALB   g/L

CRANIAL NERVES:

MOTOR:

SENSORY:

T. PROT   g/L
URATE   mmol/L
GGT   IU/L

REFLEXES	R	L	PULSES	R	L
BICEPS			FEMORAL		
TRICEPS			POPLITEAL		
SUPINATOR			DORS PEDIS		
KNEE			POST TIBIAL		
ANKLE			FEMORAL BRUIT		
PLANTARS					

CHOLESTEROL   mmol/L
UREA   mmol/L
CREAT μmol/L

DATE   / / 19

24 hour
Protein   g
Na   mmol
K   mmol
Creat. μmol

EYES	R	L	R	L
CATARACT				
MICRO ANEUR				
HAEM				
COTTON WOOL				
NEW VESSELS				
OTHER				

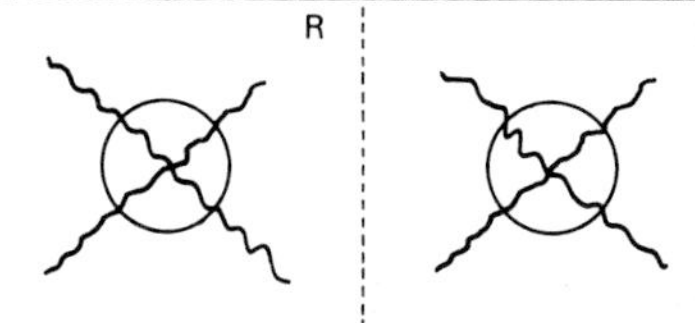

DATE   / / 19

ECG

LIST CURRENT THERAPY	THERAPY CHANGES	COMMENTS
1.		
2.		
3.		
4.		
5.		NEXT APPT.

DATE   / / 19

CXR

DATE   / / 19

OTHER

DATE   / / 19

Figure 14.5 Checklist (proforma) for the initial acceptance and annual review of diabetic clinic patients.

(type 2) diabetics.[8] They are not, however, contraindicated in insulin-dependent (type 1) cases but blood glucose levels should be monitored closely, and occasionally the dose of insulin may need to be increased by small amount. In maturity-onset diabetes the glucose intolerance may be worsened by thiazide diuretics, and when these are discontinued blood glucose levels fall. If thiazide diuretics are used then it is important to institute calorie restriction and weight loss and this may prevent a worsening of diabetic control.

It is not uncommon to encounter obese older hypertensive patients who are diagnosed as diabetic soon after thiazide treatment is started. It is difficult to be sure whether they are truly diabetic or whether they have thiazide-induced glucose intolerance. In such cases, thiazides should be stopped, calorie restriction instituted, and if necessary different antihypertensive drugs used. However, the restriction of calories and sodium intake may well normalize blood pressure and avoid problems with blood glucose.

Diazoxide—a rarely used parenteral vasodilator with a structure similar to thiazides—can precipitate profound glucose intolerance and hyperglycaemia. Nonthiazide diuretics, both loop diuretics (frusemide and bumetanide) and the potassium-sparing agents, are less diabetogenic than the thiazides and therefore preferable in treating diabetics.

Beta-blockers

Beta-blocking drugs have several theoretical disadvantages in insulin-dependent diabetics because they interfere with the autonomic and metabolic response to hypoglycaemia.[9] In hypoglycaemia glucose is mobilized from the hepatic glycogen stores in an attempt to restore normoglycaemia. The effect is under beta-2 adrenergic control, and beta-blockers reduce the response. The symptoms of impending hypoglycaemia—sweating and tachycardia—are also mediated by the beta-2 adrenergic system and this response is impaired by beta-blockers, so patients are unaware that they are becoming hypoglycaemic. In the past these problems have led clinicians to avoid beta-blockers in insulin-dependent diabetics. However, it is now known that beta-1 specific blockers (atenolol and metoprolol) have fewer effects on hypoglycaemia than nonselective blockers and can normally be used safely. They are such useful drugs, particularly in patients with coronary heart disease, that in most cases it is wrong to withhold them from this high-risk group of patients. Perhaps, though, they should be avoided in very brittle diabetics who suffer frequent hypoglycaemic attacks.

Other drugs

Most other antihypertensive drugs are safe in diabetics. The control of blood pressure is therefore along conventional lines. Vasodilating drugs such as hydralazine, the converting-enzyme inhibitors and calcium-entry antagonists are safe and useful, but there are a few anecdotal reports of glucose intolerance induced by nifedipine.

Complications of diabetes

Diabetics are particularly prone to peripheral vascular disease, and because beta-receptor blockers may aggravate or precipitate symptoms they should be used with great caution.

There is some evidence that high blood pressure aggravates the tendency of diabetics to develop both background and proliferative retinopathy. It is not certain, however, whether control of blood pressure prevents retinopathy.

Diabetics with renal damage need accurate control of blood pressure. Further deterioration of renal function can be delayed and some improvement may be achieved.

ASTHMA

In patients with asthma beta-blockers are absolutely contraindicated, as by blocking pulmonary beta-2 receptors they may cause severe bronchial constriction.[10] These patients are normally treated with beta-adrenergic agonists to reverse bronchospasm (for example, salbutamol, orciprenaline, isoprenaline). In the presence of beta-antagonists, these beta-agonists may be ineffective and bronchospasm may be irreversible. There are a number of patients with chronic obstructive airways disease who have some reversible airways obstruction but are not technically asthmatic. Where indicated for other reasons (angina or hypertension) the cardioselective beta-blockers atenolol or metoprolol can be used, but only with extreme caution. Atenolol at least does not block the response to inhaled salbutamol, whereas the nonselective blockers do. Patients who are treated with atenolol should be advised to increase the frequency of use of salbutamol inhalation.

If there is any doubt beta-blocking drugs are best avoided: calcium-entry antagonists and converting-enzyme inhibitors with the addition of a diuretic are preferable. There is some evidence that nifedipine has some bronchodilating properties, which may mean that this agent may become the drug of first choice.[11] However, alpha-blockers may be equally advantageous. The combined alpha and beta-blocking drug, labetalol, deserves mention. While the beta-blocking component of labetalol is not cardioselective and could cause bronchoconstriction, the concurrent alpha-blockade, by causing bronchodilatation, can offset the constrictor effects of beta-blockade. Thus the net effect of labetalol on airways resistance in patients with obstructive airways disease is about the same as that of the cardioselective blockers (atenolol or metoprolol).

Chronic low-dose steroid therapy may be given to patients with asthma, and this might, in theory, induce hypertension. While high-dose steroids are pressor, the evidence is that chronic low-dose therapy given for chronic airways disease or rheumatoid arthritis is not, although blood pressure should be monitored regularly.

Patients with chronic obstructive airways disease tend to develop cor pulmonale, after which they have an average life expectancy of three years. If beta-blockers are used, they may precipitate heart failure earlier, and a diuretic may have to be substituted or added.

PSYCHIATRIC DISEASE

Alcoholism
Alcoholics and heavy drinkers are more likely to be hypertensive than the general population and they should have their blood pressure monitored regularly, as they are particularly prone to develop strokes.[12]

Anxiety states
Anxious patients may develop transiently raised blood pressure, particularly with high systolic pressures. There is, however, no evidence that chronic anxiety is a cause of hypertension. In anxious patients treatment of the underlying psychiatric disease should be instituted, but because of the mild anxiolytic effects of beta-blockers these may be employed if the patient is truly hypertensive. Beta-blockers have been used in the treatment of schizophrenia.

183

Depressive disease

Once patients have been told they are hypertensive they may develop anxiety or depression about their condition. These problems may be compounded by the use of the centrally acting drugs (methyldopa, clonidine and reserpine), all of which can cause depression. These drugs should never be used in depressed patients and are best avoided in other patients. Beta-blockers do not cause depression but they may induce lethargy. This problem is particularly seen with the lipophilic beta-blockers such as propranolol, oxprenolol, metoprolol and timolol and possibly less with the hydrophilic drugs atenolol, nadolol and sotalol. It has been commented that ACE inhibitors may be associated with an improvement in well-being, although this is not well documented. Certainly the complete absence of central side-effects make them potentially useful in depressed patients.

GLAUCOMA

Rapid falls in blood pressure may aggravate glaucoma. Thus antihypertensive therapy should be given with care in patients with this condition. Beta-blockers are given topically to treat glaucoma, and a sufficient amount of the drug may be absorbed to induce systemic beta-blockade with some reduction of blood pressure.

CONNECTIVE TISSUE DISEASE

Connective tissue diseases, particularly systemic lupus erythematosus and scleroderma, cause renal damage and hypertension. In patients with scleroderma, the presence of hypertension leads to rapidly worsening renal failure. There is some recent encouraging evidence that captopril is particularly effective in this situation and may preserve renal function if given early enough. Rheumatologists should

monitor the blood pressure of all their patients with connective tissue disease. Patients receiving high doses of a corticosteroid or ACTH therapy may develop a drug-induced hypertension (see Chapter 5).

ENDOCRINOLOGY

Hypertension is common in patients with Cushing's disease, acromegaly, hyperparathyroidism, myxoedema and thyrotoxicosis (see Chapters 4 and 8).

ANAESTHESIA

Patients who undergo surgery when they have diastolic blood pressures in excess of 110 mmHg have a higher incidence of intra-operative or postoperative cardiac disease. For this reason elective surgery should not be carried out in uncontrolled hypertensives. The moments of greatest cardiovascular risk are during laryngoscopy and intubation, during hypotensive anaesthesia to aid haemostasis, and whilst the surgeon is manipulating the abdominal viscera. Spinal anaesthesia can cause profound hypotension.[13]

In view of the pressor effects of the sudden discontinuation of clonidine therapy this drug should be avoided in pre-operative patients and other drugs substituted. Sudden withdrawal of beta-blocking drugs in patients with established coronary artery disease may cause exacerbation of angina, and these drugs should not be stopped in the peri-operative period. The anaesthetist must be aware that the patient is receiving beta-blocking drugs as they impair the physiological tachycardia in response to blood loss or to atropine therapy during anaesthesia.

In the postoperative phase, while patients are resting in bed, blood pressures may remain low. Antihypertensive drugs should usually be restarted as soon as the patient is able to swallow them. Before this time, while the patient is on intravenous fluids only, intramuscular antihypertensive drugs are occasionally needed to control blood pressure.

HYPERLIPIDAEMIA

Raised blood lipid levels are independent risk factors for coronary heart disease, and probably should be corrected along dietary lines. Thiazide diuretics elevate plasma triglyceride levels as well as cholesterol. There is some doubt as to whether beta-blockers also elevate plasma lipids. All hypertensive patients on diuretic therapy should have their plasma lipid levels checked after about one year.

PRACTICAL POINTS

- Drug treatments for hypertension may have an adverse effect on accompanying conditions, so these require careful monitoring and an alteration of the regime may be necessary.

- The wide choice of antihypertensive drugs available means that there are plenty of alternatives if one sort is contraindicated.

- Most clinicians in a wide range of specialities have to manage diseases where hypertension is an additional risk factor.

15
Hypertension in the elderly

BACKGROUND

In the Western World blood pressure rises with age. If high blood pressure is defined by the WHO criteria (see Chapter 1) as a systolic pressure equal to or greater than 160 mmHg or a diastolic pressure equal to or greater than 95 mmHg at first screening, then over half the population from the age of sixty-five would be said to have high blood pressure.

Up to the age of seventy-five the height of the blood pressure is as important a risk factor as in younger people, particularly for strokes and heart failure and for renal failure (see Figure 15.1). There are now some definitive studies showing that lowering blood pressure with drugs in the elderly is of benefit. Drug treatment does appear to reduce strokes and heart attacks and to relieve the symptoms of heart failure. Our view is that treatment of high blood pressure in the elderly is justified but special efforts must be made to avoid drug side-effects, particularly postural falls in blood pressure. The elderly are particularly likely to develop such falls in pressure owing to the greater rigidity of their blood vessels and the decreased sensitivity of their baroreceptors.

THE RISE IN BLOOD PRESSURE WITH AGE

This has been discussed in Chapter 3. The rise is much greater for systolic than for diastolic pressure. Indeed, diastolic pressure may fall slightly after the age of about sixty-five. This gives rise to a

widened pulse pressure. Epidemiological evidence suggests that the height of the systolic pressure is a better determinant of risk than the diastolic pressure.

IS HIGH BLOOD PRESSURE DIFFERENT IN THE ELDERLY?

Difficulties in blood pressure measurement

In the majority of elderly patients there is no difficulty in measuring blood pressure by auscultation. However, occasionally patients are encountered, particularly those with very rigid arteries, where the blood pressure measured with a stethoscope may be falsely high compared with directly measured intra-arterial pressure. This should perhaps be suspected in patients with very high pressures who do not have evidence of target organ damage such as left ventricular hypertrophy. Clearly it is not practical to measure intra-arterial pressure in large numbers of elderly patients and it is probably not necessary.

Another problem in some patients is that no disappearance of sounds (phase 5) can be detected when measuring the diastolic pressure. Under these circumstances, phase 4 diastolic pressures (muffling) should be taken. (The topic of blood pressure measurement is covered in more detail in Chapter 6.)

Commonly, older patients have disproportionately high systolic pressures with a widened pulse pressure. In addition, isolated systolic hypertension, where the diastolic pressure is normal, is common in older people. A major problem in the elderly is the increased chance of there being other intercurrent diseases, including chronic chest disease, cancer and cardiac failure.

Renal bloodflow

Important changes in renal bloodflow occur with increasing age, both in normo-tensives and hypertensives. This leads to a decrease in the glomerular filtration rate

so that renal function declines. On average, at the age of seventy renal func-tion is about half that of a younger person. One major consequence of this is that many of the drugs used for lowering blood pressure that are excreted by the kidney may tend to accumulate.

Renin

In older people there is a decrease in the responsiveness of the renin–angiotensin system, both in normals and hyperten-

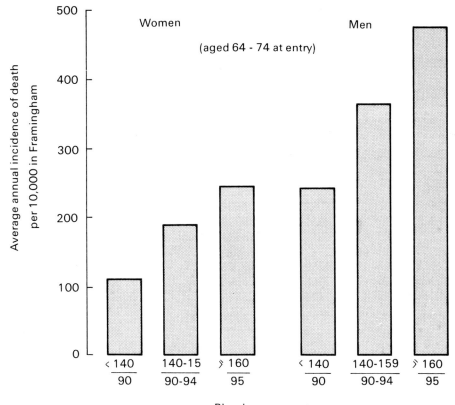

Figure 15.1 Mortality in relation to blood pressure in sixty-five to seventy-four year old men and women in Framingham (from W. B. Kannel, *Progess in Cardiovascular Disease 17*, 1974, 5–12).

sives. This is of no importance in itself but it does mean that older patients have a greater fall in blood pressure with reduction in their salt intake or with the use of diuretic therapy. This is because there is less stimulation of the renin system and therefore a smaller rise in blood levels of the powerful vasoconstrictor angiotensin II.

Catecholamines

While plasma renin levels are lower in older patients, plasma noradrenaline levels tend to be higher. The peripheral adrenoceptors are, however, less sensitive to catecholamines and are also less sensitive to beta-adrenoceptor blockers. These drugs are a little less effective in the elderly.

Cardiac output

Older hypertensives tend to have lower levels of cardiac output and lower intravascular volumes and this with the reduced renin response may explain their greater sensitivity to diuretic therapy. If cardiac failure develops, cardiac output falls even further, although extracellular fluid volume rises. Elderly hypertensive patients may be particularly sensitive to adrenergic neurone blocking agents like bethanidine, debrisoquine and guanethidine, so these drugs should never be used in the elderly because of the dangers of postural hypotension.

Secondary causes of hypertension in the elderly

As in younger patients, the vast majority of elderly hypertensives have essential hypertension. Nevertheless, secondary causes do occasionally occur. The incidence is not known exactly but it is probably somewhat lower than in younger patients. Phaeochromocytomas, adrenal

adenomas and renal artery stenosis account for no more than 1 per cent of cases but the possibility of these diagnoses should not be forgotten (see Chapter 8).

INVESTIGATION OF THE ELDERLY HYPERTENSIVE

Routine investigations that are done in the younger hypertensive should also be carried out in the elderly, irrespective of age (see Chapter 7). Older patients are more likely to have renal failure and serum urea and creatinine levels should be checked regularly, particularly if drugs are given which are excreted by the kidney. Heart failure tends to be more common, probably due to a combination of ischaemic heart disease and high blood pressure. There is also a reduction in cerebral bloodflow with increasing age as well as a resetting upwards of cerebral autoregulation. Normally, bloodflow remains constant, despite large variations in blood pressure. Older patients with hypertension are less able to regulate cerebral bloodflow if blood pressure is reduced rapidly. Blood pressure should therefore be lowered slowly. Rapid reduction precipitates strokes or, more commonly, causes patients to become confused due to cerebral ischaemia.

HOW FAR SHOULD BLOOD PRESSURE BE LOWERED?

The answer to this question is that we do not know. Clearly, in an older patient, particularly one with more rigid arteries, it may be sensible not to lower blood pressure to the so-called normal range but merely to 'take the top off' the pressure. With this in mind, we recommend that if blood pressure is to be treated, the diastolic pressure should be lowered to around 95 mmHg but no lower, and the systolic pressure should not be lowered to below 160 mmHg. It cannot be over-stressed that sudden large reductions in blood pressure in the elderly may be dangerous and more harm than good could be done by over-enthusiastic normalization of blood pressure.

About half of the antihypertensive drugs prescribed are consumed by patients over the age of sixty. While there is little doubt that there is an increased risk with raised blood pressure in patients up to the age of seventy-five, evidence that lowering the blood pressure is of benefit is not as clear-cut as in the younger age group.

Evidence of the efficacy of drug treatment

Hamilton's classic studies in 1964 did include some patients over the age of sixty-five and he showed quite clearly that drug treatment of severe hypertensives could prevent strokes.[1] More recently, the US Veterans' Administration studies in moderate hypertension (see Chapter 9) have shown that in men there was a definite benefit from drug treatment.[2] In one study there was a sub-group of eighty-one men over the age of sixty. Thirty-eight of these patients with a mean blood pressure of 174/104 mmHg were treated with drugs and were compared with a matched group of forty-three patients, who received placebo therapy. In the treated group there was a 29 per cent incidence of morbid events against 63 per cent in the untreated group, but as seen above the actual number of cases was very small. There was no difference in the incidence of heart attacks. These US Veterans were assessed as in-patients and while they were randomized on their out-patient blood pressure measurements, they almost certainly had more severe hypertension than the blood pressures before treatment would appear to indicate. Nevertheless,

they do demonstrate in small numbers, and in males only, that treatment of the elderly appears to be of some benefit against strokes and heart failure.

Evidence from the controversial HDFP study (see Chapter 9) also supports these conclusions. There were over 2000 patients aged sixty to sixty-nine years with diastolic pressures greater than 90 mmHg. Half of these were entered into a stepped care group where particular attention was paid to blood pressure reduction; the other half were referred back to their usual medical care. In the group receiving stepped care, average diastolic pressures fell to 81 mmHg and in those having their usual medical care, mean pressures fell only to 86 mmHg. With the greater fall in blood pressure there was a 16 per cent reduction in overall mortality. Despite the many criticisms of this study, it does support the suggestion that careful treatment of blood pressure in patients up to the age of seventy years may be of benefit.

In the Australian National High Blood Pressure study there was a group of 582 patients between the ages of sixty and sixty-nine (see Figure 15.2).[3] While this trial demonstrated a 39 per cent reduction in morbidity and mortality in treated cases compared with controls, the small numbers mean that only fifteen fewer cardiovascular events occurred in the treated group.

The European Working Party on Hypertension in the Elderly (EWPHE), 1985

In this largely hospital-based study in Europe, patients over the age of sixty were randomized to receive either active treatment with a thiazide combined with triamterene (plus methyldopa if blood pressure was not controlled) or placebo therapy.[4] This study has shown that blood pressure can be lowered without sig-

189

nificant adverse effects, although there were the expected metabolic changes with the use of thiazide diuretics, i.e., increases in serum uric acid and blood glucose levels.

Entry criteria for the trial included a sitting diastolic pressure on placebo treatment in the range 90 to 119 mmHg and a systolic pressure in the range 160 to 239 mmHg. Eight hundred and forty patients with an average age of seventy-two years were entered. On an overall 'intention to treat' analysis no significant difference was found in total mortality rate between the active treatment and placebo groups.

There was a significant reduction in cardiovascular mortality and a non-significant reduction in cerebrovascular mortality.

This study leaves several important questions unanswered but does confirm the benefit of treatment in elderly hypertensives (see Figure 15.3). It provides a mandate to use hypertensive drugs in patients up to the age of about seventy-five, but doubt must remain as to the value of therapy in older people. As in many other longterm studies, the choice of antihypertensive drugs is somewhat obsolete. At the doses used, thiazide diuretics are

Total number of participants	293	289
Mean age (years)	63.6	63.5
Mean blood pressure at entry	166/101	164/100

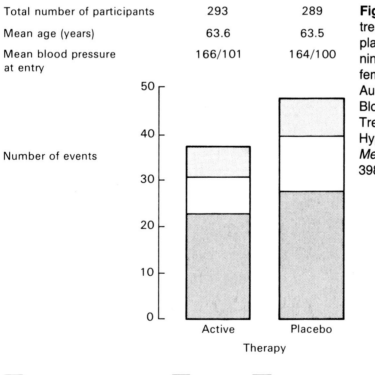

Figure 15.2 Results of treatment with thiazides or placebo in the sixty to sixty-nine year old male and female participants in the Australian National High Blood Pressure Study (from Treatment of Mild Hypertension in the Elderly *Med. J. Australia 2*, 1981, 398–402).

Ischaemic heart disease ☐ Strokes ☐ Other events

particularly likely to cause metabolic problems and methyldopa may cause postural hypotension in the elderly, as well as sedation.

Hypertension in Elderly Patients Study (HEP)[5] (see Figure 15.4) This trial was based in twelve general practices in England and Wales. Patients were randomized to receive a beta-blocker with a thiazide added if necessary, or to receive no treatment. As with the EWPHE trial there was a significant reduction in strokes but no reduction in total mortality rates when the two groups were compared. The total number of morbid events was smaller, even though the blood pressures at entry were similar to the EWPHE patients. This may reflect the fact that the EWPHE patients, being mainly hospital based, were a selected group less representative of elderly patients in the community.

The Medical Research Council in the UK is now undertaking a general practice based multicentre trial of the drug treatment of hypertension in the elderly. This should provide more information.

Isolated systolic hypertension Nearly all of the studies described above used diastolic blood pressure for the entry criteria. However, many elderly people have isolated systolic hypertension. For this reason a trial of its treatment is being started in the United States (Systolic Hypertension in the Elderly Program, SHEP).

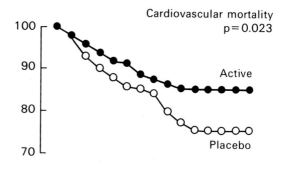

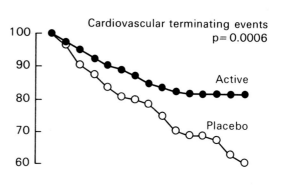

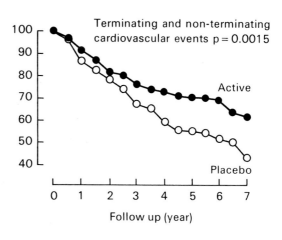

Figure 15.3 Cumulative percentage survival in patients on active or placebo treatment (from EWPHE trial).[4]

191

BLOOD PRESSURE REDUCTION (see Figure 15.5)

Non-pharmacological treatment

All elderly hypertensives should be advised about non-pharmacological treatment in the same way as younger patients (see Chapter 10), particularly since these manoeuvres are unlikely to cause postural hypotension.

- Patients who are overweight should try to reduce weight.
- Salt restriction is likely to be particularly effective in older people because of their impaired renin responsiveness. Many older people take large amounts of salt in their food because they have been accustomed to the widespread use of salt as a preservative. For this reason they may also have decreased sensitivity of salt receptors in the mouth. Our experience is that if careful explanation is given and they are told that it will take time to adjust, the elderly, like the younger patients, will find that they can get used to less salty foods.
- Many elderly patients eat inadequate amounts of potassium-rich food and

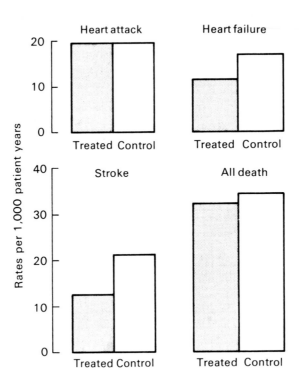

Figure 15.4 Results of the Hypertension in Elderly Patients Study.[5]

it is important to try to encourage a greater consumption of fresh fruit and vegetables. This particularly applies if diuretics are being given.

- In view of the increasing evidence that high alcohol intake can raise blood pressure, it is worth checking whether this factor is present and advising accordingly.

If these non-pharmacological approaches are not successful the question then is whether or not to use antihypertensive drugs.

The drug treatment of the elderly hypertensive

Evidence from the EWPHE clearly suggests a benefit from drug treatment. Notwithstanding this, the longterm risks of drug treatment in older patients should be very carefully considered. Rapid reduction in blood pressure may precipitate strokes, drop attacks, falls and transient cerebral ischaemic attacks. This may lead to femoral or hip fractures.

Malignant hypertension should be always treated, irrespective of age. As in the younger population, very good results have been obtained.

Patients with congestive heart failure should always be treated as there may be dramatic relief of their symptoms with a lowering in blood pressure. Beta-blockers are contraindicated until heart failure is under control, and diuretics are always necessary.

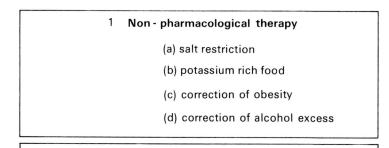

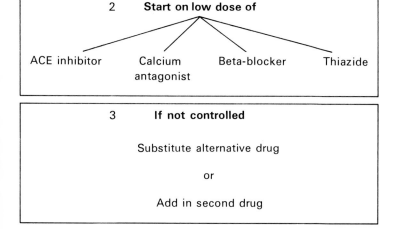

Figure 15.5 Antihypertensive therapy in the elderly.

Patients aged sixty to sixty-nine years, in our view, should be treated if they have systolic pressures consistently raised above 180 mmHg or diastolic pressures above 100 mmHg and if there are no other contraindications.

Patients aged seventy to seventy-nine years Antihypertensive treatment is justified only if diastolic pressures are consistently above 105 mmHg. Blood pressure reduction should be gradual and care taken to avoid postural hypotension.

The very old In patients over the age of eighty, there is little published evidence that antihypertensive drugs are of any benefit and they may even be harmful. Nevertheless, severe hypertension should be treated, i.e., systolic pressure greater than 220 mmHg or diastolic greater than 120 mmHg.

Which drugs?

The same drugs should be used as in younger patients (see Chapter 11), but in much smaller doses, at least initially, unless there are specific indications or contraindications (see also Table 15.1).

Thiazide diuretics These drugs are effective and generally safe in older patients. Care must be taken to monitor serum potassium and blood glucose levels.

Beta-blockers given on their own may be less effective than in younger patients. Nevertheless, it may be advisable to start with a small dose of a beta-blocker and if necessary add a low dose of a thiazide diuretic, for example, propranolol 20 mg twice daily or atenolol 50 mg once daily combined with 2.5 mg of bendrofluazide.

Most of the beta-blocker/diuretic combinations contain too high a concen-

---

Drugs that should never be used
Adrenergic neurone blockers (debrisoquine, bethanidine, guanethidine) cause postural hypotension, leading to falls and fractures

Drugs best avoided
Alpha-receptor-blockers (indoramine, prazosin, labetalol) may cause postural hypotension
Reserpine, methyldopa, cause sedation and depression

Use with care
(a) Beta-blockers may induce heart failure
Therefore use low dose
(b) Diuretics – hypokalaemia
              glucose intolerance
Therefore use low dose

Table 15.1 Drugs that are dangerous to use in the elderly.

tration of both drugs for older patients, particularly as initial treatment. Bradycardia and diuretic induced hypokalaemia are therefore potential hazards.

Calcium-entry antagonists   If the combination of a low dose of beta-blocker and diuretic is not successful or if there is a contraindication to their use such as asthma, heart failure or maturity onset of diabetes, a calcium-entry antagonist such as nifedipine, diltiazem or verapamil can be used. Claims have been made that this class of compound is particularly effective in the older age group and rarely causes postural hypotension. As with other drugs, initially a lower dose should be given than in younger patients, for example, half a nifedipine tablet (10 mg) twice daily or verapamil 40 mg three times daily.

ACE inhibitors   An alternative, especially for patients with congestive heart failure, or those who have had problems with the other drugs is to use an angiotensin-converting-enzyme inhibitor such as captopril or enalapril. These, like beta-blockers, may be less effective in older patients unless combined with sodium restriction or a diuretic.

Recent evidence suggests that both the calcium-entry antagonists and converting-enzyme inhibitors may increase cerebral bloodflow and if this is shown to be true, they may become the treatment of choice in older patients.

PRACTICAL POINTS

- There are now sufficient grounds for giving antihypertensive drugs to patients aged up to eighty whose diastolic pressures exceed 100 to 105 mmHg.

- In all elderly hypertensive patients, non-pharmacological control is the best initial approach.

- The choice of antihypertensive drugs is similar to that in younger patients, although both beta-blockers and ACE inhibitors may be relatively less effective when used alone.

16
Hypertension in pregnancy

BACKGROUND

Hypertension in pregnancy remains one of the great mysteries of obstetrics. It is the most important single cause of perinatal mortality in Westernized nations, but it is no exaggeration to say that nobody really knows why it happens. It is second only to pulmonary embolus as the commonest cause of maternal death. There is, however, evidence that good medical and obstetrical care reduce both maternal and perinatal mortality. The purpose of this chapter is to provide information on the incidence and complication rates of obstetrical hypertension, to discuss our limited understanding of its mechanisms, and to provide guidelines for the management of patients. There are some important differences in philosophy when managing pregnant and nonpregnant women and these need to be explained.

It is difficult to devise satisfactory criteria for defining the various syndromes of hypertension in pregnancy.[1] The problem is that when women first present for antenatal care in early pregnancy and are found to have raised blood pressure, they have not usually had their pressures measured in the nonpregnant state so it is not known whether they had pre-existing hypertension. If their pressures remain high three to four months after delivery, then it is usually assumed that they did indeed have pre-existing hypertension. However, the possibility that the pregnancy initiated chronic hypertension, or

at least accentuated a pre-pregnant tendency, cannot be discounted. Women who have had pre-eclampsia may have a slightly greater risk of developing long-standing hypertension, even though this may not be evident for some years.

The following classification of hypertension in pregnancy is intended to be practical rather than theoretical.

Pre-existing hypertension This implies that the mother had chronically raised blood pressure exceeding 140/90 mmHg before pregnancy. Usually this is essential hypertension, but as with all younger patients there is a greater chance of there being an underlying cause. Glomerulonephritis, pyelonephritis, renal vascular disease, systemic lupus erythematosus, primary aldosteronism or phaeochromocytoma may be present. There can also be significant proteinuria due to renal disease before the onset of pregnancy.

Pregnancy-induced hypertension When blood pressure rises to above 140/90 mmHg in the second or early third trimester, having been normal in early pregnancy, there is an increased risk of premature abortion and intra-uterine growth retardation. The risk to the mother is increased as well. In fact, if the blood pressure remains around 140/90 mmHg and does not rise, the risk is slight, but unfortunately it is not possible to anticipate whose pressures will rise and whose will not. Blood pressures in mid trimester of around 150/100 mmHg do carry a greatly increased risk to mother and fetus.

Pre-eclampsia This is defined as the syndrome of hypertension exceeding 140/90 mmHg with proteinuria and oedema, usually developing after twenty-four weeks' gestation.

A small amount of oedema in the legs is common in normal pregnancy owing to pressure of the enlarged uterus on the inferior vena cava or the iliac veins. The oedema of pre-eclampsia is more generalized in the face and hands as well as the pre-tibial area, and usually a rapid weight gain of two to four pounds (one to two kilograms) can be documented. Proteinuria, however, is not always due to pre-eclampsia; the commonest cause of mild proteinuria in pregnant women is urinary tract infection. In pre-eclampsia the proteinuria usually exceeds 0.5 g daily. Women

1 Pre-existing essential hypertension
2 Pre-existing renal disease
   a. pyelonephritis
   b. glomerulonephritis
   c. systemic lupus erythematosus
3 Pre-existing adrenal hypertension
4 Pregnancy-induced-hypertension
5 Pre-eclamptic toxaemia (PET)
6 PET on pre-existing hypertension

Table 16.1 Syndromes of hypertension in pregnancy.

with pre-existing hypertension are more prone to develop the full picture of pre-eclampsia with proteinuria and oedema.

Eclampsia This is a major obstetric emergency, with very high blood pressure, generalized convulsions, transient focal neurological signs, cerebral haemorrhage and coma. The placenta becomes small, ischaemic and haemorrhagic. The baby is growth retarded, and fetal distress or death may ensue. The mother develops disseminated intravascular coagulation and severe hypertension, and death may follow from convulsions, stroke or renal failure. The greatest mystery is that–usually but not always–within twenty-four hours of delivery of the baby, dead or alive, the syndrome of pre-eclampsia has gone. Only very rarely does the mother suffer any ill-effect after this. Odder still is the fact that a subsequent pregnancy may be totally uneventful. With good antenatal care this syndrome should become increasingly rare. If it does occur it is often due to inadequate antenatal care, which may be the fault of the doctor or of the patient who has failed to attend antenatal clinics.

Transient hypertension Some women may have a single slightly raised blood pressure reading at some stage of pregnancy, which is not confirmed on a second occasion. This is most likely to be due to incorrect methods of measuring blood pressure, but such women need careful observation. Phaeochromocytoma should be excluded.

INCIDENCE
About one quarter of all women develop a blood pressure of 140/90 mmHg or more at some stage in pregnancy; the syndrome of pre-eclampsia is fortunately

much rarer. About 50 per cent of women with raised blood pressure in early pregnancy have no known past history of hypertension, their pressures remain below 150/100 mmHg, and they do not develop proteinuria. The remaining women have severer hypertension, and a very unfavourable outlook for successful pregnancy. Looking at the figures another way, the approximate incidence of the various syndromes in pregnancy are:

Normotensive pregnancy	75 per cent
Pregnancy-induced hypertension only	13 per cent
Pre-eclampsia alone	8 per cent
Pre-eclampsia with pre-existing hypertension	2 per cent
Pre-existing hypertension only	2 per cent

While pre-eclampsia develops in about 10 per cent of women, mercifully very few progress to develop eclampsia. Hypertension in pregnancy is common in certain groups of women who need to receive

---

To the mother
Renal failure
Stroke
Eclampsia

To the baby
Placental insufficiency
Placental infarctions
Intrauterine growth retardation (IUGR)
Intrauterine death (IUD)

Table 16.2 Hazards of hypertension in pregnancy.

198

expert care at an early stage. Frequently these high-risk patients are seen in under-developed and understaffed hospitals, where facilities are scarce. It is strange that the best obstetrical facilities are often available only for the patients who need them least.

Women with a high risk of hypertensive pregnancies

Epidemiological studies have demonstrated that some women are more prone to develop pre-eclampsia than others.[2] Possibly this provides some clue to the aetiology, and it certainly implies that pre-eclampsia is at least in part preventible.

Primigravidae Nobody knows why pre-eclampsia is common in primigravidae and in particular in women aged below twenty years.

Multigravidae Women with four or more children are at greater risk, even if they have not had hypertension in previous pregnancies. This effect appears to be independent of maternal age.

Older women Women aged thirty or more have a slightly higher risk of hypertension in pregnancy.

Twin pregnancies

Rhesus isoimmunization

Diabetic pregnancies

Hydatidiform mole Fifty per cent of women with this condition develop hypertension.

New sexual partner Women with second or subsequent pregnancies from a new sexual partner have a higher risk of pre-eclampsia than those having all pregnancies by the same man.

Previous oral-contraceptive-induced hypertension Despite this weak relationship oral-contraceptive-induced hypertension is often followed by an absolutely normal pregnancy.

Obesity It is uncertain whether obesity alone is a risk factor for any condition, or is only dangerous when associated with other risk factors. This is true of both pregnant and nonpregnant patients.

Family history Patients with a family history of hypertension or pre-eclampsia.

Ethnic groups In Britain black women do not have higher perinatal death rates than whites, but by contrast the perinatal mortality in Asians is high. This is largely due to hypertension and to an increased incidence of congenital malformations. However, these may be a consequence of differences in socio-economic status rather than differences in ethnic origin.

Socio-economically depressed women The higher pre-eclampsia rates in poorer people may in part be due to some of the above mentioned variables.

Male babies The reasons for this weak association are unknown.

PERINATAL MORTALITY

In the case of hypertension in pregnancy, it is the baby's life that is at risk. Death in the mother simply should never occur. Maternal mortality is usually related to pre-existing life-threatening illnesses or severe intercurrent disease.

Pre-existing hypertension Women who enter pregnancy with pre-existing hypertension have a higher perinatal mortality. About 4 per cent of pregnancies will end with a dead baby, due either to mid or third trimester intra-uterine death or to stillbirth. The prognosis is, however, closely related to the severity of the pre-existing hypertension, and to the amount of impairment of renal function. Women with underlying renal or adrenal causes for this raised blood pressure have the worst outlook.

Pregnancy-induced hypertension only If this is mild the outlook is not bad, but if pressure rises to above 150/100 mmHg perinatal mortality rises to around 5 per cent.

Mild pre-eclampsia Women who, for the first time, after the thirty-fifth week develop a modest elevation of blood pressure from 140/90 mmHg to 150/100 mmHg with no evidence of proteinuria do not have a particularly bad outlook as long as their pressures rise no further. Perinatal mortality rates have been reported as between 1.5 to 2 per cent. The problem is that no assumptions can be made about women with mild pre-eclampsia. They may progress rapidly to develop the more florid syndrome with the associated higher perinatal death rate.

Moderate to severe pre-eclampsia When the full triad of pre-eclampsia is present—with severe hypertension, proteinuria of more than 0.5 g daily and oedema—the perinatal mortality is around 3.5 per cent. This syndrome is the main cause of total perinatal mortality. In women with pre-existing hypertension and superadded pre-eclampsia, the perinatal mortality rises to around 5 to 10 per cent. Again the severity of hypertension and the amount of renal damage are closely related to outcome. One American study reported that, taking all pregnant women with significant proteinuria, the perinatal mortality rate is as high as 9 per cent, with black patients having a particularly poor outlook.

THE MECHANISMS OF HYPERTENSION IN PREGNANCY

As stated earlier, the cause of pre-eclampsia is unknown, and investigation is confused by the fact that a great many physiological changes occur in normal pregnancy that are not themselves fully understood.[2] First we need to examine the effects on blood pressure in normal pregnancy.

Normal pregnancy: blood pressure and gestation Both systolic and diastolic blood pressure tend to fall during the first half of pregnancy, but rise again, particularly in the last trimester.

Blood pressure and posture There are very marked changes in systolic blood pressure with posture. Systolic pressure is higher in the lying than the sitting position. However, some women, when the uterus is very large, sustain a pronounced drop in pressure when lying, presumably because venous return from the lower limbs is reduced by vena caval compression.

Haemodynamics In pregnancy there is a rise in total body water of 8.5 litres and a rise of 1.5 litres in plasma volume. Cardiac output consequently rises, particularly in mid trimester, but total peripheral resistance tends to fall, so the net effect on blood pressure is small.

The renin–aldosterone system In normal pregnancy there is a marked rise in the

concentration of plasma renin substrate and a fall in renin concentration. Plasma renin activity, angiotensin II and aldosterone levels rise as a consequence of the high levels of renin substrate.

PRE-ECLAMPSIA

Plasma volume There is some contraction in plasma and extracellular fluid volume in pre-eclampsia. This may lead to reduction in utero-placental blood flow, which may cause placental insufficiency and infarction and in extreme forms ischaemia and death.

The renin–aldosterone system This is less markedly altered in pre-eclampsia pregnancy than in normal pregnancy, so it does not seem to be a cause of pre-eclampsia. However, high plasma angiotensin II levels, in a patient who is already relatively volume-depleted, may elevate the blood pressure and may also have a directly harmful effect on the fetus.

Intravascular coagulation In pre-eclampsia there is a consumptive coagulopathy, with micro-angiopathic haemolytic anaemia. Prothrombin time is prolonged, platelet counts fall and plasma fibrin degradation products rise. These might be a cause or consequence of pre-eclampsia, and may contribute to maternal renal damage.

Hyperuricaemia A decrease in tubular urate excretion occurs in pre-eclampsia before any other detectable abnormality of renal function, except perhaps proteinuria. Measurements of plasma uric acid concentrations are sometimes used as indicators of the severity of the condition. However, the use of thiazide diuretics also causes hyperuricaemia so this group of drugs should not be used in pregnancy.

Catecholamines It is possible that pre-eclampsia may be related to an increased pressor responsiveness to infused and possibly endogenous catecholamines, compared with normotensive pregnancy. Increased responsiveness to angiotensin II has also been recorded.

Prostaglandins There is some evidence that in pre-eclampsia the placenta is unable to produce local vasodilator prostaglandins. This may tie up with the increased vascular effect of both nor-adrenaline and angiotensin.

Urinary oestriol excretion This is reduced in the presence of feto-placental dysfunction. This test was once used as a method of monitoring the baby's progress before delivery, but has largely fallen from favour.

BLOOD PRESSURE MEASUREMENT

Blood pressure levels which in nonpregnant women would be considered unimportant assume great prognostic and therapeutic importance in the pregnant state. A patient whose blood pressure is above 140/90 mmHg is likely to require intensive obstetrical care. For this reason, accurate blood pressure recording is crucial. The measurement of blood pressure is so important that it is the subject of the whole of Chapter 6. There are some special problems in blood pressure measurement in pregnancy, so a few additional comments and guidelines are provided here.

1. Special efforts are needed to avoid observer error, observer bias and terminal digit preference.
2. Blood pressures measured with the patient lying flat may be falsely low.[3] Blood pressures are therefore best measured with the patient seated, but it is important that the forearm cuff is kept at the same level as the heart and that the arm is supported.
3. In hyperdynamic states such as pregnancy it is occasionally impossible to measure diastolic pressure at the disappearance of the Korotkov sounds. It is therefore generally thought that diastolic pressures should be measured at the fourth phase, the muffling of sounds. The phenomenon of the persistence of muffled diastolic sounds down to zero occurs in up to 15 per cent of pregnant women, but usually phases 4 and 5 do coincide. Practically every published report of the management of hypertension in pregnancy has employed the fourth phase, so there are good reasons for using the same technique.
4. In view of the crucial importance of relatively small deviations of blood pressure from the normal, special efforts are needed to ensure that sphygmomanometers are well maintained and accurate. Doctors and midwives should undergo special extra training to improve their accuracy.
5. In many hospitals, sphygmomanometers are so inaccurate and badly maintained, and staff are so slipshod in their techniques, that it may be better to provide the patient with her own sphygmomanometer and ask her to provide home blood pressure readings.
6. All antenatal clinics should have several 'large adult' arm cuffs for blood pressure measurement in obese mothers where arm circumference exceeds 13 in (33 cm).

THE INVESTIGATION OF HYPERTENSION IN PREGNANCY

1. As soon as a woman knows she is pregnant she should be seen by her family doctor who should measure blood pressure accurately.

2. Any women whose blood pressure is 140/90 or more should immediately be referred to an obstetric hospital or department. If the blood pressure is above 160/100 the patient should normally be admitted to hospital.

3. Obstetricians and physicians with a special interest in hypertension should establish weekly joint obstetrical hypertension clinics.

4. On arrival at the obstetrical hypertension clinic or ward a full clinical examination should be undertaken to exclude conditions such as renal disease, adrenal masses and coarctation of the aorta (see Chapter 7 for interpretation of clinical signs).

5. A full biochemical profile including serum uric acid, a haematological profile and blood glucose levels should be obtained immediately. The interpretation of the results should be as in Chapter 7. Serum uric acid levels are worth measuring serially, and any rise in late pregnancy may be associated with pre-eclampsia. It has been suggested that uric acid levels are reliable indicators of the severity of the pre-eclampsia, although there remains some doubt on this point.[4]

6. A twenty-four-hour urine save should be started to measure catecholamine metabolites, electrolytes and protein excretions.

7. An ECG should be performed. If left ventricular hypertension is present this will provide some corroborative evidence of longstanding severe hypertension.

8. Chest radiography should be carried out only in patients with suspected cardiac or chest disease.

9. Intravenous urography is contraindicated.

10. Fetal progress should be monitored in early pregnancy by serial measurements of crown–rump length (CRL) by ultrasound. In later pregnancy, fetal growth is monitored by serial measurements of biparietal diameter (BPD) (see Figure 16.1). This is the best method of diagnosing intra-uterine growth retardation.

11. At all antenatal clinic visits, weight should be monitored and urine tested for protein. History and examination may reveal evidence of oedema. If blood pressure is raised then ophthalmoscopy should be carried out. In pre-eclampsia there may be retinal artery spasm, and in chronic hypertension arterial thickening and arterio-venous nipping. In very severe hypertension with eclampsia or pre-eclampsia there may be retinal haemorrhages, cotton wool spots, hard exudates and even papilloedema.

12. Once the pregnancy has advanced beyond twenty weeks patients should be monitored by cardiotochograph (CTG – see Figure 16.2). This is a kind of fetal ECG which should demonstrate physiological beat to beat variation of fetal heart rate and the response when the baby kicks or there is a spontaneous uterine contraction.[5]

THE MANAGEMENT OF HYPERTENSION IN PREGNANCY

The drugs used to manage pre-existing

hypertension in pregnancy and to treat pre-eclampsia are largely similar. The guidelines suggested below are therefore the same for both conditions. Pre-existing hypertension may prove easy to control during the first six months of pregnancy, but in the last three months, especially if pre-eclampsia sets in, it may prove very resistant.

If the blood pressure exceeds 140/90 mmHg on two consecutive visits to the antenatal clinic, then antihypertensive drug therapy should be started. It is not necessary to admit the patient to hospital. If the blood pressure exceeds 160/100 on one occasion or proteinuria of more than 0.5 g per day develops, then usually the patient should be admitted so that blood pressure can be monitored four-hourly, proteinuria checked and measured and antihypertensive therapy started.

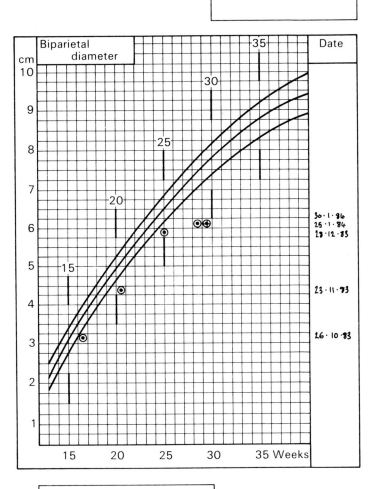

Figure 16.1 A chart for plotting serial measurements of fetal biparietal diameter (BPD). The case shown is of a thirty-nine year old patient with severe essential hypertension. The fetus which was small for dates showed intrauterine growth retardation (IUGR) at 27½ weeks and intrauterine death (IUD) at 28½ weeks. At delivery it weighed 600 gm.

Rest and sedation

Bedrest is of no value. With rest blood pressure settles, but as soon as the patient mobilizes again pressure rises and nothing has been achieved. There is no published evidence that bedrest leads to a favourable outcome in pregnancy.

Sedatives and tranquillizers are similarly of no value unless the patient is agitated or distressed. These drugs may sometimes produce an uncontrolled and prolonged fall in blood pressure and may cause hypotonia and hypothermia in the fetus. The technique of treating hypertension in pregnancy with bedrest and sedatives represents archaic obstetrical practice which is known to be useless.

Antihypertensive drugs

By prescribing antihypertensive drugs at an early stage, admission to hospital can be avoided or shortened. This saves the patient from unnecessary inconvenience and will cut the cost of antenatal care. However, there must remain a commendable reluctance to use drugs in the first twelve weeks of pregnancy. At this stage they are justified only in very severe cases. In the second and third trimesters most antihypertensive drugs are safe.[6]

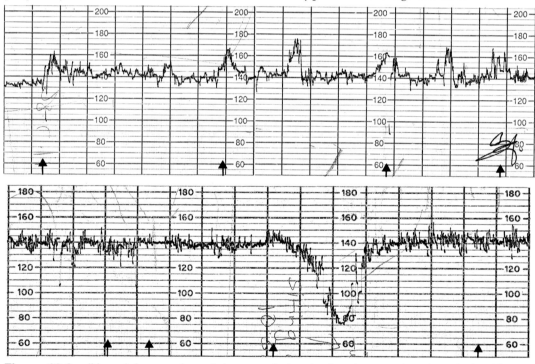

Figure 16.2 *(Upper)* A normal cardiotocograph (CTG), showing accelerations in fetal heart rate when the baby kicks (↑)

(Lower) An abnormal CTG taken from a mother with essential hypertension and super-added pre-celempsia. The fetal heart rate is unresponsive to kicking, but there is a sudden profound deceleration in heart rate, indicative of fetal distress. Within four hours a live baby was delivered by lower segment Caesarian section. While there was evidence of intrauterine growth retardation, and there were some placental infarcts, the baby did well.

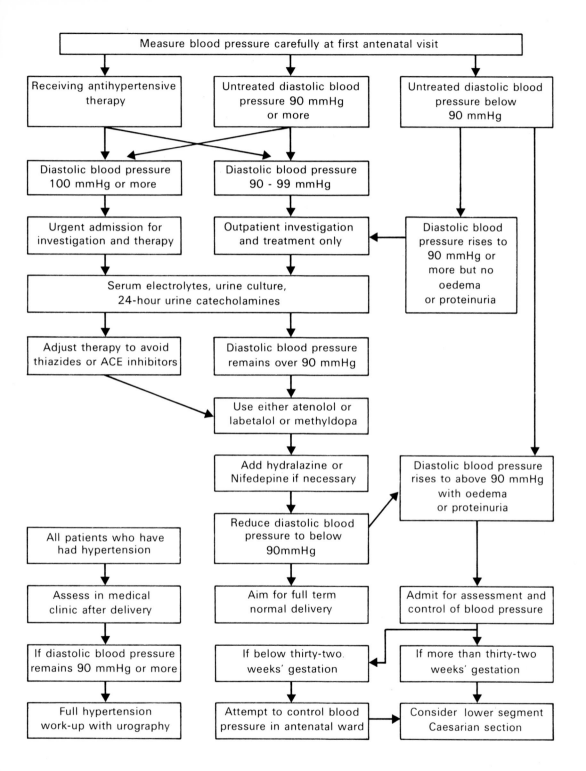

Figure 16.3 Guidelines for monitoring hypertensive patients during pregnancy.

Diuretics, including thiazides, are said to be contraindicated in pregnancy. Women with pre-eclampsia have relatively contracted plasma volumes, and diuretics will cause further contraction and worsen the impairment of utero-placental blood-flow. However, a recent review has suggested that diuretics are not as harmful as they were originally thought to be.[7] Diuretics may, of course, prove necessary if there is severe heart failure or gross fluid retention due to renal failure.

Centrally acting drugs Methyldopa has for many years been the mainstay of obstetrical antihypertensive treatment.[8] There is good evidence that it is entirely safe in pregnancy for both mother and baby, but the drug is now falling from favour because it causes severe dose-related sedation and lethargy. Methyldopa probably does remain the first-line drug in women with asthma, where beta-blockers are contraindicated. Doses of up to 2 g daily can be used, but sedation can be minimized with no more than 750 mg daily.

Beta-receptor blockers Beta-blockers and combined alpha-beta-blockers are safe in pregnancy. Atenolol, propranolol, oxprenolol and labetalol have been studied in some detail, and it is probable that the other beta-blockers are equally safe. Obstetricians have, correctly, been conservative about new antihypertensive drugs, but as beta-blockers have been available since 1965 they can be fully reassured.[9]

The worry was that beta-blockers might induce relative bradycardia in both mother and fetus, and also cause fetal hypoglycaemia. Bradycardia due to beta-blockers renders the maternal and fetal heart rates less reliable when monitoring for fetal distress. It was once felt that blockade of beta-receptors in the uterus

206

might unfavourably influence uterine contraction, causing precipitate labour. Well-conducted clinical trials can reassure us on all these points, and beta-blockers are now the drugs of first choice in obstetrics, unless there are specific contra-indications.

Atenolol can be given in a single daily dose of 50 or 100 mg. Bradycardia occurs less commonly than in nonpregnant patients. This drug may cause cold extremities and Raynaud's syndrome. If this is really a problem then oxprenolol, in a dose of 160 to 320 mg daily in a slow-release formulation, may be a reasonable alternative. Oxprenolol may cause less cold extremities because of its intrinsic sympathomimetic activity, but it may be less effective. Labetalol is effective in pregnancy and has relatively few side-effects.

Vasodilators Hydralazine (a direct arteriolar vasodilator) has been used extensively in pregnancy, and doses of 25 to 50 mg twice daily are safe. It is probably unwise to exceed 200 mg daily. This is usually regarded as a second-line drug, added to beta-blockers or methyldopa. Side-effects include tachycardia, fluid retention and headaches. The drug-induced lupus syndrome is very rare in doses below 100 mg daily.

Calcium-entry antagonists Nifedipine is a powerful antihypertensive drug, and there is some evidence that it is useful in severe pregnancy-associated hypertension.[10] Headaches and flushing are a problem, and about 10 per cent of patients cannot tolerate the drug. This must, in the present state of knowledge, be regarded as a second-line drug for use after twelve weeks' gestation. It may cause menorrhagia in the nonpregnant state, but there are no reports of increased postpartum blood loss.

ACE inhibitors Captopril and enalapril have not yet been assessed in pregnancy and must not be used. In theory they might interfere with uterine bloodflow, and in pregnant sheep an increased fetal death rate has been reported from converting-enzyme inhibitors.

Alpha-blockers These are probably safe in pregnancy, but there is so far little published evidence. Phenoxybenzamine is mandatory in patients with phaeochromocytoma, and is given in conjunction with beta-blockers.

- Teratogenicity There are no reports of an excess incidence of congenital abnormalities in babies subjected to the above drugs *in utero*. However, some uncertainty must hang over the newer drugs simply because experience world-wide is limited, and they should not be used unless other drugs have failed.

SEVERE PRE-ECLAMPSIA AND ECLAMPSIA

This condition represents a medico-obstetrical emergency, and drug treatment is urgent. Blood pressure should be monitored every fifteen minutes. Urinary protein concentration and volume output should be carefully watched. If proteinuria is present, then the prognosis is poor.

Control of convulsions Epileptiform convulsions can be prevented or controlled by intravenous diazepam in a dose of 10 mg immediately and thereafter 10 mg per hour by infusion. In Europe magnesium sulphate is also recommended, as this too may reduce platelet aggregation, which occurs in eclampsia, and lower blood pressure.

Control of blood pressure The emergency control of blood pressure is best achieved by a slow intravenous injection of hydralazine in a dose of 20 mg. This has been reported to reduce blood pressure without reducing uterine bloodflow. Other intravenous drugs, including diazoxide and labetalol, may tend to reduce uterine flow. Precipitate drops in blood pressure should be avoided as they may induce cerebral, cardiac, renal or placental ischaemia. Chronic diazoxide therapy causes diabetes mellitus. Hydralazine remains the most commonly used drug, and can be given by intravenous or intramuscular injection.

Delivery of the baby The most effective method of controlling pre-eclampsia or eclampsia is to end the pregnancy. The syndrome will then usually regress over about twenty-four hours. Advances in the quality and availability of paediatricians with special interests in neonatal care mean that it is now safer to deliver the baby after about thirty-five weeks' gestation rather than proceed with a severely hypertensive pregnancy. If the baby weighs more than about three pounds (1.5 kilograms) the outlook is very good, and babies weighing only two pounds can usually be saved.

Epidural anaesthesia During epidural anaesthesia, blood pressure falls. This is therefore a particularly satisfactory method of inducing analgesia during labour in hypertensive mothers. Care must be taken to avoid precipitate drops in pressure and concomitant parenteral antihypertensive drugs should only be used very sparingly.

POSTNATAL HYPERTENSION

Antihypertensive drugs

If hypertension is due to pre-eclampsia alone, blood pressures usually return to normal once the baby is born. Thus anti-hypertensive drugs can be withdrawn gradually over two or three days. However, blood pressure may remain mildly raised for weeks or months following delivery. Usually it is not high enough to merit drug therapy, but must be monitored carefully. If the raised blood pressure was due to pre-existing hypertension with or without pre-eclampsia therapy should be continued, although frequently the dosage of antihypertensive drugs can be reduced. As thiazides are useful antihypertensive drugs when used in combination with beta-blockers, these may be reintroduced.

Further investigation

All women who have had hypertension of any cause in pregnancy should be referred soon after delivery to a blood pressure clinic. In those women who had pure pre-eclampsia blood pressures usually return to normal, and apart from a careful history and examination no further action is needed. If blood pressures remain even slightly elevated, then a full work-up with intravenous urography is mandatory. The methods of managing such patients are covered in Chapter 7.

Further pregnancy

Women who had pure pre-eclampsia can be reassured that a further pregnancy may well not be complicated by the same troubles. However, it is important that as soon they become pregnant again they should attend a joint antenatal and blood pressure clinic. Women with pre-existing hypertension can usually be advised that it is safe to undergo a further pregnancy, but only with careful supervision as they do have an increased risk of stillbirth. Perhaps only women with hypertension complicated by chronic renal failure

should be advised to desist from further pregnancies.

SPECIAL SITUATIONS

Chronic renal disease   If the mother has pre-existing chronic renal disease, with or without hypertension, special care is necessary. Superadded pre-eclampsia is common, and it is important to measure the twenty-four-hour urinary protein content at an early stage, usually during a brief in-patient stay. Aggressive control of blood pressure is mandatory, but even then as many as 45 per cent of pregnancies may end with a dead baby. The help of a nephrologist or hypertension specialist should be sought immediately pregnancy is diagnosed.

Phaeochromocytoma   This is an important but rare cause of maternal as well as fetal death. A twenty-four-hour urine collection for urinary metanephrines or VMA should be routine in all hypertensive pregnancies. If phaeochromocytoma is suggested by this test, then abdominal ultrasound should be undertaken to locate the tumour. It is mandatory that the mother is treated with both alpha- and beta-blockers throughout the whole of pregnancy. Delivery of the baby is best by lower segment caesarian section; a surgeon should be present with a highly qualified anaesthetist as well as a physician. If all goes smoothly, it is probably best to remove the phaeochromocytoma electively a week or two after delivery, through a more appropriate abdominal incision and after CT scanning has confirmed the site of the phaeochromocytoma.

Coronary heart disease   Occasionally hypertensive women with angina become pregnant. Beta-receptor blockers with or

208

without calcium-channel blockers and nitrates are mandatory.

Asthma This is a common problem. The asthma is treated along conventional lines, with monitoring of blood theophylline levels if this drug is used. Reliance should be placed more on inhaled beta-agonists, steroids and atropine-like drugs than oral therapy. Beta-blockers should never be used, as even the most cardio-selective blockers increase airways resistance. High blood pressure should be treated with methyldopa, hydralazine or possibly nifedipine.

Oral contraceptives Women who have had raised blood pressure in pregnancy are not doomed to develop raised blood pressure when taking the oral contraceptive. However, they should be monitored carefully before starting the pill, and thereafter six-monthly.

Hypertension in later life There is some doubt as to whether women who have had pre-eclampsia are more likely to develop later essential hypertension. They should be regarded as a group to be selectively screened for hypertension in general practice, if only to settle this point.

PRACTICAL POINTS

- An active approach to hypertension in pregnancy can reduce the perinatal mortality rate from as high as 6 per cent to 1.5 per cent.

- Obstetricians should work jointly with physicians when managing this condition.

- The outlook for patients with modest elevation of pressure only is not bad, but once proteinuria develops the situation alters and the outlook for the baby is poor.

- Good antenatal care as a form of selective screening for hypertension has been routine in obstetric practice and is very worthwhile.

- With a greater use and understanding of antihypertensive drugs, there should be a further marked reduction in perinatal mortality.

17
Hypertension in children

BACKGROUND

High blood pressure in children is a neglected topic, and too little is yet known about the longterm prognosis and value of antihypertensive drug treatment.[1] These problems are due in part to the differing criteria for diagnosing raised blood pressure in various age groups. The average blood pressure of infants rises fairly sharply in the first few weeks of life.[2] It is uncertain whether the rise is any different in breast-fed compared with bottle-fed babies, or whether it is related to the time of weaning. Pressures remain relatively static until the age of about four, but then start to rise again and continue to do so steadily into adult life. There may be a slight acceleration in the rate of rise in males at the time of puberty. Along with this rise with age there is some evidence of the phenomenon of tracking, so that children whose blood pressures are in the upper part of the normal distribution tend to remain there. There is also evidence that higher blood pressures tend to rise faster.

This rise in blood pressure appears to be due to environmental factors, as it tends not to occur in non-Westernized societies. There is also a strong familial effect, as children of hypertensive parents tend to have higher pressures than children with no family history.[3] The implications for the prevention of future adult hypertension are obvious, and identification of the various environmental pressor factors is important. This topic is discussed more fully in Chapter 3.

| | SYSTOLIC BP | | DIASTOLIC BP | |
	normal mean	as percentile	normal mean	as percentile
Birth to 6 weeks	75	95	—	—
6 weeks to 4 yr	95	110	60	70
5–6yr	105	115	60	75
7–8 yr	105	120	65	80
9–10 yr	110	125	65	80
11–12 yr	115	130	65	85
13–14 yr	120	135	70	85
over 14	—	140	—	90

Table 17.1 The average blood pressures in children and the 95 percentile (above which hypertension may be diagnosed) in relation to age. There is inadequate information on diastolic blood pressure in neonates. Over the age of fourteen the average blood pressure depends on age, but at any age pressures exceeding 130/80 are abnormal by WHO criteria.

CRITERIA FOR ABNORMAL BLOOD PRESSURE

As with many other indices in childhood, clinicians usually define abnormalities of blood pressure in relation to percentiles obtained by examining large numbers of children.[4] The data for girls and boys differ slightly (see Figure 17.1). We recommend that children whose systolic or diastolic blood pressures exceed the 90th percentile should be rechecked; and those whose pressures exceed the 95th percentile should be regarded as hypertensive. This last group needs detailed investigation and should be referred to a paediatrician.

Simpler guidelines are that all blood pressures which exceed 110/75 mmHg should be considered abnormal up to the age of ten. In the teenage years any blood pressure exceeding 130/80 mmHg requires attention. Special efforts should be made to check the blood pressure in children with known renal or renal tract disease and those with a strong family history.

The main complication of hypertension in children is renal failure, and the aim of controlling blood pressure is to prevent this occurring. The next priority is to avoid future severe adult hypertension. Heart attacks and strokes are fortunately very rare, but when they do occur in children they are devastating. In particular, the risk of subarachnoid haemorrhage is greater in severely hypertensive children.

THE MEASUREMENT OF BLOOD PRESSURE

Below the age of three, the conventional auscultatory method of measuring blood pressure is difficult, and routine measurement cannot be recommended. However, infants who are ill, and particularly those with renal or renal tract disease, must have their blood pressures measured.

1. There are many Döppler blood pressure measuring devices available which should be used, but usually only systolic blood pressure can be measured reliably.

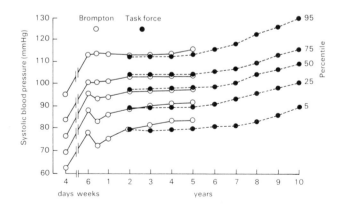

Figure 17.1 Percentiles of systolic blood pressure from ages four days to five years in the Brompton study and the Task Force for blood pressure control in children.[2]

2. There is also a flush method of estimating systolic blood pressure in infants. An elastic bandage is placed around the whole length of the arm to occlude the pulses. An infant sphygmomanometer cuff is then applied above the bandage and attached to a conventional manometer. The cuff is inflated to about 180 mmHg, and the elastic bandage is removed, leaving a white, pulseless arm. The cuff is then deflated slowly and the pressure at which the arm flushes, i.e., when blood re-enters the arm, is measured. By the end of this procedure the infant will almost certainly be crying loudly and the pressure will be falsely elevated. The procedure is only justified if other equipment is not available.

3. In children aged three and over blood pressure is measured in the same way as in adults. However, the size of the manometer cuff is crucial (see Chapter 6); it must fit snugly over the child's arm. The bladder should encircle at least two-thirds of the upper arm, but there should be no overlap. The cuff should also be about two-thirds of the length of the upper arm. All paediatricians and physicians should have a selection of cuffs at their disposal.

4. A detailed account of the methods of measurement of blood pressure is given in Chapter 6. Here a few points of special importance in children are discussed. It is important that the child is relaxed, not crying. It may be helpful to have the child seated in the mother's lap. Systolic blood pressure is taken at first appearance of sounds (phase 1), as in adults. There is some debate about which is the best estimate of diastolic pressure in children. More often than not, phase 4 and 5 coincide so there is no problem. Occasionally the gap is wide, and sometimes no fifth phase can be identified as sounds are audible even with the mercury pressure down to zero. Under both these circumstances, diastolic pressures must be taken at the phase of muffling of sounds (phase 4).

As with all blood pressure measurement the forearm cuff should be level with the heart, otherwise serious errors may occur.

Age	Width of bladder (cm)	Length of bladder (cm)
1 Newborn	2.5–4	5–10
2 6 months–3 years	6–8	12–13.5
3 3–10 years	9–10	13–22.5

Table 17.2 Cuff sizes in paediatric patients.

Leg blood pressures

Coarctation of the aorta is an important congenital abnormality causing hypertension in children, so blood pressure should always be checked in the legs if it has been found to be raised in the arms. The appropriate size of cuff is applied round the thigh with the child lying prone. The stethoscope is applied over the popliteal artery and pressures recorded in the normal way. Special thigh cuffs are available and the same rules apply as for arm cuff size; the rubber bladder should measure no less than two-thirds of the thigh circumference.

RECOMMENDATIONS FOR SCREENING

There are insufficient grounds for recommending the mass screening of children for hypertension. This may become justifiable if primary preventive measures are validated and gain more general acceptance. Until then a reasonable compromise is as follows:

1. Children who are ill enough to be referred to a paediatrician should have their blood pressure measured. In particular, children with renal disease, failure to thrive and those receiving corticosteroid therapy need careful monitoring.
2. Children admitted to hospital for any reason, including routine ear, nose or throat surgery, should have their blood pressure measured.
3. Pressures of children with a family history of hypertension should be checked. In addition, children whose parents have polycystic disease or phaeochromocytoma should be examined and the relevant tests (renal ultrasound or urine metanephrines) performed. Both these conditions may be inherited.

RECOMMENDATIONS FOR INVESTIGATING CHILDREN

Children whose blood pressures are between the 90th and 95th percentile need investigation only if there is a suspicion of some underlying disease. Children whose blood pressures are above the 95th percentile always need detailed investigation and they should preferably be referred to specialized units. The method of investigation is along similar lines to those recommended in Chapters 7 and 8. Full haematological and biochemical profile, chest x-ray, intravenous urography, ECG, urinary metanephrines or VMA and a midstream or clean-catch specimen of urine for microscopy and culture are all that is routinely needed. Further investigation depends on the results of these tests.

A good case can be made for measuring plasma renin levels routinely in all children with raised blood pressure, as this may help to detect renal hypertension.

THE AETIOLOGY OF HYPERTENSION IN CHILDREN

If the diastolic pressure exceeds 110 mmHg, it is most likely that there is an underlying renal, renovascular or adrenal cause for the hypertension. In cases where the diastolic pressure is below 100 mmHg it is most likely that no underlying cause will be found and, as in adults, such cases are classified as essential hypertensives.

There follows a brief classification of underlying causes which should be considered when investigating hypertension in children, with comment on each of the important clinical features.

Coarctation of the aorta Narrowing of the arch of the aorta occurs either immediately before, at the level of or just after the ductus arteriosus. There may also be cardiac defects including patent ductus arteriosus, bicuspid aortic valves,

213

ventricular septal defects or transposition of the great vessels. The femoral pulses may be absent or delayed and leg blood pressures are low or normal in spite of raised arm pressures.[5] Coarctation in adults carries a poor prognosis with a high risk of myocardial infarction and subarachnoid haemorrhage. For this reason surgical correction should be carried out as soon as feasible, and optimally at the age of about four. Even with early surgery blood pressure may not be normalized, so longterm follow-up is important.

Arterial disease Hypertension may occur with congenital aortic hypoplasia. Many acquired arteritic diseases may also be complicated by hypertension. These include scleroderma, systemic lupus erythematosus, juvenile rheumatoid disease and polyarteritis nodosa.

Renovascular disease In children renal artery stenosis is rarely congenital. Acquired stenosis is usually due to fibromuscular hyperplasia of renal or intrarenal arteries rather than atheroma. Detailed investigation and surgical correction is mandatory. The further investigation of renal artery stenosis is discussed in Chapter 8.

Renal disease Renal and renovascular hypertension in children are frequently associated with biochemical evidence of secondary aldosteronism, with hypokalaemia and high plasma renin and aldosterone levels. These children may present with nonspecific symptoms, including general malaise and failure to grow normally or, in babies, with failure to thrive. Hypertension may complicate acute nephritic syndrome, nephrotic syndrome, chronic glomerulonephritis, chronic pyelonephritis and obstructive or reflux uropathy with or without urinary

214

infection. Various forms of unilateral or bilateral renal hypoplasia, including the Ask–Upmark kidney (segmental renal hypoplasia), may cause hypertension, which may be very severe. Adult-type polycystic kidney disease (mendelian dominant) causes familial hypertension, renal failure and subarachnoid haemorrhage. The rarer recessively inherited form of polycystic disease is also associated with renal failure and high blood pressure.

Very rarely, a benign renin-secreting tumour (haemangiopericytoma) may be identified.[6] These are often small peripheral lesions which can usually be excised by heminephrectomy. Hypertension may also complicate malignant renal tumours (Wilms' tumour).

Endocrine disorders Both primary aldosteronism and phaeochromocytoma may present in childhood. The diagnostic lines are similar to those described in Chapter 8. In children hypertension may also complicate Cushing's syndrome, due to pituitary causes, adrenal hyperplasia, corticosteroid or ACTH therapy. The very rare congenital adrenal diseases, including 11-beta-hydroxylase deficiency and 17-alpha-hydroxylase deficiency, are associated with abnormal sexual development and hypertension which is related to mineralocorticoid excess. Hypokalaemia and renin suppression but with normal plasma aldosterone levels are strongly suggestive of this form of mineralocorticoid hypertension. As discussed in Chapter 14, hypertension may complicate diabetes, hyperparathyroidism and possibly myxoedema.

TREATMENT
The object of antihypertensive treatment should be to reduce diastolic blood pressure to below 90 mmHg. Careful monitoring of serum creatinine levels is

necessary, since the aim of treating hypertension in children is primarily to prevent the onset of renal failure.

Salt restriction with the substitution of potassium-rich foods may be sufficient to control blood pressure in some mildly hypertensive children. Even in children who are receiving antihypertensive drug therapy this dietary approach should be followed, as there is an additive effect of low-salt diet with most antihypertensive drugs. Hypertensive children often tend to be obese, and calorie restriction should be advised where this is relevant.

Drugs for juvenile hypertension

The same rules as for the treatment of adult hypertension apply, i.e., thiazide diuretics, beta-blockers, ACE inhibitors and calcium-entry antagonists. The long-term metabolic consequences of thiazides make these drugs less desirable, and they are also less effective in younger patients. Minoxidil causes hirsutism and is contra-indicated unless all other drugs have failed. The centrally acting drugs methyldopa, clonidine and reserpine may cause undue sedation. Dosages of drugs must be corrected to the weight and age of the

	Dose range in relation to body weight	Comments
Beta-blockers		All beta-blockers are safe in children, but they must not be used
Propranolol	1–2 mg/kg	in asthmatics. Smaller doses of hydrophilic beta-blockers
Oxprenolol	1 mg/kg	including atenolol if there is renal failure
Diuretics		
Hydrochlorothiazide	2·5 mg/kg	All thiazides are safe but they are not particularly effective when
Bendrofluazide	0.1 mg/kg	used alone. Thiazides are useful in combination with other agents
Spironolactone	3 mg/kg	Best reserved for cases with aldosterone excess
Frusemide	1–3 mg/kg	Best reserved for cases with renal failure
ACE inhibitors		
Captopril	0·3 to 1 mg/kg	All ACE inhibitors equally safe. Great care is necessary if there
Enalapril	unknown	is renal failure, renovascular hypertension or the patient is already receiving diuretic therapy
Calcium antagonists		
Nifedipine	unknown	There is no reason to believe that this group of drugs is not entirely safe in children
Centrally acting agents		
Methlyldopa	10 mg/kg	A safe drug but side-effects limit its use and dosage
Other agents		
Prazosin	unknown	safe in children
Hydralazine	unknown	best avoided due to risk of lupus syndrome

Table 17.3 Oral paediatric doses for five to fifteen year old children.

child as recommended in the manufacturers' literature. The pharmacy departments of most specialized paediatric hospitals are able to make up special elixirs containing very small amounts of converting-enzyme inhibitors.

PREVENTION

There is some evidence to suggest that essential hypertension is related to a genetically determined increased sensitivity to dietary salt. For this reason there is a good case to be made for restricting salt intake in children with a strong family history of hypertension.

One carefully controlled study in newborn babies has shown that those given a lower salt intake had significantly lower systolic pressure at six months of age (see Figure 17.2).[7] Since, as mentioned above, hypertensive children, or those who have above average blood pressures, tend to be obese, weight reduction is also an important preventive approach. The following measures should contribute to the prevention of adult hypertension in the community:

Definite
- The measurement of blood pressure and the regular follow-up of all children who have hypertensive parents
- Salt restriction and, where relevant, calorie restriction in children whose parents are hypertensive

Possible
- The routine measurement of blood pressure of all children over the age of ten years
- Advice on salt and calorie restriction for all children whose diastolic pressures exceed 80 mmHg

Unproven
A good case could be made for restricting the salt intake of the whole population, but no studies have been carried out that prove this to be worthwhile.

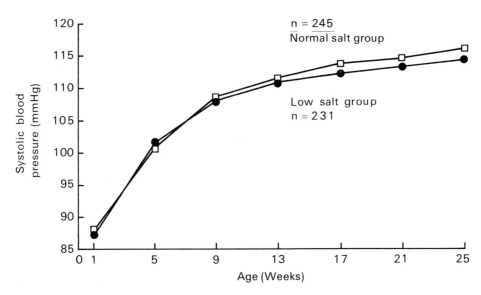

Figure 17.2 A randomized trial of low sodium intake and blood pressure in newborn infants (from A. Hofman *et al., J. Amer. Med. Ass.* **250**, 1983, 370–3).

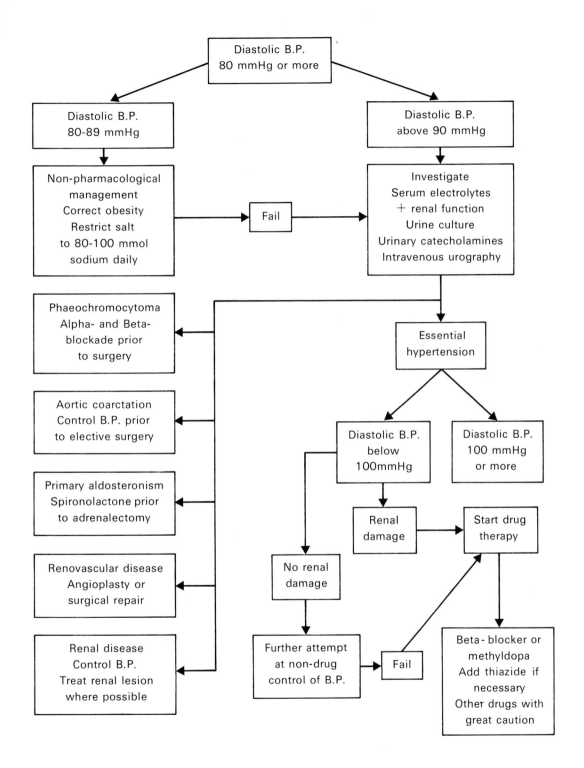

Figure 17.3 Guidelines for management of hypertension in five to fifteen year old children.

We feel there is cause for concern that many children in the developed countries now consume large quantities of salt in convenience foods including sausages, hamburgers and canned foods. The salt content of sauces and potato crisps is very high. In relation to their body weight many children in Western countries now consume as much salt as the north Japanese; a population with the highest recorded incidence of stroke. This public health issue needs further investigation and action.

PRACTICAL POINTS

- Hypertension in children is often due to underlying renal or adrenal disease.

- The main aims in controlling high blood pressure in children are to prevent renal failure and avoid future severe adult hypertension.

- Screening of children at risk is recommended.

- Salt and calorie restriction alone may be sufficient treatment for mildly hypertensive children, and are certainly desirable preventive measures for children whose diastolic pressures exceed 80 mmHg.

References

Chapter 1

1. GRIMLEY EVANS, J. and ROSE, G., 'Hypertension', *Brit. Med. Bull. 27* (1971), 37–42.
2. KANNEL, W. B., DAWBER, T. R., MCGEE, D. L. et al., 'Perspectives on systolic hypertension. The Framingham study', *Ciculation 61* (1980), 1179–82.
3. PICKERING, G., 'Hypertension, definitions, natural histories and consequences', *Am. J. Med. 52* (1982), 570–83.
4. GIFFORD, R. W., 'Isolated systolic hypertension in the elderly. Some controversial issues', *J. Am. Med. Assoc. 247* (1982), 781–5.
5. WORLD HEALTH ORGANIZATION, 'Arterial hypertension', WHO Technical Report (1978), Series 628.
6. HAWTHORNE, V. M., GREAVES, D. A. and BEEVERS, D. G., 'Blood pressure in a Scottish town', *Brit. Med. J. 3* (1974), 600–603.
7. KANNEL, W. B., 'Role of blood pressure in cardiovascular morbidity and mortality', *Prog. Cardiovasc. Dis. 17* (1974), 5–25.
8. EDITORIAL, 'Why does blood pressure rise with age?', *Lancet 2* (1981), 289–90.
9. KANNEL, W. B., 'Blood pressure and the development of cardiovascular disease in the aged' in *Cardiology in Old Age*, ed. F. I. Caird et al. (Plenum Press, New York, 1976) 146–74.
10. BEEVERS, D. G., 'Blood pressures that fall on rechecking', *Brit. Med. J. 284* (1982), 71–2.
11. HYPERTENSION DETECTION AND FOLLOW-UP PROGRAM COOPERATIVE GROUP, 'Five year findings of the Hypertension Detection and Follow-up Program I', *J. Am. Med. Assoc. 242* (1979), 2562–71.
12. PICKERING, G. W., *High Blood Pressure* (Churchill, London, 2nd edn, 1968).
13. LEW E. A., 'The insurance viewpoint. High blood pressure, other risk factors and longevity', *Am. J. Med. 55* (1973), 281–94.
14. KURJI, K. H. and HAINES, A. P., 'Detection and management of hypertension in general practices in north west London', *Brit. Med. J. 288* (1984), 903–906.

Chapter 2

1. BEILIN, L. J. and GOLDBY, F. S., 'High arterial pressure versus humoral factors in the pathogenesis of the vascular lesions of malignant hypertension. *Clin. Sci. Molec. Med. 52* (1977), 111–17.
2. HOLLANDER, W., 'Role of hypertension in atherosclerosis and cardiovascular disease', *Am. J. Cardiol. 38* (1976), 786–800.
3. ROSS RUSSELL, R. W., 'How does blood pressure cause stroke?', *Lancet 2* (1975), 1283–5.
4. KANNEL, W. B., 'Role of blood pressure in cardiovascular disease; the Framingham study', *Angiology 26* (1975), 1–14.
5. KANNEL, W. B., GORDON, T., CASTELLI, W. P. et al., 'Electrocardiographic left ventricular hypertrophy and risk of coronary heart disease', *Ann. Intern. Med. 60* (1976), 813–22.
6. SACCO, R. L., WOLD, P. A., BARUCHA, N. E. et al., 'Sub-arachnoid and intracerebral haemorrhage. Natural history, prognosis and precursive factors in the Framingham survey', *Neurology 34* (1984), 847–54.
7. SLATER, E. E. and DE SANCTIS, R. W., 'The clinical recognition of dissecting aortic aneurysm', *Am. J. Med. 60* (1976), 625–33.

8. BAUER, G. E. and HUMPHERY, T. J., 'The natural history of hypertension with moderate impairment of renal function', *Clin. Sci. Molec. Med. 45* (1973), 191s–193s.

Chapter 3

1. EDITORIAL, 'Why does blood pressure rise with age', *Lancet 2* (1981), 289–90.
2. MIALL, W. E. and CHINN, S., 'Blood pressure and ageing, results of a 15–17 year follow-up study in South Wales', *Clin. Sci. Molec. Med 45* (1973), 23s–33s.
3. STAMLER, R., STAMLER, J., RIEDLINGER, W. F., et al., 'Family (parental) history and prevalence of hypertension', *J. Am. Med. Assoc. 241* (1979), 43–6.
4. SEVER, P. S., GORDON, D., PEART, W. S. et al., 'Blood pressure and its correlates in urban and tribal Africa', *Lancet 2* (1980), 60–4.
5. BEEVERS, D. G. and CRUICKSHANK, J. K., 'Age, sex, ethnic origin and hospital admission for heart attack and stroke', *Postgrad. Med. J. 57* (1981), 763–5.
6. CRUICKSHANK, J. K., JACKSON, S. H. D., BEEVERS, D. G., et al., 'Similarity of blood pressure in blacks, whites and Asians in England', *J. Hypertension 3* (1985), 365–71.
7. MANN, G. V., 'The influence of obesity on health', *N. Eng. J. Med. 291* (1974), 178–85.
8. SIMPSON, P. O., 'Blood pressure and sodium intake' in *Handbook of Hypertension* Vol. 6, *Epidemiology of Hypertension*, ed. C. J. Bulpitt (Elsevier, Amsterdam, New York, Oxford, 1985), 275–90.
9. MENEELY, G. R. and BATTARBEE, H. D., 'High sodium – low potassium environment and hypertension', *Am. J. Cardiol. 38* (1976), 768–85.
10. KLATSKY, A. L., FRIEDMAN, G. D., SIEGELAUB, M. S. et al., 'Alcohol consumption and blood pressure. Kaiser-Permanente multiphasic health examination data', *N. Eng. J. Med. 296* (1977), 1194–1200.
11. SAUNDERS, J. B., BEEVERS, D. G. and PATON, A. 'Alcohol-induced hypertension', *Lancet 2* (1981), 653–6.
12. PUSKA, P., IACONO, J. M., NISSINEN, A. et al., 'Controlled randomised trial of the effect of dietary fat on blood pressure', *Lancet 1* (1983), 1–5.
13. KESTELOOT, H. and GEBOERS, J., 'Calcium and blood pressure', *Lancet 1* (1982), 813–15.
14. GREENE, S. B., AAVENDAL, M. J., TYROLER, H. A., DAVIS, et al., 'Smoking habits and blood pressure change. A seven year follow-up', *J. Chron. Dis. 30* (1977), 401–13.
15. BLOXHAM, C. A., BEEVERS, D. G. and WALKER, J. M., 'Malignant hypertension and cigarette smoking', *Brit. Med. J. 1*(1979), 381–83.
16. CRUICKSHANK, J. K. and BEEVERS, D. G., 'Epidemiology of hypertension: blood pressure in blacks and whites', *Clin. Sci. 62* (1982), 1–6.
17. BIER, D. M., and YOUNG, V. R., 'Exercise and blood pressure: nutritional considerations'. *Ann. Intern. Med. 98*, (1983), 864–9.
18. HARLAN, W. R., LANDIS, J. R., SCHMOUDER, R. L., et al., 'Blood lead and blood pressure', *J. Am. Med. Assoc. 253* (1985), 530–4.
19. POCOCK, S. J., SHAPER, A. G., ASHBY, D., et al., 'Blood lead concentration, blood pressure and renal function', *Brit. Med. J. 289* (1984), 872–4.

Chapter 4

1. ONESTI, G., and KIM, K. E., *Hypertension Mechanisms and Management* (Grune & Stratton, New York, 1973).
2. LUND-JOHANSSEN, P., 'Haemodynamics in essential hypertension', *Clin. Sci. 59* (1980), 343s–354s.
3. FOLKOW, B., 'Cardiovascular structural adaptation; its role in the

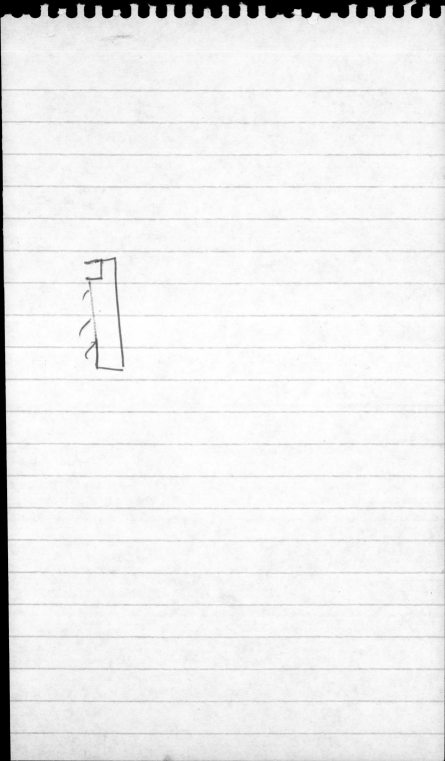

initiation and maintenance of primary hypertension', *Clin. Sci. 55* (1978), 3s–22s.

4. GOLDSTEIN, D. S., 'Plasma norepinephrine in essential hypertension; a study of the studies', *Hypertension 3* (1981), 48–52.

5. MACGREGOR, G. A. SMITH, S. J., MARKANOU, N. D., et al., 'Angiotensin converting enzyme inhibition reveals an important role for the renin system in the control of normal and high blood pressure in man', *Clin. Exp. Hypertension A5* (1983), 1367–80.

6. LARAGH, J. H., 'Vasoconstriction-volume analysis for understanding and treating hypertension: The use of renin and aldosterone profiles', *Am. J. Med. 55* (1973), 261–74.

7. DE WARDENER, H. E. and MACGREGOR, G. A., 'The relation of a circulating sodium transport inhibitor (the natriuretic hormone?) to hypertension', *Medicine* (Baltimore) *62* (1983) 310–26.

8. BLAUSTEIN, M. P. 'Sodium ions, calcium ions, blood pressure regulation and hypertension: a reassessment and a hypothesis, *Am J. Physiol. 232* (1977), C165–73.

9. BORST, J. G. G. AND BORST DE GEUS, A., 'Hypertension explained by Starling's theory of circulatory homeostasis', *Lancet 1* (1963), 667–82.

10. WEINBERGER, M. H., 'Primary aldosteronism' In: *Hypertension,* Genest, J., et al. (eds) (McGraw Hill, New York, 1983), 922–39.

11. MENARD, J., SOUBRIEK, F. BARIETY, J. et al., 'Primary reninism' In: *Hypertension,* Genest, J. et al. (eds) (McGraw Hill, New York, 1983) 1034–40.

12. KUCHEL, O., 'Pheochromocytoma', In: *Hypertension,* Genest, J., et al. (eds) (McGraw Hill, New York, 1983), 947–63.

Chapter 5

1. EDITORIAL, 'Hypertension and oral contraceptives', *Brit. Med. J. 1* (1978), 1570–1.

2. DOLL, R., HILL, I. D. and HUTTON, C. F., 'Treatment of gastric ulcer with carbenoxolone sodium and oestrogens', *Gut 6* (1965), 19–24.

3. JACKSON, S. H. D., BEEVERS, D. G. and MYERS, K., 'Does long-term low-dose corticosteroid therapy cause hypertension', *Clin. Sci. 61* (1981), 381s–383s.

4. HOROWITZ, J. D., HOWES, L. G., CHRISTOPHIDIS et al., 'Hypertensive responses induced by phenylpropanolamine in anorectic and decongestant preparations', *Lancet 1* (1980), 60–1.

5. MASSERLI, F. H. and FROHLICH, E. D., 'High blood pressure. A side effect of drugs, poisons and food', *Arch. Intern. Med. 139* (1979), 682–7.

6. PUDDEY, I. B., BEILIN, L. J., VANDONGEN R. et al., 'Differential effects of sulindac and indomethacin on blood pressure in treated essential hypertensive subjects', *Clin. Sci. 69* (1985), 327–36.

Chapter 6

1. MANEK, S., RUTHERFORD, J., JACKSON, S. H. D. et al., 'Persistence of divergent views of hospital staff in detecting and managing hypertension,' *Brit. Med. J. 289* (1984), 1433–4.

2. MAXWELL, M. H., WAKS, A. U., SCHROTH, P.C. et al., 'Error in blood pressure measurement due to incorrect cuff size in obese patients', *Lancet 2* (1982), 33–6.

3. WEBSTER, J., NEWNHAM, D., PETRIE, J. C. et al., 'Influence of arm position on measurement of blood pressure, *Brit. Med. J.,* 188 (1984), 1574–5.

4. WRIGHT, B. M. and DORE, C. F., 'A random-zero sphygmomanometer', *Lancet 1* (1970), 337–8.

5. SLOAN, P. J. M., ZEZULKA, A., DAVIES, P. et al., 'Standardized methods for

comparison of sphygmomanometers', *J. Hypertension* 2 (1984), 547–51.

6. O'BRIEN, E., FITZGERALD, D. and O'MALLEY, K., 'Blood pressure measurement: current practice and future trends', *Brit. Med. J.* 290 (1985), 729–34.

Chapter 7

1. WATERS, W. E., 'Headache and blood pressure in the community', *Brit. Med. J.* 1 (1971), 142–3.

2. RAMSAY, L. E., 'Intermittent claudication in hypertensive men', *J. Roy. Coll. Phys. London* 13 (1979), 100–102.

3. ELLIS, C. J., HAMER, D. B., HUNT, R. W. et al., 'Medical investigation of retinal vascular occlusion', *Brit. Med. J.* 2 (1964), 1093–8.

4. REES, L. H., BESSER, G. M., JEFFCOATE, W. J., GOLDIE et al., 'Alcohol induced pseudo-Cushing's syndrome', *Lancet* 1 (1977), 726–8.

5. WALSH, J. B., 'Hypertensive retinopathy, description, classification and prognosis', *Ophthalmology* 89 (1982), 1127–31.

6. KAPOOR, A., MOWBRAY, J. F., PORTER, K. A. et al., 'Significance of haematuria in hypertensive patients', *Lancet* 1 (1980), 231–2.

7. LEWIS, K. O., and PATON, A., 'ABC of alcohol: tools of detection', *Brit. Med. J.* 283 (1981), 1531–2.

8. POLANSKA, A. I. and BARON, D. N., 'Hyponatraemia associated with hydrochlorothiazide treatment', *Brit. Med. J.* (1978), 17s.

9. FERRISS, J. B. BEEVERS, D. G., BROWN, J. J. et al., 'Clinical, biochemical and pathological features of low-renin (primary) hyperaldosteronism', *Am. Heart J.* 95 (1978), 375–88.

10. KANNEL, W. B., CASTELLI, W. P., and GORDON, T., 'Cholesterol in the prediction of atherosclerotic disease', *Ann. Intern. Med.* 90 (1979), 85–91.

11. SLOAN, P. J. M. and BEEVERS, D. G., 'Hypertension and the heart. A review', *European Heart J.* 4 (1983), 215–22.

Chapter 8

1. WEINBERGER, M. H. 'Primary aldosteronism' In: *Hypertension*, Genest, J. et al., (eds) (McGraw Hill, New York, 1983), 922–39.

2. HAMET, P., 'Endocrine hypertension, Cushing's syndrome, acromegaly, hyperparathyroidism, thyrotoxicosis, and hypothyroidism' In: *Hypertension*, Genest, J. et al., (eds) (McGraw Hill, New York, 1983) 922–39.

3. KUCHEL, P., 'Adrenal medulla pheochromocytoma' In: *Hypertension*, Genest, J. et al. (eds) (McGraw Hill, New York, 1983), 947–63.

4. DE WARDENER, H. E., *The Kidney*, 5th edn (Churchill Livingstone, London, 1985).

5. GENEST, J. CARTIER, P. ROY, P. 'Renovascular hypertension' In: *Hypertension*, Genest, J. et al., (eds) (McGraw Hill, New York, 1983), 1007–34.

6. MENARD, J., SOUBRIER, F., BARIETY, J., et al., 'Primary reninism' In: *Hypertension*, Genest, J., et al., (eds) (McGraw Hill, New York, 1983) 1034–40.

Chapter 9

1. HARRINGTON, M. and ROSENHEIM, M. L., 'Hexamethonium in the treatment of hypertension', *Lancet* I (1954), 7–13.

2. HAMILTON, M., THOMSPON, E. N. and WISNIESWSKI, T. K. M., 'The role of blood pressure control in preventing complications of hypertension', *Lancet* 1 (1964), 235–8.

3. VETERANS ADMINISTRATION CO-OPERATIVE STUDY GROUP, ' Effects of treatment on morbidity in hypertension. Results in patients with diastolic blood pressures averaging 115 through 129 mmHg', *J. Am. Med. Assoc.* 202 (1967), 1028–34.

4. VETERANS ADMINISTRATION CO-OPERATIVE STUDY GROUP, 'Effects of

treatment on morbidity in hypertension. Results in patients with diastolic blood pressures averaging 90 through 114 mmHg', *J. Am. Med. Assoc. 213* (1970), 1143–52.

5. BERGLUND, G., SANNERSTEDT, R., ANDERSON, O. et al., 'Coronary heart disease after treatment of hypertension', *Lancet 1* (1978), 1–4.

6. UNITED STATES PUBLIC HEALTH HOSPITALS CO-OPERATIVE STUDY GROUP, 'Morbidity and mortality in mild essential hypertension', *Circ. Res. 30/31* (1972), supp. II 110–24.

7. AUSTRALIAN NATIONAL BLOOD PRESSURE STUDY MANAGEMENT COMMITTEE, 'The Australian therapeutic trial in mild hypertension', *Lancet 1* (1980), 1261–7.

8. HYPERTENSION DETECTION AND FOLLOW-UP PROGRAM COOPERATIVE GROUP, 'Five year findings of the hypertension detection and follow-up program (1) Reduction in mortality of persons with high blood pressure including mild hypertension', *J. Am. Med. Assoc. 242* (1979), 2562–71.

9. MULTIPLE RISK FACTOR INTERVENTION TRIAL RESEARCH GROUP, 'Risk factor changes and mortality results', Multiple Risk Factor Intervention Trial Research group, *J. Am. Med. Assoc. 248* (1982), 1465–77.

10. AMERY, A., BIRKENHAGER, W., BRIXKO, P. et al., 'Mortality and morbidity results from the European Working Party on high blood pressure in the elderly trial', *Lancet 1* (1985), 1349–54.

11. COOPE, J. R. and WARRENDER, T. S., 'Randomised trial of treatment of hypertension in elderly patients in primary care', *Brit. Med. J. 293* (1986), 1145–51.

12. MEDICAL RESEARCH COUNCIL WORKING PARTY, 'MRC trial of treatment of mild hypertension: principal results', *Brit. Med. J. 291* (1985), 97–104.

13. HULLEY, S. B., FURBERG, C. D. GURLAND, B. et al., 'Systolic Hypertension in the Elderly Program (SHEP): Antihypertensive Efficacy of Chlorthalidone', *Amer. J. Cardiol. 56* (1985), 913–20.

14. THE IPPPSH COLLABORATIVE GROUP, 'Cardiovascular risk and risk factors in a randomized trial of treatment based on the beta-blockers oxprenolol. The International Prospective Primary Prevention Study in Hypertension', *J. Hypertension 3* (1985), 379–96.

15. WILHELMSEN, L., BERGLUND, G., ELMFELT, O. et. al., 'Beta blockers versus saluretics in hypertension', *Prev. Med. 10* (1981), 38–49.

16. WHO/ISH MILD HYPERTENSION LIAISON COMMITTEE, 'Trials of the treatment of mild hypertension. An interim analysis', *Lancet 1* (1982), 149–56.

17. BEEVERS, D. G. JOHNSTON, J., DEVINE, B. L. et al., 'Relation between prognosis and the blood pressure before and during treatment of hypertensive patients *Clin. Sci. Molec, Med. 55* (1978), 333s–36s.

Chapter 10

1. MRC WORKING PARTY ON MILD TO MODERATE HYPERTENSION, 'Randomised controlled trial of treatment for mild hypertension: design and pilot trial', *Brit. Med. J. 2* (1977) 1437–40.

2. MACGREGOR, G. A. 'Sodium is more important than calcium in essential hypertension,' *Hypertension 7* (1985), 628–37.

3. AMBARD, L. and BEAUJARD, E., 'Causes de l'hypertension arterielle', *Arch. Gen. Med. 1* (1904), 520–33.

4. KEMPNER, W. 'Treatment of hypertensive vascular disease with rice diet', *Am. J. Med. 4* (1948), 545–77.

5. MACGREGOR, G. A. MARKANOU, N. D. BEJY, F. E. et al., 'Double-blind randomised crossover trial of moderate sodium restriction in essen-

tial hypertension', *Lancet 1* (1982), 351–5.

6. MACGREGOR, G. A., *The Salt-Free Diet Book* (Martin Dunitz, London, 1984).

7. MACGREGOR, G. A., SMITH, S. J., MARKANOU, N. D., et al. Moderate potassium supplementation in essential hypertension', *Lancet 2*, (1982), 567–70.

8. CAPPUCCIO, F. P., MARKANOU, N. D., BEYNON, G. W., et al. 'Lack of effect of oral magnesium on high blood pressure: a double blind study', *Brit. Med. J. 291* (1985), 235–8.

9. PUSKA, P., IACONO, J. A., NISSENEN, A., et al., 'Controlled randomised trial of the effect of dietary fat on blood pressure', *Lancet 1* (1983), 1–5.

10. WRIGHT, A., BURSTYN, P. G., and GIBNEY, M. J., 'Dietary fibre and blood pressure', *Brit. Med. J.2* (1979), 1541–3.

11. REISIN, E., ABEL, R., MODAN, M. et. al., 'Effect of weight loss without salt restriction in the reduction of blood pressure in overweight hypertensive patients', *New Eng. J. Med. 298* (1978), 1–6.

12. POTTER, J. F. and BEEVERS, D. G. 'The pressor effect of alcohol in hypertension', *Lancet 1* (1984), 119–22.

13. PATEL, C., MARMOT, M. G. and TERRY, D. G. 'Controlled trial of biofeedback-aided behavioural methods in reducing mild hypertension', *Brit. Med. J. 282* (1981), 2005–2008.

Chapter 11

1. AMES, R. P., 'Negative effects of diuretic drugs on metabolic risk factors for coronary heart disease', *Am. J. Card. 51* (1983), 632–8.

2. MEDICAL RESEARCH COUNCIL WORKING PARTY ON MILD TO MODERATE HYPERTENSION, 'Ventricular extrasystoles during thiazide treatment. Sub-Study on MRC Mild

Hypertension Trial', *Brit. Med. J. 287* (1983) 1249–53

3. PRICHARD, B. N. C. and OWENS, C. W. I., 'Drug treatment of hypertension' In: *Hypertension*, Genest, J. et al. (eds) (McGraw Hill, New York, 1983), 1186–94.

4. 'Calcium antagonists in hypertension – Focus on verapamil', *Am. J. Card. 57*, (1986), 1D–106D.

5. 'Calcium antagonists in the treatment of hypertension', Murphy, M. B. and Dollery, C. (eds) In: *Hypertension 5* (1983), Supplement: II-1–II-129.

6. POOL, P. E. MASSIE, B. M. and VENKATARAMAN, K., 'Diltiazem as monotherapy for systemic hypertension. A multicenter randomised placebo-controlled trial', *Am. J. Card. 57* (1986), 212–17.

7. EDWARDS, C. R. W. and PADFIELD, P. L. 'Angiotensin, converting enzyme inhibitors – past, present and bright future', *Lancet 1* (1985), 30–4.

8. CROOG, S. H. LEVINE, S., TESTA, M. A. et al., 'The effects of antihypertensive therapy on the quality of life', *New Eng. J. Med. 314* (1986), 1657–64.

Chapter 12

1. *British National Formulary*, Number 11 (1986), 67–104.

2. BERGLUND, G., and ANDERSON, O. 'Low doses of hydrochlorothiazide in hypertension: antihypertensive and metabolic effects', *Eur. J. of Clin. Pharmacol. 10* (1976), 177–82.

3. WILCOX, R. G., 'Randomised study of six beta-blockers and a thiazide diuretic in essential hypertension', *Brit. Med. J. 2* (1978), 383–5.

4. 'Calcium antagonists in the treatment of hypertension', Murphy, M. B. and Dollery, C. (eds) In: *Hypertension 5* (1983), Supplement: II-1–II-129.

5. CROOG, S. H., LEVINE, S., TESTA, M. A.

et al., 'The effects of antihypertensive therapy on the quality of life', *New Eng. J. Med. 314* (1986), 1657–64.

6. EDWARDS, C. R. W. and PADFIELD, P. L. 'Angiotensin converting enzyme inhibitors: past, present and bright future', *Lancet 1* (1985), 30–4.

7. BALL, S. G. and ROBERTSON, J. I. S., 'A need for new converting enzyme inhibitors?' *Brit. Med. J. 290* (1985), 180–1.

8. MCAREAVEY, D. RAMSEY, L. E., LATHAM, L. et al., 'Third drug trial comparative study of antihypertensive agents added to treatment when blood pressure remains uncontrolled by beta-blocker plus thiazide diuretic', *Brit. Med. J. 288*: (1984), 106–11.

9. BANNAN, L. T. and BEEVERS, D. G., 'Emergency treatment of high blood pressure with oral atenolol', *Brit. Med. J. 282* (1981), 1757–8.

Chapter 13

1. COOPE, J. R., 'Hypertension in general practice: what is to be done?', *Brit. Med. J. 288* (1984), 880–1.

2. BARBER, J. H., BEEVERS, D. G., FIFE, R. et al., 'Blood pressure screening and supervision in general practice', *Brit. Med. J. 1.* (1979), 843–6.

3. COOPE, J. R., 'Management of hypertension in general practice', *Brit Med. J. 282* (1981), 1380–2.

4. OSBOURNE, V. L. and BEEVERS, D. G., 'A comparison of hospital and general practice blood pressure readings using a shared care record card', *J. Roy. Coll. Gen. Pract. 31* (1981), 345–50.

5. SILVERBERG, D. S., BALTUCH, L., HERMONI, Y. et al., 'Control of hypertension in family practice by the doctor-nurse team', *J. Roy. Coll. Gen. Pract. 32* (1982), 184–6.

6. PETRIE, J. C., ROBB, O. J., WEBSTER, J. et al., 'Computer assisted shared care in hypertension', *Brit. Med. J. 290* (1985), 1960–2.

7. FOLSOM, A. R., LEUPKER, R. V., GILLUM, R. F. et al., 'Improvement in hypertension detection and control from 1973–1974 to 1980–1981', *J. Am. Med. Assoc. 250* (1983), 916–21.

Chapter 14

1. BABER, N. S. and LEWIS, J. A., 'Confidence in results of beta-blocker post infarction trials', *Brit. Med. J. 284* (1982), 1749–50.

2. BEEVERS, D. G., FAIRMAN, M., J., HAMILTON, M. et al., 'Antihypertensive treatment in the course of established cerebral vascular disease', *Lancet 1* (1973), 1407–1408.

3. NEIL-DWYER, G., WALTER, P., CRUICKSHANK, J. M. et al., 'Beta-blockade and subarachnoid haemorrhage', *Drugs 25* (1983) supp. 2, 273–7.

4. O'MALLEY, K., O'CALLAGHAN, W. G., LAHER, M. S., et al., 'Beta-adrenoreceptor blocking drugs and renal blood flow with special reference to the elderly', *Drugs 25* (1983) supp. 2, 103.

5. SCHALEKAMP, M. A., BEEVERS, D. G., BRIGGS J. D. et al., 'Hypertension in chronic renal failure, an abnormal relation between sodium and the renin-angiotensin system', *Am. J. Med. 55* (1973), 379–90.

6. CHRISTLIEB, A. R., 'The hypertension of diabetes', *Diabetes Care 5* (1982), 50–8.

7. PACY, P. J., DODSON, P. M., KUBICKI, A. J., et al., 'Comparison of the hypotensive and metabolic effects of metoprolol therapy with a high fibre low sodium low fat diet in hypertensive type 2 diabetic subjects', *Diabetes Res. 1* (1984), 201–207.

8. MURPHY, M. B. LEWIS, P. J., KOHNER, E. et al., 'Glucose intolerance in hypertensive patients treated with diuretics; a fourteen year follow up', *Lancet 2* (1982), 1293–5.

9. BARNETT, A. H., LESLIE, D. and WATKINS, P. J., 'Can insulin treated diabetics be given beta-adrenergic blocking drugs', *Brit. Med. J. 280* (1980), 976–8.

10. DECLAMER, P. B. S., CHATERJEE, S. S., CRUICKSHANK, J. M., et al., 'Beta-blockers and asthma', *Brit. Heart J. 40* (1978), 184–9.

11. LEVER, A. M. L. CORMIS, P. A. and GIBSON, G. J., 'Nifedipine enhances the bronchodilator effect of salbutamol', *Thorax 39* (1984), 576–8.

12. POTTER, J. F., BANNAN, L. T. and BEEVERS, D. G., 'Alcohol and hypertension', *Brit. J. Addiction 79* (1984), 365–72.

13. PRYS-ROBERTS, C., 'Anaesthesia and hypertension', *Brit. J. Anaesth., 56* (1984), 711–24.

Chapter 15

1. HAMILTON, M., THOMPSON, E. N. and WISNIEWSKI, T. K. M., 'The role of blood pressure control in preventing complications of hypertension', *Lancet 1* (1964), 235–8.

2. VETERANS ADMINISTRATION CO-OPERATIVE STUDY GROUP, 'Effects of treatment on morbidity in hypertension II. Results in patients with diastolic blood pressure averaging 90 through 114 mmHg', *J. Am. Med. Assoc. 213* (1970), 1143–52.

3. AUSTRALIAN NATIONAL BLOOD PRESSURE STUDY MANAGEMENT COMMITTEE, 'The Australian therapeutic trial in mild hypertension', *Lancet 1* (1980) 1261–7.

4. AMERY, A. BIRKENHAGER, W. BRIXKO, P. et al., 'Mortality and morbidity results from the European Working Party on high blood pressure in the elderly trial', *Lancet 1* (1985), 1349–54.

5. COOPE, J. R. and WARRENDER, T. S., 'Randomised trial of treatment of hypertension in elderly patients in primary care', *Brit. Med. J. 293* (1986), 1145–51.

Chapter 16

1. MACGILLIVRAY, I., 'Hypertension in pregnancy and its consequences', *Brit. J. Obstet. Gynaecol. 68* (1961), 557–69.

2. MACGILLIVRAY, I., 'Raised blood pressure in pregnancy. Aetiology of pre-eclampsia', *Brit. J. Hosp. Med. 26*, (1981), 110–19.

3. VAN DONGEN, P. W. J., ESKES, T. K. A. B., MARTIN, C. B. et al., 'Postural blood pressure differences in pregnancy', *Am. J. Obstet. Gynecol. 138* (1980), 1–5.

4. OBIEKWE, B. C., CHARD, T., STURDEE, D. W. et al., 'Serial measurement of serum uric acid as an indicator of fetal wellbeing in late pregnancy', *J. Obstet. Gynaecol. 5* (1984), 17–20.

5. CURZEN, P., BEKIR, J. S., MCLINTOCK, D. G. et al., 'Reliability of cardiotocography in predicting baby's condition at birth', *Brit. Med. J. 289* (1984), 1345–7.

6. DE SWIET, M., 'Antihypertensive drugs in pregnancy', *Brit. Med. J. 291* (1985), 365–6.

7. COLLINS, R., YUSUF, S. and PETO, R., 'Overview of randomised trials of diuretics in pregnancy', *Brit. Med. J. 290* (1985), 17–23.

8. REDMAN, C. W. G., BEILIN, L. J., BONNAR, J. et al., 'Fetal outcome in trial of antihypertensive treatment in pregnancy', *Lancet 2* (1976) 753–6.

9. RUBIN, P. C., BUTTERS, L. CLARK, D. M.

et al., 'Placebo controlled trial of atenolol in treatment of pregnancy associated hypertension', *Lancet 1* (1983), 431–4.

10. WALTERS, B. N. J. and REDMAN, C. W. G., 'Treatment of severe pregnancy associated hypertension with the calcium antagonist nifedipine', *Brit. J. Obstet. Gynaecol. 91* (1984), 330–6.

Chapter 17

1. ILSLEY, C. D. and MILLAR, J. A., 'Hypertension in children', *Brit. Med. J. 290* (1985), 1451–2.

2. DE SWIET, M., FAYERS, P. M. and SHINEBOURNE, E. A., 'Blood pressure in four and five-year-old children: the effects of environment and other factors on its measurement. The Brompton study', *J. Hypertension 2* (1984), 501–505.

3. SZKLO, M., 'Epidemiologic patterns of blood pressure in children', *Epidemiological Rev. 1* (1979), 143–69.

4. NATIONAL HEART, LUNG AND BLOOD INSTITUTE, 'Report of the task force on blood pressure control in children', *Paediatrics 59* (1977) supp., 797–820.

5. ALPORT, B. S., BAIN, H. H., BALFE, J. W. et al., 'Role of the renin-angiotensin-aldosterone system in hypertensive children with coarctation of the aorta', *Am. J. Cardiol. 43* (1979), 828–34.

6. BROWN, J. J., FRASER, R., LEVER. A. F. et al., 'Hypertension and secondary hyperaldosteronism associated with a renin-secreting renal juxtaglomerular cell tumour', *Lancet 2* (1973), 1228–32.

7. HOFMAN, A., 'Blood pressure in childhood: an epidemiological approach to the aetiology of hypertension', *J. Hypertension 2* (1984), 323–8.

Acknowledgments

The authors and publishers are grateful to the following for their assistance: Mrs D. Thomas for line drawings and figures, Dr P. M. Dodson for his advice on hypertension in diabetes and Mrs V. Stewart for secretarial assistance.

For loan of and permission to reproduce illustrations: Miss J. McCulloch, Department of Photography, Dudley Road Hospital (Figures 6.3, 6.4, 6.6, 7.1, 7.3, 7.4, 8.5); Miss G. Plant, Department of Cardiology, Dudley Road Hospital (Figures 7.10, 14.1, 14.2); Miss A. L. Reynolds (Figures 16.1, 16.2); Dr G. Sagar (Figures 2.6, 2.7); Dr K. G. Taylor (Figure 7.2); Dr J. P. Wingate (Figures 2.4, 2.8, 8.2, 8.4, 8.9); Department of Clinical Chemistry, Dudley Road Hospital (Figure 8.1); Department of Haematology, Dudley Road Hospital (Figure 7.7); Department of Medical Illustration, Charing Cross and Westminster Medical School (Figure 10.3); Gower Medical Publishers, *Slide Atlas of Hypertension* (Figures 8.3, 8.5); ICI/Inderal (Figures 7.5 (i), (ii)).

Index

Page numbers in *italic* refer to the illustrations

229